Exiles in a Land of Liberty

Studies in Religion

Charles H. Long, Editor
Syracuse University

Editorial Board

Giles B. Gunn
University of California at Santa Barbara

Van A. Harvey
Stanford University

Wendy Doniger O'Flaherty
The University of Chicago

Ninian Smart
*University of California at Santa Barbara
and the University of Lancaster*

Exiles in a Land of Liberty

Mormons in America, 1830–1846

by Kenneth H. Winn

The University of North Carolina Press

Chapel Hill and London

© 1989 The University of North Carolina Press
All rights reserved
Manufactured in the United States of America

The paper in this book meets the guidelines for permanence
and durability of the Committee on Production Guidelines
for Book Longevity of the Council on Library Resources.

93 92 91 90 89   5 4 3 2 1

Library of Congress Cataloging-in-Publication Data

Winn, Kenneth H.
  Exiles in a land of liberty: Mormons in America, 1830–1846 / by
Kenneth H. Winn.
    p.   cm. — (Studies in religion)
    Bibliography: p.
    Includes index.
    ISBN 0-8078-1829-1 (alk. paper)
    1. Mormons—United States—History—19th century. 2. United
States—History—1815–1861. 3. United States—Church history—19th
century. I. Title. II. Series: Studies in religion (Chapel Hill,
N.C.)
  E184.M8W56   1989   88-23291
  973.5′088283—dc 19   CIP

for Karen,
mi corazón

Contents

Acknowledgments

$\mathbf{I}$t is a pleasure to thank the many fine people and institutions that helped me in the writing of this book. Before historians can engage in serious research and writing they must be free from basic economic worry. To that end I benefited from a fellowship from the Charlotte W. Newcombe Foundation and a Doctoral Dissertation Fellowship from Washington University in St. Louis. For both awards I am grateful. More recently, my friend Peter J. Michel and the Missouri Historical Society have provided me with the time and support necessary to put the final touches on the manuscript.

I am also happy to acknowledge research assistance from the staffs of the special collections departments of the Newberry Library, the Chicago Historical Society, the Missouri Historical Society, the Utah State Historical Society, the Salt Lake City Public Library, the Olin Library and Inter-Library Loan at Washington University, the Lovejoy Library at Southern Illinois University at Edwardsville, and the History Office and Archives of the Church of Jesus Christ of Latter-Day Saints. I owe a special debt to Mary Schnitker Kiessling and Bevene Bona of the Church History Office. Mary, in particular, went beyond the call of duty to make my lengthy research trips to Salt Lake City not only profitable, but pleasant. I remember her and the rest of the staff fondly.

At an early stage of my research I received useful advice from Linda Wilcox and Stephen C. LeSueur. Many other people have been helpful along the way. Jean Baker and Robert Shalhope gave me a number of useful comments on my third chapter. I hope they can find reason to like the rest. More generally, I would be remiss if I did not express my admiration for the practitioners of the "New Mormon History" (although, like the "New Social History," the New Mormon History is not very new anymore). I have littered my footnotes with references to their work, but even that fails to demonstrate my respect for their skill and the sophistication with which they approach their subject or, for many of them, their faith.

My friends and colleagues at Washington University have aided me in so many different ways that I am loath to single out any one of them. The personal and professional support rendered by Mark Kornbluh and Henry Berger, however, transcends this urge and is most gratefully acknowledged. I also owe a word of thanks to a number of student research assistants, especially Jennifer N. Toth, Amy M. Pfeiffenberger, and Anne K. Hamilton, for their help in preparing this manuscript for publication. Bette Marbs, Patricia Pinter, Carolyn Brown, and Dora Arky all helped with the final typing.

Rowland Berthoff, who directed my doctoral dissertation, gets his own paragraph, but deserves more. His patient reading of the manuscript revealed implications I had missed and saved me from a number of foolish errors. I, alas, am responsible for the foolish errors that remain. I cherish our continuing relationship.

In deference to scholarly tradition I have saved my most important debts for last. My parents, J. Hugh and Elaine S. Winn, have been rocks of uncritical support for these many years. My wife, Karen, greatly improved the language of the manuscript, endured endless (and often repetitive) discussions of early Mormonism, and importantly, took considerable time away from her own work and leisure to help me see this project through. Fortunately I owe her more than she dimly suspects. By contrast, my daughter, Alice, the best girl in all of North America, possibly the whole world, helped to drag things out.

Exiles in a Land of Liberty

Introduction

When the Book of Mormon first appeared on March 26, 1830, it verified what most Americans already knew. It was God who had delivered the United States from British monarchy and endowed it with republican liberties. Speaking in the Lord's name, the pre-Columbian Mormon prophet Jacob proclaimed that America would "be a land of liberty unto the Gentiles" and promised that there would "be no kings upon the land."[1] Jacksonian Mormons gloried in these sentiments. Over the next few years, they indulged in all the conventional slogans of American self-praise, waxing fervent over the illustrious signers of the sacred compact of 1776 who, guided by God, had created an asylum for the oppressed where all could enjoy the rights of freemen under our happy form of government.[2]

Fifteen years after the publication of the Book of Mormon, however, Mormon expressions of hatred and contempt for the United States were commonplace. On September 26, 1845, Brigham Young announced that he did not "intend to winter again in the United States." Denouncing Americans as "corrupt as hell from the president down clean through the priests and the people," he concluded that Mormons did "not owe this country a single sermon."[3] Accordingly, on February 5, 1846, the "Camp of Israel" began their fabled exodus from the Mormon settlement at Nauvoo, Illinois, for an unknown destination outside the territorial limits of the United States. There, they believed, they would build the kingdom of God and await the collapse of "Babylon" under the weight of its own iniquity.

The trek west notwithstanding, the Mormons felt not so much that they had left the United States as that it had left them. They still celebrated God's gift of liberty; it was the majority of Americans who did not. This conviction came as a result of sixteen years of bitter conflict with their neighbors. Between 1830 and 1846 persecution hastened or forced the church's departure from six separate gathering places within the states of New York, Ohio, Missouri, and Illinois. Clashes between the church and its enemies took perhaps hundreds of lives, cost millions of dollars in property losses, and inflicted untold psychological damage. The Mormons reaped the overwhelming majority of these losses. As the years of unrelieved hostility progressed, the Mormons grew increasingly weary of their country. On June 27, 1844, an angry anti-Mormon mob stormed the jail in Carthage, Illinois, and murdered the Mormon founder and prophet Joseph Smith and his brother Hyrum. The assassination of the hated Smith did not dampen anti-Mormon hostility. After a brief respite, armed bands of the original inhabitants (called "old citizens" or "old settlers") initiated guerrilla-style warfare against isolated church settlements. By the fall of 1845, the Mormons had had enough. There were no gentile neighbors to shoot them in the Great Salt Basin, and this alone was enough to make it a promised land.

The oldest and most interesting debate about early Mormon history attempts to determine the church's relationship to American culture. This study reexamines this debate and endeavors to bring fresh answers to it by employing what other historians have called "republican ideology."[4] In recent years, historians have seen Aristotle as the "unmoved mover" of republican thought. From him, the meandering descent of republican tradition winds its way through Western Civilization transformed and refined in the works of the Renaissance philosopher Niccolo Machiavelli, James Harrington and the thinkers of the English Revolution, the writers of the English "Country" opposition to Prime Minister Robert Walpole, and finally taken over by the American revolutionaries. Republican ideology, as conceived by these men, dichotomized political life into a struggle between the forces of virtue and corruption. A strong republic rested upon the foundation of a virtuous citizenry composed of independent property-owning men whose self-reliance, civic spirit, and hardy disdain for enfeebling luxury separated them from the very wealthy and the very poor. Property ownership, because it was generally understood as farm ownership, meant self-sufficiency, so the property owner, beholden to none, could exercise his free and independent judgment about what was good for his community. Yet while possession of the basic necessities of life engendered good citizenship, opulence did not. The republican citizen scorned luxury because it fostered a lust for fine things and encouraged the citizen to put his private advantage ahead of his public duty. Threats were, in fact, omnipresent. Republican government balanced precariously between anarchy and tyranny. Good citizens were expected to arm themselves, form militias, and exercise constant vigilance in putting down challenges that threatened to upset this fragile equilibrium.

Although republican theorists dreaded both anarchy and tyranny, they felt that corruption of civic virtue ultimately led to the latter. The forces of anarchy just walked a more crooked path to get there. Americans constantly feared that a republic was not strong enough to defend itself. Anarchy reared its head when the rabble, generally men with no stake in society, or a set of "designing men" fractured the body politic into unrestrained factions. Republicans knew that the people would never tolerate chaos and feared they would turn to the champion on the white horse who brought the order of the sword. It was the ambitious strong man, or perhaps a "secret combination" of men, who walked the straighter road to tyranny. Through wealth or political power such men reduced other citizens to dependent status, forced them to do their will, and thereby transformed the public interest into private interest. For this reason, women, children, slaves, and propertyless men were classically considered unfit for the franchise because they were seen as dependents having no will of their own. When citizens prostrated their own independent judgment to that of others, liberty was imperiled.

Preservation of a republic necessitated a stable, even static, society. Accordingly, patriotic Americans guarded against political innovation and, through the "republican jeremiad," expressed their foreboding about change and loss of virtue.[5] The legacy of Puritanism played a major role in reinforcing many republican values, such as thrift, self-discipline, and a regard for the commonwealth.[6] The Puritan jeremiad had lamented the declension from righteousness and exhorted the people to reformation. Republican Americans converted this act into a ritual bemoaning of the near extinction of liberty unless a speedy return to virtue took place.

In the Jacksonian era, the scheme of republican ideology developed by the Founding Fathers remained basically intact, although it took on an increasingly libertarian cast. The rapid change and severe social dislocation of the period caused Americans to invoke their jeremianic concerns over the loss of republican liberties at an unusually high pitch. Whigs and Democrats, Masons and anti-Masons, as well as Mormons and anti-Mormons, bewailed the country's impending ruin. The opponents of each, of course, had caused this sad decline. Emphasis on farm ownership, or even property ownership, as the sine qua non of civic virtue had declined. Merchants, manufacturers, and laborers were all now tacitly welcomed aboard the ship of republic virtue. Increasingly, republicans accepted those qualities associated with Victorian America—sobriety, thrift, punctuality, and self-discipline—as sufficient badges of civic virtue.[7]

Many an antebellum forest must have fallen to supply all the paper the Mormons and their opponents used to proclaim themselves good republicans and their opponents antirepublicans. This ideological quarrel, however, remains largely uncommented on by historians. There are probably two reasons for this. First, many scholars unfamiliar with the concept of republican ideology often assume that words like "tyranny," "mobocracy," "vice," "virtue," "luxury," "corruption," as well as "republicanism," possess a timeless meaning when, as we have seen, they are code words of a specific ideology that has pervaded American history from at least as early as the American Revolution. Second, Mormon and anti-Mormon concern about republicanism seems easy to dismiss as mere rhetoric. True enough, since the days of the Founding Fathers, a wide chasm has existed between American political ideals and practice, even among more conventional patriots. Yet Mormons and anti-Mormons alike thought that they measured up to republican standards and that their opponents did not. While many felt uneasy about the actions they took, they reassured themselves in their diaries, in their letters to family and friends, and in the newspaper to the community at large, that in defense of republican liberties they stood shoulder to shoulder with Thomas Jefferson.

If historians have not seen the conflict between the Mormons and their gentile neighbors explicitly in terms of republicanism, they have extensively addressed the question of Mormon "Americanism." For various reasons, scholars, who can agree upon little else, have magnified Mormonism's exceptionalism—sometimes to emphasize its specialness as a religion, at other times to characterize it as an oddity of antebellum social disorder.[8] Many of these historians reason that Mormonism, with its novel doctrines and dissent from mainstream religions, must have represented an ideological counterculture subversive to larger society. If not, why did it attract such brutal violence?

Mormonism first emerged as a protest movement decrying the religious anarchy created by the "priestcraft" of major denominations and, implicitly, the growing economic inegalitarianism of Jacksonian society. The Mormons framed their critique within the context of republican ideology. The solutions the Mormons devised for these problems, in turn, brought swift reaction from the gentile communities where they settled. Non-Mormons recoiled from the church members' slavish devotion to their prophet Joseph Smith and their economic and political unity. The attacks that came from fearful anti-Mormons, however, only increased Mormon apprehensiveness of mobocracy and their fears that America had fallen into irredeemable corruption. Both Mormons and anti-Mormons accused each other of being antirepublican and, not surprisingly, each group betrayed a keener eye for their opponent's lack of virtue than their own. Curiously, Mormons charged gentiles with inciting anarchy, while gentiles accused the church of the other antirepublican evil of tyranny. In point of fact, the Mormons did subvert and distort the political and social institutions, republican or not, where they settled. This resulted partially from beliefs inherent within Mormonism and partially from a defense against gentile attacks. Anti-Mormons, numerically superior in number, punished the church for grievances, real and imagined, and for not accepting their version of republican ideology. Those historians who believe that Mormon values were rejected by the majority of their neighbors as being antirepublican are, in effect, accepting the interpretation of the contemporary anti-Mormons themselves.

chapter 1

The Origins of Mormonism

Mormonism represented no retreating sign of the oppressed, but an angry indictment of early nineteenth-century America. It is a curious fact, then, that by all accounts its creator, Joseph Smith, was not a thundering, long-faced Isaiah, but a man possessed of a remarkably cheerful, optimistic disposition. However, Smith had reason for dissatisfaction. Years of injustice suffered by his family and a broad sensitivity to the advancing disintegration of the larger social structure alienated him from the mainstream of American life. Yet while thousands of people in similar circumstances simply floundered, the recognition of a gap between what was and what should be sparked in him a call to prophethood. Like the prophets of old, however, Joseph demanded not so much a new world as repentance and a return to virtues lost. When he attacked American society, he did so by measuring it against its own ideals, reworking the distinctive American language of republican ideology into an expression of his anger and aspirations. In doing so, he struck a responsive chord in others, and at the age of twenty-five, he founded America's most successful indigenous religion.

Joseph Smith, Jr., was born in Sharon, Vermont, on December 23, 1805, to Joseph and Lucy Mack Smith, both of old New England stock. Joseph's ancestors had prospered in the New World. The Smith line had accumulated a substantial amount of property, and a number of family members had achieved political distinction in state and local offices. The Macks had also obtained a measure of success, many filling Congregational pulpits. The first break with this general good fortune came during the lifetime of Joseph's two grandfathers. Asael Smith, his paternal grandfather, left his ancestral home in Topsfield, Massachusetts, to rebuild his fortune as a pioneer in the wilds of

Vermont. Solomon Mack, his maternal grandfather, led a life of wild military and economic misadventure and never achieved economic security. Still, both of these men managed to instill a keen sense of respectability into their children.[1]

When Joseph and Lucy married on January 24, 1796, their prospects looked promising. They had a farm in Tunbridge, Vermont, and Lucy's brother, Stephen, had presented her with the handsome wedding gift of a thousand dollars from himself and his business partner. Unfortunately, one financial disaster followed another. The farm proved barren and rocky; an unscrupulous partner in a ginseng speculation absconded with their substantial investment. Before many years had passed, the Smiths were living an impoverished, nomadic life, endlessly searching for the fresh start that would bring them financial security.[2]

The Smiths were not alone in their misfortunes. Farmers throughout New England had found that extracting a living from their unproductive soil was a marginal enterprise at best. Capricious weather, erratic economic conditions, and competition from more fertile lands further west ruined thousands of farmers, and they too left New England in search of better prospects. The productive land surrounding the Genesee and Mohawk rivers in upstate New York and the prospect of thriving commerce held out by the new Erie Canal lured many of these New Englanders. In 1816, the Smiths migrated to the region and settled near the village of Palmyra. Unluckily, by the time they arrived, the best land had long since been taken; and the boom had subsided into the hard times that culminated in the Panic of 1819. Too poor and perhaps not enterprising enough to push further west, they decided to try to make the best of things farming an inferior piece of land.[3]

As class lines sharpened in the 1820s, the Smiths' consciousness of their lowly status deepened. After seven moves in twenty years, they were poorer than the day they married, richer only by nine children. Life under these circumstances became an unceasing struggle to shore up family finances. The Smith children, consequently, received scant schooling, as everyone old enough to work quickly joined the struggle to stave off poverty.[4] Many of the Smiths' more well-to-do neighbors looked down on them as mere riffraff. Years later, a hostile anti-Mormon investigator had no trouble eliciting affidavits testifying to, among other things, their indigent condition. One neighbor, Roswell Nichols, charged that "for breach of contracts, the non-payment of debts and borrowed money, and for duplicity with their neighbors, the [Smith] family was notorious." In his financial desperation, Joseph Smith, Sr., allegedly once "confessed that it was sometimes necessary for him to tell an honest lie, in order to live."[5] Typically, the Smiths' detractors charged the family's poverty to a want of industry. Joseph Capron, for instance, noted with scorn that "the whole family of Smiths, were notorious for indolence, foolery, and falsehood. Their great object appeared to be, to live without work."[6]

These and other similar remarks were made after the founding of the Mormon church, and they betray hostility to what the Smiths became. Yet there can be no doubt that these sentiments antedated the advent of Mormonism. Irrespective of the fairness of these assessments of the Smith family, the smug social superiority shown by some of their neighbors rubbed salt in the economic wounds they suffered long before the publication of the Book of Mormon. This humiliation probably took its greatest toll on the fiercely proud and socially ambitious Lucy, but undoubtedly the whole family felt it keenly. It certainly affected Lucy's son, Joseph, who was bitter over what he described as "being persecuted by those who ought to have been my friends, and to have treated me kindly."[7] The Smiths had once held a respected place among their neighbors; now they received snubs from people they considered their social equals. But the residents of Palmyra cared little about successful ancestors or former social status; they simply saw the Smiths' present poverty. Mormonism, with its economic egalitarianism and its denunciation of the haughty rich, distinctly reflects Joseph's indignation at his family's treatment at the hands of their neighbors.[8]

The Smiths were, on the whole, good, decent, hard-working people who should have fared better, but did not. They had lost the social status of their forebears through misfortune and poor judgment; in their poverty-induced rootlessness, they felt a painful separation from their larger community. They knew they deserved a respectable place in society, but found themselves instead neglected and scorned by their economic "betters," even while they struggled to maintain the middle-class virtues that separated them from the idle poor. As Mormonism grew, the charges leveled at the Smiths in New York would be systematized into a general accusation that they had violated the republican moral code. Yet the Smiths did not reject republican principles. They exemplified the virtues of hard work, thrift, independence, and a concern for the community as much as their more prosperous neighbors did. They, likewise, shunned the vices of idleness and selfishness, and abhorred the condition of dependence. The social and religious rebellion Joseph Smith, Jr., eventually led burst forth not as a rejection of republican values, but as an attempt to restore them. What began as anger toward his family's exclusion from their proper place as worthy upholders of these standards became transformed into a counteraccusation: it was not the Smith family and their friends who had rejected the principles of republican virtue, but their opponents.

Obviously, Mormonism was a religious revolt, not simply a social protest movement. Yet it is nearly impossible to extricate the secular from the religious elements in early Mormonism. To the modern mind, bad economic conditions and social fragmentation are secular problems, but such a perception had only just gained ascendance in the antebellum period. Joseph Smith and his followers rejected the tendency toward secularization, refusing to bifurcate their lives into separate spheres of the sacred and the profane.

Smith had a religious tradition of family heterodoxy to draw upon in his eventual dissent from the existing churches. Both his grandfathers had broken away from the traditional churches of New England. Although Asael Smith had his children baptized in the Congregational church, he eventually decided that its doctrines, and those of the other long-standing churches, coincided with neither Scripture nor reason. His religious views, however, were quite pronounced. His reading of the millennial prophecies in the Book of Daniel convinced him that the American Revolution signified the beginning of God's destruction of all ecclesiastical and monarchical tyranny, and the advent of His kingdom. On the other hand, Solomon Mack, by his own account, abandoned not only the Congregationalism of his minister father, but all other thoughts of religion as well. Then, during an illness at the age of seventy-seven, he had an intense mystical experience. As a result, he spent the remaining years of his life warning his fellow countrymen against lusting after worldly goods or ignoring their God.[9]

Like their parents, Joseph, Sr., and Lucy Smith held fervent religious beliefs yet could find no home among the organized churches. Instead, like many other unchurched people, they embraced the doctrines of "Christian primitivism," the belief that the innovations of the churches down through the ages had corrupted the original religion of Jesus. Accordingly, they demanded a return to "true" Christianity as they interpreted it in their simple, common-sense reading of the Bible. This meant a special emphasis on a lay ministry, the baptism of believers by immersion, gifts of the spirit, and the authority to act in God's name. These doctrines had their origins in the backlash against the divisive elements of the Second Great Awakening. Many people hoped that an appeal to the Bible as the sole source of authority would undercut the rivalry of denominational competition. If they could not find a particular precept in the Bible, it must be disavowed; if they could, it must be accepted as truth. The Smiths found none of these principles of primitivism in practice in the churches they visited, and Joseph, Sr., in particular, refused to join a church until he found one that preached the restored gospel.[10]

Joseph, Sr., had not always made such a staunch stand against the old-line churches; but around 1811, he had a number of dreams that finally settled his opinion against them. For the Smith family, like many others, God was the author of dreams; if properly understood, they could bring enlightenment and guidance.[11] In one of these dreams, an attendant spirit showed Joseph a box representing "true religion." When Joseph opened its lid, wild animals symbolizing the various religious sects rushed to attack him, forcing him to drop the box. The meaning of the dream was clear to Joseph: the churches knew nothing of true religion, and kept others from discovering it.[12]

In a second, more important dream, an attendant spirit took Joseph through a land of desolation into a pleasant valley. There he gathered his family around a beautiful tree bearing fruit "delicious beyond all description." The scene so affected him that he fell into an intense rapture. The spirit guide then informed him that the fruit represented "the pure love of God, shed abroad in the hearts of all those who love him, and keep his commandments." Joseph's bliss, however, was interrupted by the observation of a large and spacious building filled with finely dressed men and women. These people laughed at Joseph and his family, "pointing the finger of scorn" at them and "treat[ing them] with all manner of contempt." When he inquired of his guide as to the meaning of the spacious building, the spirit replied, "It is Babylon, it is Babylon, and it must fall. The people in the doors and windows are the inhabitants thereof, who scorn and despise the Saints of God, because of their humility." The answer so delighted Joseph that he told of awakening and "clapping my hands together for joy."[13]

Joseph's interpretation of his dreams contains the essential Christian primitivist critique at the heart of early Mormonism. From the first dream came the assurance that all the various denominations are wrong and malicious in their attempts to keep people from the true gospel. The second dream exhibited strong class-conscious, perhaps republican, feelings of disdain for the haughty rich who heap scorn upon humble people; people who in reality are the true saints of God. As messages from the Lord, the Smiths understandably placed great value on these dreams. Lucy could still remember her husband's description of them in vivid detail forty years after they occurred. Much more important, Joseph Smith, Jr., not only knew the dreams intimately, but incorporated a version of the second dream into the Book of Mormon.[14]

Although the Smiths found little to their liking in the conventional churches, Lucy felt troubled over their failure to join a congregation and waged an intermittent battle to get the family to join, first the Methodist, and then the Presbyterian church.[15] In the religious fervor stimulated by the Second Great Awakening, the churches mounted an awesome crusade to revitalize their members and capture the hearts and minds of the unchurched. In large part, women played the role of God's fifth column in this movement, subverting irreligion in the household.[16] Lucy proved no exception to this general pattern. On several occasions, she apparently persuaded her son Joseph to attend church with her, but he did not find the experience edifying. Joseph later claimed he wanted to jump and shout at revivals and "get religion" just like everyone else, but found he just could not feel "the spirit." Lucy and several of her children finally decided to put aside doctrinal objections for the greater good of church attendance and joined the Presbyterians. Her husband, meanwhile, stayed at home unrepentant in his scorn of organized religion. Joseph, Jr., fell somewhere between his parents, holding himself aloof from the churches, yet admitting a preference for the Methodists.[17] Throughout the 1820s, the Smith family remained divided over religion until Joseph founded the Mormon church.

The family quarrels over church attendance, their never-ending economic insecurity, and the injustice of their social position tormented Joseph, Jr. In these circumstances, it is hardly surprising he should come to crave some form of certainty. Unfortunately, as a teenager, he could do little to resolve these problems: he worked for his father, supplemented his family's income by hiring out his labor to neighbors, and participated in a series of quixotic searches for hidden treasure. More important, instead of retreating into sullenness in the face of social rejection, he cultivated a prodigious personal charm—a quality that would serve him well as a prophet of God. However, Joseph eventually subsumed his economic and social worries into his overriding concern for religious security. He felt a principled repugnance for the fierce denominational struggle for membership. For a man who came to believe that unity and harmony represented the sine qua non of religious life, revivalism seemed more like "rivalism." At one point, the tangle of religious conflict drove him to the very verge of skepticism.[18] The inordinate stress each sect placed on its differences from the others served merely to confuse him. The religious divisions within his family intensified this confusion and made it all the more urgent that he resolve it. "In the midst of this war of words and tumult of opinions . . . " he asked himself, "what is to be done? Who of all these parties are right?"[19] According to the canonical version of the story, sometime in 1820 Joseph, now fourteen years of age, turned to the Bible in search of answers. In doing so, he came upon the Epistle of James and read James's injunction to those who lack wisdom to ask God for guidance (1:5). In obedience, Joseph went into the woods and prayed. Quite remarkably, both God and Jesus appeared in answer to his prayer. By his own account, Joseph then "asked the personages who stood above me in the light, which of all the sects was right—and which I should join. I was answered that I must join none of them, for they were all wrong, and the personage who addressed me said that all their creeds were an abomination in His sight: that those professors were all corrupt; that they draw near to me with their lips, but their hearts are far from me; they teach for doctrines the commandments of men: having a form of godliness, but they deny the power thereof. He again forbade me to join any of them."[20] When the epiphany ended, Joseph knew his father's Christian primitivism had been right after all, but it took nearly ten years before he could end his family's religious divisions by reuniting them in the "true church."

In the meantime, Joseph embarked upon another career. In 1822, he discovered a "seer stone" while digging a well. This stone, he claimed, gave him power to see hidden treasures buried in the earth; and for the next four years, he led sporadic money-digging expeditions in search of them. Few things he ever did would prove so harmful to his reputation. Both his subsequent opponents and many later historians have used this episode in his life to defame him as a smooth-talking charlatan who, poor but too lazy to work, conned the credulous out of money and property in wild-goose chases after easy wealth. Joseph's creation of Mormonism, they argued, simply represented a more sophisticated and profitable method of fleecing the gullible.

In a sense, Joseph's critics were right to see connections between Mormonism and his money digging. Like his invention of Mormonism, his money digging displayed, albeit in a lesser way, his powerful gift of persuasion, his concern for his family's welfare, and his religious inclination. Although Joseph never discovered treasure in the course of his money-digging adventures, he convinced men, some of them several times his age, of his power. In fact, he acquired a far-flung fame for his unusual talent. In 1826, a well-to-do farmer named Josiah Stowell traveled all the way from Bainbridge (now Afton), Pennsylvania, to seek Joseph's assistance in finding money he believed buried on his land. Joseph never found any money in Pennsylvania, but he did find his future wife, Emma Hale, whom he soon married. He also found trouble. Stowell's relatives watched dubiously as the prosperous farmer threw away their inheritance on what they considered a fantasy. In their eyes, Joseph was merely a confidence man; and, to put an end to things, they had him arrested. Historians still do not know with certainty on what charge he was arrested (probably as a "disorderly person") nor whether or not he was convicted (although it is likely), but Joseph clearly found the experience disagreeable, and his money-digging career abruptly ended.[21]

Yet if Smith's pursuits as a money digger did not lend credit to his career as a religious leader, they were not inconsistent with it. Marvin Hill has convincingly demonstrated that a taste for seer-stones and money digging were in no way singular to Smith, but enjoyed a widespread folk popularity throughout the rural northeastern United States. Hill notes, as well, that not just the Smiths, but a number of early Mormons, such as Oliver Cowdery, Martin Harris, Orrin P. Rockwell, Joseph Knight, and Josiah Stowell, at one time or another tried their hand at money digging or divining before joining Joseph's church. Both Mormons and non-Mormons thought of these unusual powers in religious terms and explained them as spiritual gifts. Joseph's father understood his son's ability to peer into the earth as a "wonderful gift which God had so remarkably given" and lamented only its use "in search of filthy lucre."[22] When Smith repudiated money digging after 1826, he did not repudiate his seer-stone, but used it to translate part of the Book of Mormon and apparently prized it long afterwards.[23] Furthermore, it is probably unfair of his critics to charge Joseph with using money digging as a replacement for hard work. If he was as "lounging" and "idle" in his youth as some have characterized him, he must have subsequently undergone a striking transformation for, in his calling as a prophet he evinced a prodigious capacity for work. His family, however, did need money; and, as usual, Smith simply blended his hopes for wealth with his religious inclination. His preoccupation with finding hidden money appears to have been a "mystical means of acquiring money (and status) which the family sorely needed."[24]

Joseph's search for buried treasure served as a method by which he might solve his family's troubles. Mormonism was another. Yet while money digging, if successful, might allow the Smith family to take a rightful place in their society, Mormonism challenged that society's legitimacy and instead offered the Smiths a prominent place in a new order. Joseph's first vision marked the initial step in this direction. Even as he strove to improve his family's position in the existing society, a part of his mind turned toward overthrowing it altogether.

On the night of September 21, 1823, about a year after he found his seer-stone, Joseph retired to bed laden with a guilty conscience because of his "weakness and imperfections." According to his account, he prayed to God for the "forgiveness of all my sins and follies, and also for a manifestation to me, that I might know of my state and standing before Him."[25] In the midst of this supplication, an intense light flooded the room, and he saw a white-robed angel who identified himself as Moroni, a messenger from God. Moroni told Joseph that the Lord had work for him to do. This honor brought peril, as well as glory, Moroni warned, for Joseph's "name should be had for good and evil among all nations, kindred, and tongues."[26] Moroni then informed Joseph he must bring to the knowledge of the world a book "written upon golden plates, giving an account of the former inhabitants of this continent, and the sources from whence they sprang. He also said that the fullness of the everlasting Gospel was contained in it, as delivered by the Savior to the ancient inhabitants; also that there were two stones in sliver bows—and these stones, fastened to a breastplate, constituted what is called the Urim and Thumnin—deposited with the plates; and the possession and use of these stones were what constituted 'Seers' in ancient or former times; and that God had prepared them for the purpose of translating the book."²⁷ Moroni appeared twice more during the night, repeating the identical message of his first visitation.

Joseph's worries about his family's troubled financial condition played a central part, if not the sole part, in stimulating his creation of Mormonism. He himself left a record of how the two things were interconnected in his mind, although, to the degree to which he recognized this connection, it only served to further his anxieties and fill him with self-reproach. On Moroni's third visit, Joseph stated, the angel had cautioned him, warning "that Satan would try to tempt me, (in consequence of the indigent circumstances of my father's family,) to get the plates for the purpose of getting rich. This he forbade me, saying that I must have no other object in view in getting the plates but to glorify God, and must not be influenced by any other motive than that of building up His kingdom; otherwise I could not get them."²⁸

Joseph's family expressed an unfeigned joy on the following day when he told them of Moroni's visit. Yet while everyone looked forward with great excitement to his recovery of the plates, it would take another four years before he could announce that he had found them. Smith explained the delay as a period of testing he had to endure before the Lord deemed him worthy to possess them. Joseph knew the plates lay somewhere in an old Indian mound (the "Hill Cumorah" in the Book of Mormon) near his family's farm; and every year on the anniversary of Moroni's visit, he repaired there to try and unearth them once more. Moroni's admonition to him not to regard the plates as a means to wealth was well-advised. Joseph reported that on his first visit to Cumorah he did not find them because Satan tempted him to seek "the Plates to obtain riches" and not "the glory of God."²⁹ Lucy, similarly, recorded that on his second trip he managed to secure the box containing the plates, but then "the unhappy thought darted through his mind that there was probably something else inside the box besides the plates, which would bring some pecuniary advantage to him."³⁰ When he put down the box and turned away for a moment, it disappeared. Of possibly greater significance was Joseph's reaction in 1826 when his family's fortune plunged to its nadir. With only a single mortgage payment outstanding, the Smiths lost their farm. It was a tragic loss, deeply felt by all. Not long afterward, Joseph announced his severe chastisement by an angel for not having "been engaged enough in the work of the Lord; that the time had come for the Record to be brought forth."[31] He received the plates on the next anniversary of Moroni's visit. In the end, the plates did bring economic security to his family, although not in the crude fashion Smith earlier envisioned. Years later, as the successful prophet of the Mormon church, Joseph reminded his troublesome younger brother, William, "You know the doctrine I teach is true, and you know that God has blessed me. I brought salvation to my father's house, as an instrument of God when they were in a miserable condition."[32]

Joseph finally proclaimed his acquisition of the plates on September 22, 1827. This date marks the formal beginning of his rebellion against the religious and social injustice his family had suffered. Ironically, however, the young prophet soon swirled in a vortex of controversy that far exceeded the hated disorder of the past decade. Despite the Smith family's attempt at secrecy, word of the "golden bible" spread quickly throughout the area. Even before the publication of the Book of Mormon, public reaction was loud and sharply divided. Joseph found willing believers, but many more scoffers. The contempt in which many of their neighbors had always held the Smiths now poured forth in open hostility. More seriously, the family's creditors vigorously pressed for the payment of debts. At one point, a creditor offered Joseph's penniless father a choice between disavowing his son's religious claims or imprisonment for debt. He chose jail.[33] Joseph himself lived in constant physical peril and plunged into a highly dramatic life of subterfuge and narrow escape. People made frequent attempts to steal the plates from him: some in hope of riches, others with the aim of exposing fraud. The persecution finally became so intolerable that Joseph fled with his new bride, Emma, back to her home territory of Susquehanna, Pennsylvania. Thus, he undertook the first of his many flights under the threat of persecution.

In Pennsylvania, Joseph hoped to find the peace to "translate" what he termed the "reformed Egyptian" of the golden plates into English. Toward that end, a wealthy New York farmer named Martin Harris had provided the funds for his flight and he, with Emma, served as Joseph's scribe. Nevertheless, the writing went slowly. Harris, as he would ever after, proved a mixed blessing for the prophet. After dictating 116 pages of manuscript, Joseph was cajoled into letting Harris take them back to New York to show his skeptical wife. The result was a disaster, for the manuscript disappeared. While historians do not know what happened for certain, it is generally suspected that Harris's wife destroyed the manuscript. Joseph fell into despair upon learning this, knowing that he could not make an exact reproduction of the earlier portion. Charges of fraud seemed inevitable if the missing pages should later come to light and be compared for discrepancies with any second version. It took a revelation from God to right the situation. Joseph would not rewrite the first section, but rely on another abridged version of the same material included with the plates. Understandably, the Lord also strictly commanded him to not allow the new manuscript out of his possession.

Joseph went back to New York, and in April 1829 acquired a new scribe, a bright young school teacher named Oliver Cowdery. With the aid of the able Cowdery, Joseph now began dictating at an amazing pace, completing work on the volume in ninety days. As Klaus Hansen points out, this meant, roughly, an output of around three thousand words a day.[34] Upon finishing the manuscript, Joseph invited eleven friends and family members to view the heretofore unseen plates and, with divine aid, affirm the accuracy of his translation. Martin Harris, one of these witnesses, atoned for his past sins by offering his farm as surety on the profits of publications. On March 26, 1830, 5,000 copies were made available to a candid public.

The Book of Mormon was Joseph Smith's clarion call against the world he grew up in. In his long-suffering family's torment, he found in microcosm the bitter fruit of a society going bad. On poor land with meager resources, the Smiths had labored desperately against the press of poverty year after year with only scant effect. Scornful neighbors denigrated these efforts, more ready to grind the faces of the poor than extend the hand of charity. Worst of all, the churches had fallen away from the true religion of Christ. They had abandoned the humble saints of God when they should have played the leading role in binding up society's wounds. Instead, hireling priests gave sanction to social oppression in their lust for personal gain and fostered divisions rather than harmony. In the Book of Mormon, Joseph systematized all these inchoate discontents of his family into one coherent protest.

chapter 2

The Book of Mormon as a Republican Document

Republican sentiments were not the cause of Joseph Smith's dissatisfaction with American society; that came from a specific sense of religious, social, and economic oppression. Yet the values of republicanism offered him a framework within which to analyze his feelings of injury, and to plot his course of action. In the Book of Mormon, he fused the religious and republican values that he and an entire subculture of American society held into an urgent expression of their fears and aspirations. God, Smith said, had chosen Americans to be His people, to redeem themselves and ultimately humanity. Americans, in fact, had gladly shouldered this burden up through the time of the Founding Fathers. Unfortunately, by Smith's day, they had turned away from building the just and holy society, and were embracing all manner of vice and wickedness. The entire society seemed to teeter on the brink of irredeemable corruption. If Americans would not return to godly ways, they were doomed. Only speedy repentance, Smith warned, could stay God's wrathful destruction of this new American Babylon.

Ostensibly, the Book of Mormon has little to do with the America of 1830. Its plot opens in 600 B.C., when God forewarned a Hebrew prophet named Lehi of the impending Babylonian captivity. Lehi accordingly gathered his family and followers together and fled Jerusalem. For a number of years, they wandered through wilderness until they reached the sea. There, under divine guidance, they built a ship and commenced an arduous ocean voyage that eventually deposited them on the shores of what is now called America. Upon their arrival, long simmering family arguments finally divided Lehi's sons into two irreconcilable factions. Those who faithfully followed God, obeyed the

Law of Moses, and anxiously awaited the Messiah became known as Nephites, after Lehi's righteous son, the young prophet Nephi. Those who chose the way of darkness and irreligion were called Lamanites, after Lehi's wicked son, Laman. The largest portion of the Book of Mormon recounts the incessant warfare between these two peoples. The Nephites strove for virtue, labored industriously, and lived according to their religious principles. Not infrequently, however, their very success seduced them into spiritual complacency, and their religious zeal waned. The constant labor of a series of prophets recalled them to faith. The Lamanites, on the other hand, became an idle, fierce, dark-skinned people, aroused from indolence only in expectation of plunder. When the Nephite prophets failed to reawaken the slumbering virtue of their people, God permitted the Lamanites to wage successful war against the Nephites until they remembered in their desperation the religion of their fathers. This cycle of virtue, fall, and religious rebirth continued until the advent of Christ, who came to his "other sheep" after His crucifixion in Jerusalem. In America, Jesus reunited the Nephites and Lamanites, chose twelve disciples, delivered teachings similar to those of the New Testament, and set in motion a two-hundred-year period of peace, prosperity, and righteousness. Unfortunately, the harmony Christ inspired gradually faded. One thousand years after Lehi landed in America, both branches of his descendants had become hopelessly corrupt. In a war of extinction, the Lamanites finally vanquished their ancient foes. In the twilight of Nephite civilization, the prophet Mormon hastily engraved upon golden plates an abridged version of a history kept by the prophets since Nephi. Shortly before his death, Mormon entrusted these plates to his son, Moroni, who added some words of his own and buried the plates in the Hill Cumorah before he too was killed. This Moroni, of course, was the angel who informed Joseph of the existence of the plates in 1823. At the end of the Book of Mormon, without the benefit of contact with Nephite society, the Lamanites grew more fierce, dark-skinned, and "loathsome" than ever before. Eventually they forgot their own history, and it is the descendants of these people, the Indians, whom Columbus discovered on his voyages to the New World.

The Book of Mormon is the masterpiece of a most uncommon common man. Despite his awkward writing style, wooden characters, and tediously chronic warfare, Joseph Smith not only voiced the protest of his less articulate countrymen but provided them with comprehensive and purportedly divine answers to their problems. In the oft-quoted words of the founder of the Disciples of Christ, Alexander Campbell, the Book of Mormon contains "every error and almost every truth discussed in N. York for the last ten years. He [Smith] decides all the great controversies—infant baptism, ordination, the trinity, regeneration, repentance, the fall of man, the atonement, transubstantiation, fasting, penance, church government, religious experience, the call of the ministry, the general resurrection, eternal punishment, who may baptize, and even the question of freemasonry, republican government and the rights of man."[1]

Obviously, the Book of Mormon is a seminal work, and its contents can be explored from diverse approaches. Yet even as it purports to relate the religious history of ancient America, it in fact proffers a stirring, if veiled, critique of Jacksonian America. Smith's critique in biblical tones at times sounds almost subversive to American society, but his argument on its most fundamental level employs the language and ideals of republican ideology generally shared by all Americans. Republican ideology, it will be recalled, characterized the ideal society as one composed of independent, industrious, self-reliant citizens. These citizens exemplified simplicity, frugality, and civic virtue and shunned luxury and dependence which demoralized society and led to threats of tyranny and anarchy. Having inherited similar biases toward wealth and labor from Puritan thought, Americans appropriated the Puritan jeremiad to voice their fears that society would collapse if they abandoned republican virtue. Thus the Book of Mormon with its cycle of virtue, decline, and reawakening displays a striking similarity to the canons of republican literature.[2]

The positive ideals of republicanism shine forth most clearly in the moral character Smith attributed to the Nephites. At their godly best, they exhibit the personal qualities of industriousness, self-restraint, and humble fidelity to the other divine precepts that most Americans deemed necessary both for individual success and for the maintenance of the republic. The prophet Nephi, for instance, recorded that shortly after his followers separated from the wicked Lamanites, "I did cause my people that they should be industrious, and that they should labor with their hands": a practice they continued as long as they remained worthy of God's favor.[3] Similarly, the Jaredites, a godly band of immigrants to America from the Tower of Babel, "were exceeding industrious," so much so that there "never could be a people more blessed than they, and more prospered by the Lord."⁴ Even groups of Lamanites, who on occasion converted to the Nephite religion, marked their change of heart by quickly abandoning their indolent ways and beginning to "labor exceedingly."⁵

Not only did Smith cast his exemplars of godly virtue as industrious and diligent workers, he also, like a good republican, commended certain occupations as productive and denounced others as parasitical. Lawyers and merchants, for example, he condemned as economic oppressors. He sometimes praised craftsmen adept at metal work, carpentry, or weaving, but he reserved his strongest approbation for farmers. Americans generally extolled the yeoman farmer as the epitome of industriousness, independence, and civic virtue, and so it is in the Book of Mormon. Thus, the righteous refugees who followed the great Nephite prophet, Alma, out of the clutches of the tyrannical King Noah had no sooner reached safety than they "pitched their tents, and began to till the ground, and began to build buildings, &c.; yea, they were industrious, and did labor exceedingly."⁶ The converted Lamanites, too, abjured their wild nomadic past and began "tilling the ground, raising all manner of grain, and flocks, and herds of every kind."⁷

The diligence the Nephite brought to his labor made for earthly success but, ironically, also threatened to ruin him. Republicans insisted that if wealth became the ultimate end of a citizen's striving, he fell prey to corruption and imperiled his independence; allegiance to the republican moral code ensured society's well-being. So, too, in the Book of Mormon with obedience to the commandments of God. The Nephites, like good republicans, understood both the blessings and temptations of wealth. They often succumbed to temptation, but in the wake of the consequent disaster, they remembered the Lord, and their religious rebirth fostered a new commitment to industry and revived prosperity. In one such case after a series of disastrous wars

> the people of Nephi began to prosper again in the land, and began to multiply and to wax exceeding strong again in the land. And they began to grow exceeding rich; but notwithstanding their riches, or their strength, or their prosperity, they were not lifted up in pride of their eyes; neither were they slow to remember the Lord their God; but they did humble themselves exceedingly before him; yea, they did remember how great things the Lord had done for them, that he

had delivered them death, and from bonds, and from prisons, and from all manner of afflictions; and he had delivered them out of the hands of their enemies. And they did pray to the Lord their God continually, insomuch that the Lord did bless them, according to his word, so that they did wax strong, and prosper in the land.[8]

Not only the common Nephite, but also his leaders, tilled the earth. For the Nephites' rulers to live by "glutting in the labors of the people" would be immoral.[9] Republicans believed that such specialization in a society weakened its elements; only by remaining absolutely independent would each citizen preserve his own virtue and that of the republic. Similarly, the Nephite prophets, as special agents of God, were not common people, but they were expected to live like them. Good King Benjamin, who spent his days in service to his people, personifies this attitude: "[I] sought [neither] gold nor silver, nor no manner of riches of you." He did not cast them into prison and make them into slaves, but encouraged the highest morals and obedience to God. "I, myself," he continued, "have labored with mine own hands, that I might serve you, and that ye should not be laden with taxes."[10] Benjamin exhorted his followers to go and do likewise. One of those who did so was Benjamin's son, King Mosiah, who "did cause his people to till the earth. And he also, himself did till the earth, that thereby he might not become burdensome to his people."[11] Joseph Smith, who angrily denounced the "priests" of his day as idle parasites sponging off their flocks, portrayed the Nephite prophets as commanding their priests not to act similarly. Thus, the prophet Alma enjoins his priests "not to depend upon the people for their support," but to "labor with their own hands."[12] There would be no idle luxury-loving aristocrats among the people of Nephi.

The "priestcraft" practiced by Protestant ministers seemed to Smith only a single facet, albeit an important one, of American society's growing inegalitarianism and dedication to self-seeking. Although Smith's words of protest at times curiously presage Karl Marx, he did not so much forge revolutionary religious ideals as resurrect older New England values of subservience to authority and communalism. In the Book of Mormon, Smith has the prophet Alma command "that the people of the Church should impart of their substance, every one according to what he hath; if he hath more abundantly, he should impart more abundantly; he that hath little, but little should be required; and to him that hath not should be given. And thus they should impart of their substance, of their own free will and desires toward God, and to those priests who stood in need, yea, and to every needy naked soul."[13] Smith, through King Mosiah, anticipated the argument of the haughty rich man who might argue that the poor deserved their poverty: "Perhaps thou shalt say, the man hath brought upon himself his misery, therefore I will not give unto him of my food or impart unto him of my substance, that he may not suffer, for his punishments are just." Mosiah responded to this by asserting that we are all beggars. Our wealth and our life depend upon God. If He gives to us, should we not give sustenance to our fellow children of God? To condemn the poor is to risk our own condemnation by the Lord.[14]

Despite Smith's strong empathy for the poor, he did not romanticize them. "There are three kinds of poor," he later explained, "the Lord's poor, the devil's poor, and the poor devils."[15] The Mormon commitment to the work ethic is legendary, and Smith fully expected those in need to be worthy of charity. After Mosiah pressed the claim of the poor upon the rich man, he lectured the poor man to labor assiduously on his own behalf, "that he might win the prize."[16] The picture of the ideal citizen in the Book of Mormon bears an unmistakable resemblance to that drawn by republican ideologists. The model Nephite is not the poor man, but an industrious, self-reliant, middling farmer who disdains luxury and self-seeking at the expense of others and at the same time displays a sensitive concern for his community and the poor.

The political state in the Book of Mormon is not formally a republic but a theocracy, ruled first by kings and then by judges. Nevertheless, the political sentiments espoused by the Nephites rang just as familiarly in the ears of Jacksonians as did their social values. When King Mosiah decided to end monarchy in favor of popularly elected judges, he spoke in terms of equal rights and privileges. "This inequality" of kingship, said Mosiah, "should be no more in this land especially among this my people; but I desire that this be a land of liberty, and every man may enjoy his rights and privileges alike, so long as the Lord sees fit, that we may live and inherit the land; yea, even as long as any of our posterity remaineth on the face of the land."[17] The prophet Alma, whose son would win election as the first chief judge, spoke for God Himself in denouncing monarchy, saying, "Behold, it is not expedient you have a king; for thus saith the Lord: Ye shall not esteem one flesh above another."[18] Monarchy, then, is not only unjust, but akin to idolatry.

Yet Smith has even these men, who destroy kingship in the land of the Nephites, cast a wistful glance back at monarchy. At the same moment that Alma pronounced the Lord's repugnance for kingship, he informed his followers, "If it were possible that ye could always have just men to be your kings, it would be well for you to have a king."[19] Even Mosiah, as he led the attack on monarchy as inherently inegalitarian, told the Nephites that if they could always have good kings like his father Benjamin, "it would be expedient that ye should always have kings to rule over you."[20] Smith created Mormonism, in large part, as a conservative response to anarchistic aspects of society, and he clearly entertained a certain romanticism about a righteous, almost Hobbesian, ruler, who dispenses justice above Society's fray. Even after he ends monarchy in the Book of Mormon, his chief judges continue in this mode; and he, no doubt, viewed his own role as prophet on comparable lines.

When Alma and Mosiah sighed over the demise of monarchy, they knew it was the odd bad king who spoiled it for everybody. In the American Revolution, patriots deemed George III a tyrant bent on enslaving the colonists through the usurpation of their liberties, the imposition of oppressive taxes, and the spread of corruption through royal patronage and placement. The New England clergy feared the spread of religious error through the anticipated installation of an Anglican bishop in Boston. Mosiah, likewise, noted that evil kings "teareth up the laws," lead their citizens into bondage, spread religious abominations, and enforce their will through their "friends in iniquity."[21] "How much iniquity," he exclaimed, "doth one wicked king cause to be committed! Yea, and what destruction!"[22] Mosiah suggested, however, that the price of bloodshed and contention to overthrow a tyrannical king was too high even in the unlikely event of successful revolution. It would be better to have no kings at all than to suffer through the occasional bad ones.

In the literary overthrow of monarchy, Smith has his Nephite society embrace rule by "the voice of the people" in its stead. That he entertained some ambivalence about democracy seems clear from the favorable remarks he put in the mouths of his prophets concerning kingship. Smith's endorsement of democracy in the Book of Mormon has a backhanded quality in the same spirit as Winston Churchill's quip that democracy was the worst possible form of government—except for all the rest. Smith, for instance, allows Mosiah, the leading architect of the Nephites' republican government, only a guarded, provisional approval of popular rule: "Now it is not common that the voice of the people desireth any thing contrary to that which is right; but it is common for the lesser part of the people to desire that which is not right; therefore this ye shall observe, and make it your law to do business by the voice of the people. And if the time cometh that the voice of the people choose iniquity, then is the time that judgments of God will come upon you."[23] Although Smith cast his vote on the side of majorities, he knew, and would later come to know even better, that democracy does not ensure righteousness.

Smith, however, does not abandon the evils of monarchy for the evils of isocracy. He instead has the Nephites create a government by judges who rule in an almost kingly fashion. Still, judicial government in the Book of Mormon works in roughly the same manner as it does in the American legal system. There exists a series of higher and lower courts, and a litigant could appeal an unfavorable decision all the way up to the chief judge, who ultimately governed the nation. Judges served a life tenure with good behavior; but, if a higher judge was found to be unrighteous, a body of lower judges could impeach him and the "voice of the people," the jury, would decide his fate.[24]

Although the election of judges and the impeachment process in the Book of Mormon fail to meet traditional American standards, Smith clearly portrays them as republican procedures. For example, when the wicked Amlici wished to overturn the rule of judges and establish himself as king, he offered himself to the people as a political candidate. Soon both his followers and opponents launched what has the appearance of political conventions, for and against his election. Finally, "it came to pass that the people assembled themselves together throughout all the land, every man according to his mind, whether it were for or against Amlici, in separate bodies, having much dispute and wonderful contentions one with another; and thus they did assemble themselves together, to cast their voices concerning the matter: and they were laid before the judges. And it came to pass that the voice of the people came against Amlici, that he was not made king over the people."[25] In another instance, three sons of a deceased chief judge named Paharon, Paanchi, and Pacumeni "did contend for the judgment seat, which did also cause the people to contend."²⁶ In the election that followed, "Paharon was appointed by the voice of the people to be a Chief Judge and a governor over the people of Nephi." Pacumeni acted as a member of the loyal opposition: "When he saw that he could not obtain the judgment seat, he did unite with the voice of the people."²⁷ His brother Paanchi, however, resisted the election returns and unsuccessfully tried to raise a rebellion. For his treason, he "was tried according to the voice of the people, and condemned to death, for he had raised up in rebellion and sought to destroy the liberty of the people."²⁸ The point worth noting here is the emphasis on "the voice of the people" as the final political authority. Despite their "princely" status, neither an eldest son nor any son had any special right to the judgment seat. Elections in this and in the previous case were decided between candidates and serious issues and did not appear merely as a formality, as the traditional acclamation of a king usually was.²⁹

Similarly, despite the fact that Smith gave very little attention to political procedure in the Book of Mormon, there is an account of an attempted impeachment, the outline of which seems consistent with republican values. Some Nephites demanded that "a few particular points of the law should be altered." Chief Judge Paharon, who perceived the wicked nature of these changes, refused, and a warm dispute ensued. Those who wished for the changes, known as "king-men," began calling for Paharon's removal from the judgment seat. Those opposing the alterations, "freemen," labored to support the chief judge. It is true that no body of lower judges sought to impeach him, but the passage is brief and silent as to any mode of removal attempted. On the other hand, "the voice of the people" that constituted the jury in impeachment trials decided the matter on the side of the freemen.³⁰ While this impeachment episode does not explain operative methods, it is no vaguer than the other political processes in the Book of Mormon. Most of the religious principles promulgated in the Book of Mormon would be dead letters if subjected to a similar standard.

The drama of war caught Joseph Smith's imagination far more than the machinations of bureaucracy. The Nephites, however, never fought wars of aggression and always justified their fighting by principles Jacksonian republicans would have acknowledged as just. Once when fighting against desperate odds, the Nephites nevertheless managed to carry the day against the Lamanites because they "were inspired by a better cause; for they were not fighting for monarchy nor power; but they were fighting for their homes, and their liberties, their wives, their children, and their all; yea for their rights of worship and their church; and they were doing that which they felt it was the duty which they owed to their God."[31]

In a series of protracted wars with domestic opponents and the Lamanites, there emerged a great Nephite hero named Moroni, whose martial prowess and inspirational character make him the most outstanding of the many warriors in the Book of Mormon. General Moroni, however, is no humble figure of republican virtue, but of republican *virtù*; that is, he had the will and energy to shape his own destiny and win his independence. Like Andrew Jackson, he could cut through formal legal niceties to establish or maintain liberty in an aggressive, dynamic fashion. Yet Smith made it plain that despite his fierce eagerness for battle, Moroni fought for his country's freedom and religion. He did not, wrote Smith, "delight in bloodshed; a man whose soul did joy in liberty and the freedom of his country, and his brethren from bondage and slavery; yea, a man whose heart did swell with thanksgiving to God, for the many privileges and blessings which he bestowed upon his people; a man who did labor exceedingly for the welfare and safety of his people; yea, and he was a man firm in the faith of Christ, and he had sworn with an oath, to defend his people, his rights, and his country, and his religion, even to the loss of his blood."[32]

One of Moroni's most famous battles began when Amaliciah, a man of strong monarchist ambitions, succeeded in fomenting a revolt against the government. Moroni quickly sprang to his government's defense and in a fit of passion "rent his coat; and took a piece thereof, and wrote upon it, In the memory of our God, our religion, and freedom, and our peace, our wives, and our children; he fastened it upon the end of a pole thereof . . . (and he called it the title of liberty.)"[33] The Nephites soon rallied around his standard and the battle was engaged.[34]

In another case, Moroni anticipates Frederick Jackson Turner and many a grumbling nineteenth-century pioneer. In a letter to Chief Judge Paharon, Moroni complained that, unlike the men on the frontier, the Nephites in the secure eastern region had grown complacent in the cause of freedom. They consequently failed to provide the necessary support for those actively fighting and dying for liberty on the

Lamanite borders. This indifference, charged Moroni, amounted to nothing less than treason. If the people of the heartland did not soon manifest "the true spirit of freedom," the general warned, "I will stir up insurrections among you, even until those who hath desires to usurp power and authority, shall become extinct."[35] Paharon, in response, apologized for Moroni's problems and affirmed his dedication to "the rights and liberty of my people." Yet Paharon had troubles too, for Moroni had accurately sensed a waning devotion to freedom among certain of his countrymen. Monarchists, the perennial disrupter of Nephite domestic harmony, had risen in revolt and made their stronghold Zarahemla, the capital and largest city in the land. Upon receiving this intelligence, Moroni returned from his campaign against the Lamanites. He soon crushed the rebellion and, after a "trial, according to law," duly executed those found guilty of subverting "the cause of freedom."[36]

In these events, Moroni and his followers seem the stock figures American revolutionary theorists had in mind when discoursing on the necessary character of citizens of a republic. Living a spartan life on the frontier, they had not become debilitated by the luxury and vices available to their countrymen. Under the constant threat of having their liberty taken from them by the Lamanites, they exerted the eternal vigilance necessary for its preservation. It is likewise appropriate, although perhaps fortuitous in the story, that the monarchists inhabit the safe settled regions of the country, for cities in the republican canon generally represented dens of luxury, vice, corruption, and all things antithetical to republicans.

The Book of Mormon's positive vision of society falls readily into republican categories. The godly Nephite labors assiduously, usually at tilling the soil; he idealizes social and political egalitarianism; and he goes to war for traditionally republican reasons. But the Book of Mormon is a work of protest; and for every word in praise of the godly life, ten criticize corrupt practices. Indeed, even more than in its prescription for righteous conduct, the Book of Mormon's denunciation of unvirtuous behavior demonstrates its fidelity to the canons of republicanism.

This is true of nothing so much as Smith's attack on luxury. Classical theorists feared that the republican virtues of simplicity, economy, and industry would ironically result in the amassing of the large fortunes necessary to cater to luxurious desires. In turn, the widespread satisfaction of these desires would endanger the republic. A man who desired more than he needed could be tempted to sell his political liberties for material advantage. By the same token, the very wealthy citizen had the wherewithal to undermine the civic virtue of others by reducing them to dependence on himself. When the public good was ignored in favor of private interest, the republic would be at an end.

In America the legacy of Puritanism strengthened the republican fears of luxury. Edmund Morgan, in tracing the Puritan ethic in the thought of the American revolutionaries, has observed that the

> Puritans were always uncomfortable in the presence of prosperity. Although they constantly sought it, although hard work combined with frugality could scarcely fail in the New World to bring it, the Puritans always felt more at ease when adversity made them tighten their belts. They knew that they must be thankful for prosperity, and that like everything good in the world it came from God. But they also knew that God could use it as a temptation, that it could lead to idleness, sloth, and extravagance. These were vices, not simply because they in turn led to poverty, but because God forbade them. Adversity, on the other hand, though a sign of God's displeasure, and therefore a cause of worry, was also God's means of recalling a people to him. When God showed anger man knew he must repent and do something about it. In times of drought, disease, and disaster a man could renew his faith by exercising frugality and industry, which were good not simply because they would lead to a restoration of prosperity, but because God demanded them.[37]

This passage is worth quoting at length because in almost every particular Joseph Smith shared the opinion of his New England forebears and portrayed the Nephites struggling with the temptation of luxury along lines Puritans and republicans would have readily understood.

Strictly speaking, both Nephites and republicans agreed that there was nothing wrong with wealth so long as its possessors continued to retain their civic spirit and walk humbly with God. The problem in the Book of Mormon is that they never do. No Solomon appears who keeps his relationship with the Lord as well as his wealth and glory. The successful Nephite prophet always lives simply, labors with his hands, and makes generous worldly sacrifices to spread the gospel. Whenever Smith declared the Nephites industrious and in the midst of prosperity, it was certain that disaster lay in the offing. In a passage typical of many in its description of the evils of luxury, Smith wrote, "It came to pass in the eighth year of the reign of Judges, that the people of the church began to wax proud, because of their exceeding riches, and their fine silks, and their fine twined linen, and because of their many flocks and herds, and their gold, and their silver, and all manner of precious things, which they had obtained by their industry; and in all these things were they lifted up in the pride of their eyes, for they began to wear costly apparel."[38]

Inevitably, the Nephites' sinful pride in their worldly possessions led to further sin. Perhaps reflecting the dire poverty of his youth and the scorn his family received from its more prosperous neighbors, Smith dwelt at considerable length on the sins of the wealthy and the threat they posed to society. The rich in the Book of Mormon never remained content merely to enjoy their wealth, but took delight in grinding the faces of the poor. Those in the church obsessed with "the vain things of the world" frequently worked to transform the public good into their private interest by "persecut[ing] those that did not believe according to their will and pleasure."[39]

Smith often specified merchants and lawyers as the persecutors of the poor in the Book of Mormon. This accords with the republican view that not all occupations merited equal approval. Traditionally, theorists feared that, unlike farmers, merchants and lawyers might not possess sufficient allegiance to republicanism because they pandered to luxury, lived parasitically upon the troubles and desires of others, and held no attachment to the land. Smith demonstrated similar prejudices, sometimes implying that the mere presence of these professions was a symptom of social decadence. In the twenty-ninth year of the reign of Judges, he wrote, "there began to be some disputing among the people; and some lifted up into pride and boasting, because of their exceeding riches, yea, even unto great persecutions: for there were many merchants in the land, and also many lawyers and many officers."[40] Similarly, in the Book of Mormon's most extended treatment of lawyers, Smith pictured them as self-seeking men who craftily oppose repentance and deny truth for selfish advantage. The sole "object of these Lawyers," wrote Smith, "was to get gain."[41]

If lusting after "gain" represented an occupational hazard for lawyers and merchants and threatened the harmony of Nephite society, "priestcraft" menaced the Nephites with "their entire destruction."[42] Nehor, its archetypal practitioner, would preach any doctrine for money even if it imperiled the souls of his listeners. Smith believed priestcraft the leading sin of the churches in his own day and took aim particularly at Universalists when he had Nehor declare unto the people that every priest and teacher had ought to become popular; and they ought not to labor with their own hands, but that they had ought to be supported by the people; and he also testified unto the people that all mankind should be saved at the last day, and that they need not fear nor tremble, but that they might lift up their heads and rejoice: for the Lord had created all men, and had also re-deemed all men; and in the end, all men should have eternal life. And it came to pass that he did teach these things so much, that many did believe on his words, even so many that they began to support him and give him money; and he began to be lifted up in the pride of his heart, and to wear very costly apparel; yea, and even began to establish a church, after the manner of his preaching.[43]

Nehor later tried to enforce his priestcraft by the sword, slaying a true man of God he could not defeat with words. Before Chief Judge Alma executed him, Nehor recanted his words, but priestcraft persisted in Nephite society.[44]

Throughout the Book of Mormon, the Nephites are generally ruled by godly prophets, judges, and kings impervious to the temptations of luxury, but they do have one would-be tyrant of major significance named King Noah. No other figure in the volume is more corrupt or corrupting of others. Noah stands for everything a good republican despises. He holds no regard for the commandments of God or the community over which he rules, "but he did walk after the desires of his own heart." Noah passed "his time in riotous living with his wives and concubines" and gathered around himself wicked priests who had a taste for the same. These debauchees were "supported in their lazi-ness, and in their idolatry, and in their whoredom, by the taxes which King Noah had put upon his people; thus did the people labor exceed-ingly, to support iniquity."[45] The people, however, did not complain about Noah's Bacchanalian way of life because they too became cor-rupted by the king's words and example. When Noah turned the pub-lic interest into his private interest, the spread of corruption under-mined his once virtuous state. As a republican might have predicted, Noah's kingdom fell into ruin and his people became the slaves of the Lamanites. The recitation of Noah's career provided Joseph Smith with his platform to denounce the evils of monarchy. Alma revealed the Lord's strictures against kingship while a refugee from Noah's persecution, and Mosiah cited Noah's example to support government by "the voice of the people."

Nephite society faced greater challenges to its civic virtue, however, from "secret combinations" bent on internal subversion than from tyrants like King Noah. Smith introduced a number of secret organizations in the Book of Mormon, but none so famous as the "Gadiantons." Traditionally, non-Mormon historians have viewed the Freemasons as Smith's model for the Gadianton Robbers. Smith had the inspiration for such a portrait at hand: in September 1826, not far from Smith's home in upstate New York, William Morgan, an ex-Mason, was kidnapped and never seen again. Since Morgan had just completed writing an exposé of the secrets of Freemasonry, many people assumed the Masons had murdered him for his betrayal of their society. When it later appeared that the Masons had successfully used their political influence to thwart attempts to bring Morgan's murderers to justice, the countryside exploded in righteous indignation. During the next three years, roughly corresponding to the period of Smith's writing of the Book of Mormon, the local outrage over Morgan's alleged murder grew into a formidable anti-Masonry movement that had political repercussions throughout the entire northern half of the United States. With crusading fervor the anti-Masons trumpeted that the secret society endangered the existence of the republic. When each Mason swore a secret oath binding him to his order, he forfeited the political independence of mind necessary for the exercise of civic virtue: loyalty to Masonry replaced loyalty to the general community. In case after case, anti-Masons perceived a pattern of Masonic collusion to secure political and economic preferment in spite of the just claims of the community. Only the eradication of this insidious conspiracy, they argued, could save the republic from internal subversion.

Historians might contend, with perhaps some reason, that Masons, such as Andrew Jackson, did succeed in subverting the republic. In the Book of Mormon, however, Smith has the Masonlike Gadiantons play a far less cryptic role in undermining Nephite society for their private advantage. At the outset, Smith makes their Masonic character clear. Forgetting for a moment his attempt at a Jacobean biblical style, his description could easily pass for a contemporary republican critique of Freemasonry. When Nephites joined the Gadiantons, they

> did enter into their covenants, and their oaths, that they would protect and preserve one another, in whatsoever difficult circumstances they should be placed in, that should they should not suffer for their murders, and their plunderings, and their stealings.

And it came to pass that they did have their signs, yea, their secret signs, and their secret words; and this that they might distinguish a brother who had entered into the covenant, that whatsoever wickedness his brother should do, he should not be injured by his brother, nor by those who did belong to his band, who had taken this covenant; and thus they might murder, and plunder, and steal, and commit whoredoms, and all manner of wickedness, contrary to the laws of their country, and also to the laws of their God; and whosoever of those which belonged to their band, should reveal unto the world of their wickedness and abominations, should be tried, not according to the laws of their country, but according to the laws of their wickedness.[46]

What made the Gadiantons serious ideological opponents of republicanism rather than mere thugs were their political ambitions. Cynics have called government "organized theft," and the Gadiantons took this principle to its logical extreme. Hiding in the mountains, they terrorized peaceful communities, murdered four chief judges, and after substantial numbers of corrupted Nephites joined their band, "did obtain sole management of the government."[47]

The Nephites' complacency toward luxury brought on the scourge of the Gadiantons. Like other republicans, the time of ultimate danger to them lay not in periods of adversity, but when the going got too easy. Since the practice of republican virtue often led to wealth, and wealth to the evils of luxury, the Gadiantons emerged in a society corrupted by its own success. In explaining this point, Smith wrote that God had blessed the Nephites "so long with the riches of the world, that they had not been stirred up to anger, to wars, nor to bloodshed; therefore they began to set their hearts upon their riches; yea, they began to seek gain, that they might be lifted above one another; therefore they began to commit secret murders, and to rob, and to plunder, that they might get gain.—And now behold, those murderers and plunderers were a band which had been formed by Kishkumen and Gadianton."[48] The Gadianton tyranny came to an end and republican principles were restored only after severe chastisement from the Lord brought the Nephites to repentance. The Gadiantons' mischief, however, did not end with their removal from power. Smith had them return at the conclusion of the Book of Mormon to spark the war of extermination that brought Nephite civilization to a close.

Once morally debilitating luxury set in, republicans knew that only a speedy return to first principles could save their country. In the Jacksonian era, unprecedented economic change left most Americans better off than ever before but at a cost of equally unprecedented social disorder. In echoing the jeremiad of their Puritan ancestors, republicans warned of America's imminent fall unless they recaptured the heroic virtues of the revolutionary generation. Joseph Smith, no less than his fellow countrymen, employed the jeremiad both to warn his own generation of its corruption and, as the instrument wielded by his Nephite prophets, to arouse the slumbering virtues of their people. Alma, for instance, expressed his jeremianic concerns, demanding to know if his people would continue to

> trample the holy one under your feet; yea, can ye be puffed up in the pride of your hearts; ye still persist in the wearing of costly apparel, and setting your hearts upon the vain things of the world, upon your riches; yea, will ye persist in supposing [*sic*] that ye are better one than another; yea, will you persist in the persecutions of your brethren, who humble themselves, and do walk after the holy order of God . . . yea, and will you persist in turning your backs upon the poor, and the needy, and in withholding your substance from them? And finally, all ye that will persist in your wickedness, I say unto you, that these are they which shall be hewn down and cast into the fire, except they speedily repent.[49]

Similarly, when the people under Noah set their hearts on riches and became corrupt, God sent the prophet Abinadi to exhort them to repentance. Slavery, as every republican knew, was the ultimate price paid for the loss of civic virtue, and in accordance with his republican predilections, Smith has Abinadi warn that God would inflict them with "bondage" if they did not repent their wickedness.[50]

The lot of a Nephite prophet was a hard one; the people rarely listened to him. Abinadi, for instance, was executed for his pains. Smith routinely referred to the Nephites as a stubborn, "stiff-necked" people, and they are nothing if not ingrates. When God does "all things for the welfare and happiness of his people," wrote Smith, "they do harden their hearts, and do forget their Lord . . . because of their exceeding prosperity." This forces God to coerce their return to virtue by other means when His prophets fail to change the hearts of the people: "And thus we see, that except the Lord doth chasten his people with many afflictions, yea, except he doth visit them with death, and with terror, and with famine, and with all manner of pestilences, they will not remember him.[51] His Puritan forefathers interpreted natural disasters as divine warnings against sin; Smith actually inflicted them upon the erring Nephites.

Disease, pestilence, and famine were not the only means by which God recalled His people to Him. He assigned that role to the Lamanites as well. Early in the Book of Mormon when the children of Lehi split into two bands, the Lord informed the prophet Nephi that He would use the Lamanites as a "scourge unto thy seed, to store them up in remembrance of me."[52] Whereas the Nephites' self-satisfied complacency led them into the perils of overcivilization and tyranny, the Lamanites lived in anarchy, possessing few restraining influences of civilization at all. As "a loathsome people," whom God had cursed with dark skin, the Lamanites had no republican attachment to the land, but lived a nomadic life in tents. Wild, idolatrous, and ferocious, the Lamanites' chief occupation was plundering and murdering the Nephites. Though tireless in war, they were a "very indolent people" who fought for riches "so they might not labor for them with their own hands."[53] On this same principle, they introduced slavery and, in the words of the Nephite leader Zeniff, brought the people "into bondage that they might glut themselves upon the flocks of our fields."[54] Interestingly enough, as white Americans were sometimes attracted to the unrepublican characteristics of Indian life, members of the Nephites occasionally converted to Lamanite ways. When this occurred, the converted Nephites discarded all pretense to republican virtue and became "even more hardened and impenitent, and more wild, wicked, and ferocious, than the Lamanites; drinking in with all the traditions of the Lamanites; giving way to indolence and all manner of lasciviousness; yea, entirely forgetting the Lord their God."[55]

American political theorists believed that a republic was the best form of government, but it was also the frailest and most difficult to preserve. They saw the maintenance of civic virtue as a heroic task and felt by no means certain of the people's ability to hold fast against the constant threat of corruption. Thus, republican ideologists would have expressed little surprise at the conclusion of the Book of Mormon when the whole Nephite society fell into irredeemable corruption. Once they had lost their will for freedom, the Lamanites swept Nephite "republicanism" from the earth.

Clearly, Smith made God's values republican values. Like all creative thinkers, Smith tended to emphasize certain aspects of his ideology at the expense of others, but the Book of Mormon fits easily into a republican framework. God loves those who live simply, work hard, have an attachment to the land, and shun luxury. While the righteous jealously guard their independence, they are compassionate to the poor and deferential to their godly republican leaders and to the Lord Himself. To the Nephites who maintained these virtues, the Lord gave freedom, peace, and prosperity. Conversely, God does not love those who shun labor, or who have no attachment to the land; nor does He love those who use their wealth to corrupt the virtue of others or who are corrupted by their desire for wealth. Smith exemplified these vices in the grasping tyranny of King Noah, on the one hand, and in the anarchistic ways of the Lamanites, on the other. To such sinners, God sent prophets to call for a rebirth of virtue.

If the heart of the Book of Mormon was intended as a history of ancient America, illustrating timeless principles of religion and its foes, the volume begins and ends with a novel history of Christendom and a disquisition on the state of affairs in Joseph Smith's own day. According to Smith, the Devil destroyed the true religion of Jesus and his apostles by founding the Catholic church—a view not unfamiliar to American Protestants. The Pope and his minions held dear the same unrepublican values as King Noah: they lived in riotous debauchery, lusted after great wealth, and exerted themselves mainly in the persecution of the true saints of God.[56] Through their wicked measures, the "great and abominable church" had succeeded in enslaving all of Europe. God, however, was not without His own resources to aid His saints. The Lord had purposely hidden America from the world so that He might create a land of inheritance for His people, and it was He who inspired Columbus's discovery of this new "land of promise."[57] The immigrants who landed on these shores did not come randomly, but were actually "led out of other countries, by the hand of the Lord."[58] When these immigrants rose in rebellion against the efforts of "their mother Gentiles" to place them in captivity, God was with them and prospered their cause.[59] Between the destruction of the Nephites and the American Revolution, the Lord had lost none of His republican ardor. He still insisted, however, on virtue as the price of freedom and promised if Americans would "serve him according to the commandments which he hath given, it shall be a land of liberty unto them; wherefore they shall never be brought down into captivity."[60] God promised that monarchy would not rise in America because "I the Lord, King of Heaven, will be their king."[61]

Smith repeatedly referred to America as "a land which is choice above all others" in the eyes of God.[62] Yet despite the United States' special relationship with the Lord, it had come perilously close to losing His blessing by Smith's day. Fifty years after the Revolution, Americans were acting out the now familiar story of a corrupted people. They unconsciously followed in the footsteps of the fallen Nephites, turning their backs on righteousness. Americans set their hearts on wealth, scorned and oppressed the poor, and persecuted the humble saints of God. They had also permitted the growth of "secret combinations"—the Devil's method of "overthrow[ing] the freedom of all lands, nations, and countries."[63] All of these sins, however, paled in comparison to the corruption of the churches. Ministers not only sanctioned society's wickedness but practiced priestcraft, "set[ting] themselves up for a light unto the world, that they may get gain, and praise of the world; but they seek not the welfare of Zion."[64] The doctrinal acrimony spawned by denominational competition amounted to little more than a bidding war to win a flock to fleece. Sinfully, these "hireling priests" turned their backs on the godly poor who could not afford their favor.[65]

Smith held out America as the world's last best hope in the Book of Mormon. When it, too, began to share in the world's corruption, Smith knew it was a harbinger of the millennium. An angel warned readers of the Book of Mormon,

> If the Gentiles repent, it shall be well with them . . . whoso repenteth not, must perish; therefore, woe be unto the Gentiles, if it so be that they harden their hearts against the Lamb of God: for the time cometh, saith the Lamb of God, that I will work a great and marvellous work among the children of men; a work which shall be everlasting, either on the one hand or on the other; either to the convincing of them unto peace and life eternal, or unto the deliverance of them to the hardness of their hearts and blindness of their minds, unto their being brought down into captivity, and also onto destruction, both temporally and spiritually, according to the captivity of the Devil, of which I have spoken.[66]

God could not tolerate such wickedness much longer, especially from a people He claimed as His own. At the advent of the millennium, the Jews would return to Israel and convert to Christianity. Simultaneously, the other covenanted people, the Indians (Lamanites), would learn of their ancestors' history and find religious rebirth. If the gentiles persisted in unrighteousness, God would send the Indians to war against them, tearing them to pieces "as a young lion among flocks of sheep," a prophecy that angered and frightened gentiles on the frontier when Mormons began preaching to their Indian neighbors.[67]

God demanded repentance from Americans; but He mercifully intended to help them in their task. The Lord would raise a "choice seer" to guide them through the tumult of the "last days."[68] Smith, with an eye to his own ambition, resurrected the Biblical Joseph to declaim that the choice seer's "name shall be called after me; and it shall be after the name of his father."[69] In the days when the Catholic church held exclusive control over the Bible, it had removed "many plain and precious things . . . from the Book . . . causing an exceeding great many to stumble" and had given Satan power over them. The seer Joseph would restore these "plain and precious things" earlier lost by bringing "out of the earth" the record of the Nephites.[70] By this, of course, Smith meant the Book of Mormon that he claimed to have unearthed in the Hill Cumorah.

Yet while Smith extended to Americans the possibility of staying the Lord's wrath with speedy repentance, he doubted that many would grasp the opportunity. Smith placed his faith instead in a gathering of God's true saints. Jesus promised to enter into a covenant with these and reestablish His true church. Together they would "build a city, which shall assist my people that they may be gathered in, which are scattered upon all the face of the land, in unto the New Jerusalem. And then shall the power of heaven come down among them; and I also will be in the midst: and then shall the words of the Father commence, at that day even when this Gospel shall be preached among the remnant of this people."[71] Many Americans had long viewed the founding of the United States as the birth of the New Jerusalem. Joseph Smith, doubting that his countrymen would be either spiritually or civically reborn, transformed this general expectation into the actual building of a holy city like Jerusalem of old.

Joseph Smith inextricably fused his old-fashioned religious and republican values—as did most Americans. Yet, in practice, he was a radical. Most of his countrymen took a celebratory view of their society, extolling their own republicanism as a harbinger to the millennium. Americans often punished specific groups, such as Masons, for their allegedly antirepublican behavior; but most people understood these groups to be aberrant and serenely contemplated the general virtue of their fellow citizens. Smith considered the entire American mainstream of society as an aberration that had deserted the republican morality of its forefathers. In the guise of a prophet of the coming millennium, Smith in effect posed as the conservative defender of an older America crumbling under the social pressures of Jacksonian America. In the Book of Mormon, Smith filled new bottles with old wine; and thousands of socially rootless, economically insecure, and religiously confused Americans soon found they could savor the vintage.

Social Disorder and the Resurrection of Communal Republicanism among the Mormons

Both the Mormons and other Americans in the 1830s looked back upon the revolutionary era with nostalgic admiration. The Founding Fathers had not merely been heroic amidst grave peril; they embodied the personal qualities that enabled people to rise above their individual interests to act for the benefit of the common good. Their virtue had made the creation of an American republic possible; people now feared that they themselves might lack the virtue simply to maintain the Republic. The pursuit of self-interest had mounted to the point of rapaciousness; patriots feared it was sapping the moral fiber of the rest of the country. Only a return to the ways of the Founders, they warned, would stave off the Republic's incipient ruin.

The Edenic virtue and social harmony that antebellum Americans espied in the late eighteenth century had never existed, of course. The revolutionaries had their share of social, economic, and political troubles; and they, no less than their descendants, mourned the extinction of the social virtues of their fathers. Nevertheless, Jacksonian Americans accurately detected a social cohesiveness in the world of the Founders that was absent in their own. Although revolutionary America was never really the community of independent yeomen prescribed by republican ideology, it is remarkable just how close it had come in Jacksonian retrospect.[1] Rich and poor certainly existed, yet given the wide availability of land, the middling sort of farmers made up the vast majority of Americans. Furthermore, despite broad economic shifts in the late eighteenth century, Americans of the revolutionary era experienced little of the type of wrenching economic change inflicted upon early nineteenth-century Americans. Paradoxically, however, in the midst of their rough equality of condition, they still retained a lingering attachment to older views of social hierarchy. Americans understood their country or, more typically, their locality as an organic commonwealth in which society accorded to a natural aristocracy of uncommon men the benevolent rule of their humbler neighbors. Similarly, the master of each household held a responsibility for the general conduct and welfare of his dependents—his wife, children, servants, apprentices, or farm hands—irrespective of his own convenience. On Sunday, if he was a churchgoer, the master led his dependents to the Congregational, Presbyterian, or perhaps Episcopal church, where a learned divine affirmed that a stern, if no longer angry, God had ordained the social arrangement. Naturally these social relationships did not always result in harmony; masters could, and sometimes did, act like cruel tyrants; servants sometimes did not serve. Yet these ties, if occasionally oppressive, effectively provided a certain sense of social unity and harmony. Thus, if the Jacksonians' ancestor worship falsely turned the men and women of the revolutionary era into demigods, they were at least right in feeling that an older, more coherent social structure had crumbled without generating significant new social forms to take its place.

Between the passing of the revolutionary generation and the publication of the Book of Mormon in 1830, the old inherited colonial institutions and customs faltered under the onslaught of a massive economic upheaval and the uneasy applications of republicanism.[2] In 1776, the United States had consisted of little more than a narrow band of farms and towns hugging the Atlantic coast. By 1830, it spanned half the continent. New towns and farming communities quickly sprang up; new states were admitted as Americans on the move scurried to claim their share of the newly opened lands in the West. A transportation revolution in this period helped to stimulate the growth of a market economy as new roads, canals, and steamboats carried finished products west and returned east laden with the agricultural produce of the pioneers. In New England, the dawn of industrialization broke forth as entrepreneurs molded the men and women of rural areas, and later European immigrants, into a new proletarian labor force.

This change made most Americans more prosperous than their parents; some even became quite rich. Yet the cost to society was great. The wildly erratic economic climate filled many people with anxiety about the future. Their fortunes seemed less secure than in previous generations. Part of the problem stemmed from the process of settling the West. The frequent movement of families from one area to another left many people feeling rootless and isolated, a feeling exacerbated by the fact that these removals inhibited the growth of stabilizing institutions. To a person who would move on further west in a few years, civic concern often degenerated into the mere matter of a real estate transaction. Despite their troubles, however, westerners managed to produce cheap foodstuffs in such abundance that they undermined the marginal economic position of thousands of farmers who tilled the rocky soil of the Northeast. Many New England farmers sought to stave off disaster by sending their daughters to the new textile mills at places like Lowell or Waltham. When the even more desperate European immigrants, primarily those from Ireland, began flooding into the United States after the War of 1812, they replaced older Americans in the factories and other less desirable occupations. This new immigration had other important economic consequences. For instance, the new addition to the work force transformed America's habitual labor shortage into a sudden excess; indeed, an unemployment problem. Even the social structure of the older, larger eastern seaboard cities groaned under the impact of the dramatic influx of diverse groups of people. The problems of economic insecurity and social isolation, of course, only represented the direct costs of the ongoing economic revolution. The spreading epidemics of crime, alcoholism, and other social ills made manifest the inability of American institutions to cope with the fundamental shifts in the economic substructure of American life.

While the exploding economy was most directly responsible for creating social disarray, the egalitarian, individualistic thrust of the American Revolution exacerbated it. Curiously, while Americans between 1776 and 1830 let slip the republican ideal of approximate equality of condition in favor of the unrepublican reality of great disparities in wealth, they also exchanged the older undemocratic notions of elite rule for equal privilege. The embrace of republicanism proved to have leveling implications: old leaders, traditions, and patterns of deference came under fire. No longer did employers or employees need to govern the behavior of others or have their behavior governed; all should govern themselves. Increasingly, personal qualities of self-discipline, such as thrift, industry, sobriety, punctuality, and piety, served as sufficient proofs of good republican character.[3] These self-imposed values would not only make a person wealthy but benefit the country as a whole as well. The egalitarian sentiments that made both employers and their laborers' opinions equal before the ballot garnered a respect formerly reserved for the learned and social elite for the opinions of common folk in other areas of life, such as economics, theology, and even medicine. Men and women of humbler station now listened less to the traditional leaders of society and more to each other. A proliferation of newspapers, almanacs, and public spokesmen gave open expression to folk ideas long repressed. In religion, the Second Great Awakening spurred Americans to attend church in greater numbers than had their parents; but converts, now more obedient to their own consciences and stirred by denominational competition, fractured church bodies into a vast array of schismatic branches.[4] In the end, America's developing egalitarian individualism proved a mixed blessing. While it unquestionably gave more dignity and a greater social role to average citizens, it also weakened any potential source of leadership that might have contended more successfully with the problems that beset them. The ensuing confusion and social fragmentation only served to undermine the already shaky institutions battered by the nation's economic dislocations.[5]

Americans, of course, did not suffer the ravages of social disorder without a murmur. Jeremiads rang out across the land, warning that an unholy combination of vices—indolence, selfishness, luxury, and irreligion—all menaced the republic. Yet despite the omnipresent predictions of the nation's imminent fall, it is doubtful that many Jacksonians sincerely believed it would occur. They truly feared for their country, but they felt that the course of history had not yet slipped from their control. The real purpose of the jeremiad was to awaken a supposedly slumbering people to the necessity of social reform; indeed, a plethora of organizations soon sprang into existence to set the country aright. Missionary societies set out to convert the heathen in the West. Temperance reformers sought to reclaim the drunkard. Criminologists designed model prisons to remake wrongdoers into godly republican citizens. A host of fraternal orders and improvement societies shared problems and offered mutual support. These and many other groups offered positive, if not always effective, solutions to the nation's troubles. Unfortunately, this so-called explosion of "freedom's ferment" possessed its negative side as well. For some Americans, the word "reform" meant persecuting Irish-Americans, Masons, free blacks, or any other group they deemed insufficient in republican virtue. If these people lacked a proper respect for individualism, steady habits, and democratic institutions, guardians of republican values demonstrated an eagerness to teach them, even if it sometimes meant literally beating these values into their heads.

Many Americans wished to reform the Mormons in the same manner they wished to reform the Irish Catholics. Yet, ironically, the Mormon church itself came into existence as a conservative response to the perceived moral crisis gripping the nation. When on April 6, 1830, in Fayette, New York, Joseph Smith and five other men ordained each other the first elders in the Church of Christ, they saw themselves as initiating a "restoration movement" that would sweep away the corruptions of Babylon with the true gospel of the Savior.[6] No doubt these beginnings must have appeared unpropitious to all but Smith and his handful of devotees. After all, untold numbers of religious sects were being founded and forgotten all through the Northeast. Yet if the new church failed to fulfill the millennial expectations of its first adherents, the exponential growth of membership during its first decade was impressive. At the end of 1830, Smith had won the allegiance of about 190 followers in New York. In the following year, after the church's migration to Ohio and Missouri, membership climbed to around 2,000. By 1839, when the governor of Missouri ordered the expulsion of all Mormons from the state, over 10,000 men, women, and children fled to Illinois for safety. Clearly, Mormon doctrines and institutions spoke to a yearning within many troubled Americans that conventional churches left unmet.

To these thousands of anxious Americans, Mormonism meant, above all, a flight from anarchy—social, economic, but especially religious, anarchy. On the face of it, the religious background of Mormon converts does not reveal an especially zealous people thirsting after spiritual peace. For example, a study of those Mormons who converted prior to 1845 discloses that nearly a third belonged to no church at all before gathering with the Saints,[7] and more than half had belonged to the conventional churches typical of rural America in the period—Baptist, Presbyterian, Methodist, and Disciples of Christ. Why then did future Mormons choose to separate themselves from other religious Americans? The answer, at least initially, lies in the disgust they felt with the increasing reliance these mainstream churches placed on the revival and the doctrines that lay behind it.

By 1830, the revival had become the main technique of rousing religious enthusiasm in the movement known as the Second Great Awakening. The New England phase of the Awakening began in the late 1790s when the older Calvinist clergy led by Jedidiah Morse, Timothy Dwight, and Nathaniel Taylor grew fearful that foreign infidelity, deism, and Jeffersonianism (all synonymous terms) were sweeping the country. In an effort to stave off this looming threat of irreligion, these divines launched an ambitious crusade to recall their countrymen to the faith of their fathers. While they fulfilled some of their original aims, the movement eventually slipped from their control and took on other purposes. By the 1820s, revival-minded clergymen like Lyman Beecher in New England and Charles Finney in the West had shifted the goals of the Awakening from defending their exhausted Calvinist heritage to aggressively driving infidels to conversion. These men set their listeners on fire with dreams of millennial empire. Finney, in particular, preached doctrines of perfectionism, holding out the prospect of sinless lives and a sinless America if Christians would bring the ways of the Savior into their every action.

All of these efforts to harangue the citizenry into godliness created a substantial backlash against the Awakening in a significant minority of Americans. A large measure of this stemmed from the distaste people who considered themselves devout Christians had for being characterized as infidels. Yet the Mormons, and the many others who dissented from the mainstream of the Awakening, rejected not merely the doctrines preached, but those whose interests the doctrines served. At the time of the Revolution, the established churches certainly exhibited little hostile opposition to the secular realm. They did, however, possess a certain legitimate claim to having a special role in the nation's leadership. In the half century that followed, the dissenting churches and their allies effectively invoked the leveling sentiments sanctified by the Revolution to pull down the state-supported churches from their pedestals of special privilege. Ironically, the desired goal of equal competition among churches for the voluntary allegiance of members had the unintended consequence of further eroding their independent stance. As denominational rivalry heated up, ministers were increasingly forced to curry the favor of their congregations. Like businessmen, they loudly extolled the particular merits of their continually new and improved gospel while they simultaneously ran down the competition. The system worked well for supersalesmen like Finney, but the average clergyman could only cling desperately to the notoriously uncertain economic favor of his parishioners. Protestantism, always sensitive to the needs of the layman, now truckled to his opinions and prejudices.[8]

It was not just any member of the church that the economically dependent minister listened to.[9] The person who paid the piper was generally someone who was benefiting from the massive economic changes transforming America—and who had little in common with most of those who became Mormons. As the market economy developed during the course of the early nineteenth century, the masters gradually severed their traditional ties with their laborers. In an effort to place their affairs on a more rational, self-interested footing, they moved toward the cash nexus as the basis for all their employee relationships. This freed them to hire or fire workers seasonally, or at will. Similarly, they closed the ranks of their households to exclude non-family members in search of greater privacy. Thus, in New York by the 1820s, the older feelings of community and benevolent paternalism had broken down. When the faltering economy further sharpened class lines during the decade, relations between the well-to-do and those less fortunate became strained. While new entrepreneurs marched toward a brighter world lit by laissez-faire capitalism, the poor floundered in economic uncertainty. This fragmentation of the older order led to other social ills such as crime and drunkenness. When these disorders finally reached frightening proportions, the economic elite turned to religion for an explanation of their community's breakdown. Here the revival, with its emphasis on the individual's internal religious experience, came to their rescue, absolving them from guilt for abandoning their traditional roles. Disorderly workers released from the paternal governance of their masters were no longer God's erring children but sinners whose salvation lay in their own hands. Indeed, the very behavior most useful to the emerging economic order found sanctification in the revival. Personal traits, like independence, thrift, punctuality, and sobriety, that already possessed strong legitimation as republican values received religious reinforcement, but they were bereft of their communal context.

The Mormons staunchly defended older communal beliefs and customs in the face of these innovations. More than other Americans, they were caught within the web of the religious, economic, and social uncertainties that plagued their day. Frequent moves in search of economic betterment, like those experienced by the Smiths, spread church members further across the northern states; Mormonism exerted its greatest appeal upon persons of New England ancestry, the region strongest in that communal tradition the church was defending. Although converts were often economically struggling and rootless, this is not to say the church recruited its members from the most degraded and impoverished ranks of society. The majority of those who became Mormons still clung to the marginal edge of respectable society. In fact, the overwhelming number of the prophet's followers were simply young men and women who had not yet succeeded in establishing themselves. Marvin Hill has determined that over 80 percent of those Mormons who converted before 1846 were under thirty years of age, with the median age falling somewhere between twenty and twenty-five years.[10] While most of these church members had little education, three years at a common school being perhaps typical, they had enough learning to read the Bible and the Book of Mormon, and to function within an agricultural community.[11] The trouble was, of course, that the agricultural community, especially in the Northeast, no longer needed these young people. When the changing economic climate squeezed them out of their traditional role as small farmers, they became forced to sell their labor to their more prosperous neighbors. This loss of economic security came hard, but those who hired them made it galling by repudiating the older paternal obligations toward those dependent upon them. Even worse, the balm of religious comfort was denied these benighted people. The ministers who had once exhorted masters to act as good fathers to their laborers now gave their approbation to the master's callousness and blamed the plight of poverty on the poor man's sins.

Thus, many future Mormons found revivalistic religion, with its message of individual responsibility for one's own fate and salvation, to be menacing. Still, even as they spurned the revival of those churches most intimately associated with it, they nevertheless caught the religious fervor of the Awakening.[12] Most, in fact, absorbed the same millennialist-perfectionist doctrines as their more conventional neighbors. These doctrines, however, instead of bringing them spiritual relief, stimulated a powerful and unfulfilled religious urge in those who would later become Mormons. How could they join a church in which the clergy and parishioners were clearly so removed from the undefiled Christianity of Jesus? Before the existence of the Mormon church resolved this dilemma, the future Saints flocked to the Christian primitivist movement, joining others in their quest to restore the principles of the Apostolic church.

The American Christian primitivist movement arose prior to the Second Great Awakening, around 1790, but it grew precipitously as the numbers of religious casualties in the Awakening mounted. The primitivist movement was national in scope and, to the degree it was organized, found leaders in Elias Smith in New England, Alexander Campbell in Pennsylvania, and Barton Stone in Kentucky. The American Revolution exerted an enormous sway on the thinking of these men, for whom revolutionary ideals not only heralded the political liberation of humanity, but the religious liberation as well.[13] In yoking republicanism and religion, it might seem that the primitivists did little more than other churchmen. Yet where the Calvinist clergy, for instance, had extolled republicanism for preserving their Puritan heritage from foreign infidelity, the primitivists rejected the colonial past completely. In the eyes of the primitivists, the churches Americans had inherited from Europe expounded a gospel tainted by monarchical thought and practice. Only by casting them down, as patriots had cast down Old World political institutions, could a religion fit for a republic be born. Ironically, the clergy now discovered the weapons of Christian republicanism they had forged in the war with Great Britain now turned on them. As self-appointed champions of the people, the primitivists attacked learned ministers as decadent, power-hungry, money-grubbing tyrants whose priestcraft kept their flocks servile and their pockets full.

Mormon converts after 1830 employed the same standards of religious republicanism as the primitivists to judge the shortcomings of their changing society. They could not, however, share the primitivists' unalloyed faith in the people. For them, the religious and economic leaders of society not only had shunned disinterested civic virtue for a single-minded pursuit of their own gain, but had gulled other Americans into imitating them. As deeply religious people, Mormons found greatest fault with the clergy. John Whitmer, one of the eleven witnesses to the Book of Mormon, was typical of most Saints when he charged, "This generation abounds in ignorance, superstition, selfishness, and priestcraft; for this generation is truly led by . . . hireling priests whose God is the substance of the world's goods."[14] But Mormons made it clear that it was not merely "the priests" who led others into corruption. In the greatest proselytizing tract in Mormon history, *The Voice of Warning* (1837), Parley Pratt derided Americans for their obsession with private ends: "Yea behold the narrow-minded, calculating, trading, overreaching, penurious sycophant of the nineteenth century, who dreams of nothing here but how to increase his goods, or take advantage of his neighbor, and whose only religious exercises or duties consist of going to meeting, paying the priest his hire, or praying to his God, without expecting to be heard or answered, supposing God has been deaf and dumb for many centuries, or altogether stupid and indifferent like himself."[15] God could not be expected to tolerate such wickedness. In a revelation given to Joseph Smith in 1833, the Lord condemned "every man that walketh his own way, and after the image of his own god, whose image is the likeness of the world."[16]

Given their troubles, it is perhaps understandable that Mormons drew a more pessimistic conclusion about the meaning of their country's ills than did their fellow citizens. The self-seeking of Americans threatened to plunge their lives into an intolerable anarchy. As republicans, Mormons knew that their flight from virtue could eventually sweep away whatever was good about their country. In March 1833, the Mormon newspaper editor William Phelps surveyed the nation and found little to alleviate the gloom of his brethren. With an eye to the republican cycle of virtue and corruption endured by the ancient Nephites in the Book of Mormon, he observed that "the continent of America is a choice land above all others, and ever since men have dwelt upon it, if they have been virtuous, and have walked uprightly before the Lord, they have been blessed. When they have not done so, they have been visited with calamities. Perhaps few are aware, that the situation of the country, is still the same, for God is the same yesterday, today, and forever."[17] A world wracked with wars, pestilence, famine, earthquake, and other disasters has made up the stock imagery for millenarians throughout history, and the Mormons dutifully noted their appearance. Yet they admonished Americans that these troubles would come not only to foreign lands, but to their own. God Himself had said as much: "Ye hear of wars in foreign lands, but behold I say unto you that they are nigh unto your doors, and not many years shall pass hence ye shall hear of wars in your own lands."[18]

Whereas the majority of Americans saw God working through their efforts to regenerate the sinful, the Mormons saw God about to destroy the sinful majority. Yet despite this ominous cloud that hung over humanity, the country was not beyond redemption. Unlike the despairing followers of William Miller, the Mormons did not simply wait for Jesus to take them to Heaven while the Lord destroyed the world. Americans still had a chance to mend their ways, for God promised, "If this generation harden not their hearts, I will work a reformation among them."[19] It was the duty of the Saints to offer this chance for repentance to all people. While they did not really expect everyone to grasp it, they knew some would; and they sent out an army of missionaries to find them. Those who heeded the call would separate themselves from "the world" and build a kingdom fit for Christ upon His return.

As fugitives from the pervasive anarchy of Jacksonian America, the Mormon image of the kingdom of God was nothing if not orderly. Every important Mormon doctrine at its root betrays this craving for security. The precondition for this orderly kingdom was, of course, an orderly religion. Truth to the Mormon mind was singular, and the burgeoning religious pluralism of the era confused and offended it. "God," wrote Orson Pratt, "is not the author of jarring and discordant systems. The gospel dispensation revealed and established *one* Lord, *one* faith, *one* baptism, *one* Holy Spirit: in short *one* system of religion, *one* church, or assembly of worshippers, united in their doctrine, and built upon the TRUTH, and all bearing the name SAINTS."[20] "Indeed," wrote Orson's brother Parley, "while mankind are left at liberty to transform, spiritualize, or give any uncertain or private interpretation to the word of God, all is uncertainty."[21]

The Mormons' interpretation of religious order came, in part, from their Christian primitivist heritage.[22] The primitivists had promised not only to humble the proud, but to end the religious confusion engendered by priestcraft. The people, they insisted, should shun the priests and become their own ministers. Any person with a Bible and the ability to read could learn the plain self-evident truths of Christianity. If a particular doctrine or practice could be located in Scripture, it was Christian; if it could not, then Christians must spurn it. Thus, with one fell swoop, the primitivists sought to excise all dogma and church organization that had grown up between the days of the apostles and the early nineteenth century. By strict adherence to what was biblical and common to all Christians, sectarian strife would wither away—or so they hoped. Unfortunately, as Joseph Smith realized, when every man becomes his own theologian, religious anarchy does not abate, but intensifies. Soon every reader of seemingly self-evident biblical passages discovers that he or she alone understands their true meaning. What originally distinguished Smith from other primitivists was his ability to cut the Gordian knot of religious uncertainty by backing his "literal" reading of the Bible with an appeal to an authority none could challenge—that of direct revelation from God. For thousands of men and women troubled by religious disarray, the Christian primitivism preached by Alexander Campbell and others proved in the end only a way station on the road to greater security in Mormonism.

When converts accepted Smith's claims to be the revelator of God's will, their religious confusion and distress ended. Smith's greatest work of revelation, the translation of the Book of Mormon, provided his followers with definitive answers to the most hotly disputed religious controversies of their day. Similarly, the revelations that followed over the next fourteen years provided anxious men and women with continuing guidance for the path to salvation. It mattered little to Mormons that Smith's revelations were sometimes demonstrably false, nor did the great body of Saints complain when he subsequently altered revelations to fit changed circumstances.[23] Smith, in fact, never claimed perfect accuracy for his revelations. "Some revelations," he once said, "are of God: some revelations are of man: and some revelations are of the devil."[24] This is not to say most Mormons doubted that Smith's communications with God were both accurate and divine. Those who had doubts either quickly suppressed them or left the church. The Saints derived too great a benefit from the prophet's communications with the Lord to deny their truth. In exchange for their refusal to subject the authenticity of revelations to a too-careful scrutiny, the Mormons received a religious assurance they could have obtained in no other manner.

The Saints acquired religious security from revelation; they gained added self-confidence from their identity as God's chosen people. The Mormon interpretation of religious history chronicles the variable fortunes of the peoples who covenanted with the Lord. The Jews lost God's favor when they rejected Christ, and the Lord then shone his light upon the gentiles. The true Church of Christ, however, flourished only briefly in the days of the apostles. It soon fell under Satanic influence in the guise of the Roman Catholic church, beginning the period of "the great apostasy." The Protestant Reformation liberated Christians from this captivity; but because the Bible had become distorted in Catholic hands, it no longer served as a reliable guide for religious belief. The effort to make it so splintered Protestants into numerous warring factions, none of which had God's authority to support its views. By the early nineteenth century, religious confusion had degenerated into complete corruption. The Lord's once-beloved gentiles had forsaken Him, twisting what relics of the pure gospel they possessed into doctrines countenancing all manner of sin. In His wrath, God determined to bring the world to its apocalyptic conclusion. Not all people, however, were to fall under His judgment. A righteous remnant of the gentiles still faithfully labored to obey His commandments, and upon these He would bestow His mercy. For these saints, the Lord had hidden the continent of America from the world until the "latter days" when it became necessary to guide them there out of other nations. To end the honest religious misunderstandings among them, God raised up a seer, Joseph Smith, to whom He revealed the undenied gospel of Christ as delivered to an ancient American people called the Nephites. Together, these saints would build a New Jerusalem providing them with sanctuary amidst Babylon's fall.[25]

As a self-consciously biblical people, the Mormons modeled their behavior upon that of other covenanted people. On one level, for instance, they identified with Israel's flight out of Egypt and its search for a promised land. On another level, they aspired to emulate the holy practices of the primitive church. Yet in reality, the Mormons unconsciously patterned themselves on no people more closely than their New England grandfathers. Remarkably, Robert Kelley's recent description of the cultural republicanism of these older New Englanders might serve nearly as well for their Mormon descendants:

> New England republicans were above everything, a pious and moralistic people. Believing in the politics of virtue, they looked to the building of a Christian sparta, a universal Yankee nation, in the new United States. They thought of the nation at large as they did of the Puritan villages: as an organic community to be bound together in a shared way of life. The moral purity of the whole society, as an offering to God and an example to the fallen world, was their central concern. In their eyes government was a divine institution which, like the Calvinist God Himself, should be strong and active. It should guide the nation toward economic as well as moral health by direct intervention. Thus it would foster godly living and industrious habits. The American people should be self-disciplined, self-denying, hard-working, but not corrupted by affluence; they should be energetic, upright, and engaged in furthering God's business.[26]

In the widening social stratification of Jacksonian America, these values were being lost. By resurrecting the communal republicanism of their ancestors, Mormons meant to reseal the growing fissures of their society.

Conversion to Mormonism thus meant not only a sweet release from religious confusion, but from social uncertainty as well. Before joining the church, most Mormons felt themselves in futile struggle against a treacherous world. Once in the fold, the brethren relieved the converts of their solitary burdens with a sense of shared enterprise. The price of this support, however, was high. Mormonism demanded of its adherents total absorption into the group.[27] During the early years of the church, members "consecrated" all of their worldly goods to the church in exchange for a stewardship over property to which they had, at least technically, surrendered all rights of ownership. Nor could converts call their time their own. Most members donated enormous amounts of time to labor on church projects, such as construction of the temple, and nearly all sacrificed years of their lives to build up the kingdom as missionaries. Converts relinquished, as well, all considerations of private life. A member's work, marriage, child-rearing, relations with his or her neighbors, even food and drink were considered either to hinder or hasten the building of Christ's kingdom. The church accordingly expected a member to give or receive counsel on all such matters. God explicitly demanded union of the Saints: "If ye are not one, ye are not mine."[28]

The Mormon church's control over its members seemed an intolerable infringement of personal freedom to many contemporary observers. Periodically, some converts thought so too and left the church. But for the overwhelming majority of the Saints, the new social arrangement could not have been more satisfactory. One reason they accepted it so easily was that it coincided with their desire that a church be like a large extended family. The Mormons considered themselves children of God and, as such, embraced one another as "brothers" and "sisters." Converts who had wearied of the impersonal relationships of the marketplace, or had come from shattered rootless families, found solace in these expressions of kinship.[29] Brothers and sisters do not ask each other what they have done to deserve their dinner that day. They may recognize each other's frailties and occasionally even bicker, but they acknowledge each other's right to family membership and support. The Mormons singled out the aged for special attention as well, addressing them as "father" or "mother." This attention did not necessarily give the elderly greater authority over younger members, but it showed that the church respected their years and continued to value their membership. The real fathers of Mormonism, of course, were men like "Brother" Joseph, "Brother" Brigham, and "Brother" Sidney. These fraternal salutations projected the image that made rank-and-file church members equals of those who, in fact, ruled them. Mormons found little hypocrisy in this. On the contrary, the Saints clung tenaciously to the older New England belief that authorities were their divinely appointed guardians.[30] Children do not always like what their parents direct them to do; but, ideally, they obey, believing that their father or mother has their best interest at heart.

If Mormonism radiated goodwill from within, to all outside appearances the Saints in Ohio and Missouri still lived in the same rude cabins, wore the same rough clothes, and fought the same desperate battle for subsistence they did before joining the church. Yet Mormonism had alchemized the hardscrabble existence of converts into a glorious sacrifice for the preparation of the kingdom of God. They had surrendered themselves to something larger than their own existence. Mormon settlements bustled with energy and enthusiasm. The converts cast their eyes not on the miserable present, but on their vision of the millennium.[31] When the world finally crumbled under the weight of the Lord's judgment, the Saints would rule with Christ and finally receive the recognition they merited. A column entitled "Signs of the Times" frequently appeared in Mormon newspapers joyfully warming Mormon hearts with tales of earthquakes, riots, plagues, and wars from around the world. In a similar vein, one Mormon writer heralded the last days, proclaiming,

> We live in a great time; one of the most eventful periods that has ever been; it is not only the time when the captivity of Jacob's tents will return, but it is the time when the wicked shall be destroyed; when the earth shall be restored to its former beauty and goodness, and shall yield its increase, when plagues shall be sent to humble the haughty, and bring them, if they will, to a knowledge of God: yea, it is a time when the wicked can not expect to see the next generation; yea, it is that great time, when none shall live in the next generation unless they are pure in heart.[32]

The heart-rending troubles the converts had experienced now became occasions for celebration.

The Saints rooted their millennial hopes in the firm ground of practical activity. Daily Mormon life revolved around an endless cycle of sermons, church school gatherings, ordinance ceremonies, judicial meetings, and missionary work, all run by the Mormon priesthood. The priesthood began simply enough with Joseph Smith's presiding over the church simply as "first elder," but titles and offices soon burgeoned.[33] By 1835, the prophet had created a priesthood divided into the Aaronic, or "lesser," order and the Melchizedek, or "higher," order. Within these two bodies was a whole plethora of graded offices. In the Aaronic priesthood, the new convert gradually rose from deacon to teacher to priest. If he passed these trials of authority, he won acceptance into the Melchizedek order as an elder. A few went on from there to become high priests. All senior authorities of the Mormon church—apostles, stake presidents, bishops, seventies, and patriarchs—were members of the High Priesthood. Joseph Smith, with two counselors, stood at their head as the First Presidency, and Smith claimed charismatic authority over the whole church as "Prophet, Seer, and Revelator."

The spirit behind the Mormon priesthood was a curious blend of older hierarchical notions and democratic practice. No man was left out of the business of building the kingdom. Every male member in good standing received ordination to the priesthood, in accordance with the Mormon belief in lay leadership. Although Smith and his lieutenants ruled over the church, they remained officially only the first among equals. In granting religious understanding, Mormons argued, God was "no respecter of persons, and . . . every man in every nation has equal privilege" before Him.[34] In their scorn of learned priests, the Saints democratically threw open the door to any man who felt the prompting of the Holy Ghost—something that converts possessed in ample supply. In a circumscribed manner, even revelations were not the exclusive property of the prophet—each member could receive them according to his official station. Smith, therefore, learned God's will for the whole church, lesser authorities for their calling, fathers for their families, and individuals for themselves.[35] Thus, the evangelical antinomianism inherent in revivalism found expression among the Saints, but its anarchic tendency was contained within the order of church discipline.

The Saints modified these egalitarian sentiments, however, with a strong attachment to rank, as indicated by their numerous and intricately graded church offices. Fawn Brodie has described the Mormon priesthood as a pyramid resting on a broad base of priestly foot soldiers and gradually narrowing to the prophet at its peak.[36] Yet perhaps the old medieval analogy comparing society to the human body better characterizes its intent. All members held different "gifts," from the prophet at its head who possessed them all to the lowliest deacon at the foot who had but one.[37] In church conferences, reminiscent of New England meetings, members could debate any issue and even technically overrule the prophet, or even depose him. But these powers were more apparent than real. Ultimate authority lay with the man who could reveal God's will. Decision making remained with the head, and the body carried out its decision. The Mormon church, as Thomas O'Dea has noted, "was a democracy in participation and an oligarchy of decision-making and command."[38] Better positions within the body, however, were not closed to the average member. By improving upon their gifts, seniority, and loyalty, men advanced through the ranks supporting their leaders as they patiently waited their turn to rule.

Membership in the priesthood enhanced the self-esteem of men denied authority and influence within larger American society. That each man held some measure of authority gave him a sense of common ownership and responsibility for the church's success; yet the feeling of comradeship and solidarity within the priesthood mitigated the risks of competition and failure. While church offices were largely designed to carry out explicitly practical goals, the same impulses that drove other citizens into the mushrooming voluntary societies of the era stimulated the creation of new positions in the church as well. Voluntary societies and fraternal organizations softened the harshness of American individualism by offering their initiates good fellowship, mutual aid, and special recognition to those who lived otherwise humdrum lives outside the lodge. But as satisfying as it must have been for members to assume impressive titles and conduct elaborate ceremonies in ritual dress, lodge members were forced, however reluctantly, to recognize the fantastic quality of the performance. By contrast, as Klaus Hansen points out, for Mormons this was the real world. Their titles and ceremonies had God's sanction behind them; and building the kingdom, as frivolous or frightening as it may have seemed to outsiders, was a serious business.[39]

Mormon leaders deemed it necessary to separate themselves physically from the world in order to build the kingdom of God upon righteous principles. Separation meant not only an escape from sectarian wickedness, but relief from the brutal uncertainties of the market economy. The Saints responded to the anarchy inherent in the Jacksonian abandonment of political control over the economy by idealizing self-sufficient communitarianism. Paradoxically, both Mormons and non-Mormons drew upon republican tradition to justify their actions. The latter extolled their destruction of economic controls as creating equality of opportunity, while the former labored to insure equality of result. Constant communion with the Lord and His angels did not keep Joseph Smith from a thoroughgoing interest in the material well-being of his followers in the here and now. Once when a convert inquired about his opinion of Swedenborgians, Smith replied, "Emanuel Swedenborg has a view of the world to come[,] but for daily food he perished."[40] Smith did not, of course, mean daily food in a literal sense, but he might as well have. Of the prophet's 112 published revelations, 88 dwelt in part or wholly with matters of an economic nature.[41]

As an economically injured group of New England heritage, it is perhaps not surprising that the Mormons turned instinctively to some form of overt control of the economy. Their Christian primitivism, however, helped to transform these inchoate feelings into a commitment to communitarianism. They had read in their Bibles how the apostles "had all things in common; and sold their possessions and goods and parted them to all men, as every man needed."[42] This combination of economic need and biblical analogy worked powerfully upon their views. The prophet's alter ego during the 1830s, Sidney Rigdon, had earlier led his followers out of the Disciples of Christ over Alexander Campbell's refusal to base his church on communitarian principles.[43] Shortly thereafter, a part of Rigdon's band, known as "The Family," established communitarian living arrangements. Rigdon's conversion to Mormonism, in fact, may have resulted from his reading the communitarian sentiments that permeate the Book of Mormon. In one such passage, Smith clearly echoes the language of the Acts of the Apostles. The Nephites, immediately following Christ's visit, had "all things common among them; therefore there were not rich and poor, bond and free, but they were all made free, and partakers of the heavenly gift."[44] There are important differences between the two passages, however. In the quotation from Acts, the apostles share their poverty—they have sold all of their goods. By contrast, the passage from the Book of Mormon reveals Smith's allegiance to republican ideals—the Nephites were not divided into rich and poor, bond and free. All subsequent Mormon economic experiments proceeded from this essentially republican vision.

On January 2, 1831, Joseph Smith received a revelation directing the

New York Saints to sell their property and unite with Rigdon's followers in Kirtland, Ohio. When Smith arrived about a month later, he found Rigdon's "Family" in tatters. Speedy action was necessary to save communitarianism from an abrupt and ignominious end. On February 9, the prophet promulgated the "law of consecration and stewardship," the first in a series of revelations that would guide church economic practices during the 1830s.[45]

The earth, according to these revelations, belongs to God; and men are only its temporary stewards. No man had any more right to a greater portion of its fruits than another. If the Saints were "not equal in earthly things," warned the Lord, they could not "be equal in obtaining heavenly things."[46] In the revelation on consecration and stewardship, God commanded all church members to consecrate (deed) both their real and personal property to their presiding bishop. The bishop would then grant each family or individual a stewardship in proportion to their just needs and wants. In implementing the revelation, the Saints hoped to balance the tyrannical temptations inherent within the bishop's position with the steward's natural tendency to antisocial selfishness in formal negotiations. In an 1833 letter the church presidency observed, "The matter of consecration must be done by the mutual consent of both parties; for to give the Bishop power to say how much every man shall have, and he be obliged to comply with the Bishop's judgment, is giving to the Bishop more power than a king has; and upon the other hand, to let every man say how much he needs, and the Bishop be obliged to comply with his judgment, is to throw Zion into confusion, and make a slave of the Bishop. The fact is, there must be a balance or equilibrium of power, between the Bishop and the people, and thus harmony and good will may be preserved among you."[47] If, for some reason, the bishop and the steward could not reach a settlement, they would place the matter before a council of twelve high priests.

Once individual stewardships were settled, the difference that accrued to the church would be used in two ways. First, the poor would receive assistance in bringing their stewardships up to a level of equality with others. Second, any remaining surplus would be used to promote church projects in the common interest. The system insured future equality through annual consecration of surplus income, which would again be redistributed.

Over the next decade, the church communitarian system underwent a number of modifications. The most important of these was the introduction of the "inferior" law of consecration and stewardship in 1838. This law required the Saints to consecrate only those properties deemed surplus at the time of conversion rather than make a formal gift of their entire property. The amount of annual consecration was also changed to an arbitrary 10 percent of each member's income. Another important economic experiment, the creation of United Firms, also occurred in 1838. These firms were essentially voluntary agricultural cooperatives. In a manner strikingly reminiscent of the high medieval yeomanry, three groups of Mormon farmers banded together to cultivate large common fields that lay outside their villages. A fourth firm, never implemented, envisioned the union of mechanics, shopkeepers, and laborers inside the towns. All of these experiments, however, came to an abrupt end with the Mormon expulsion from Missouri during the winter of 1838–39. The Saints made no further effort to revive communitarianism in their new settlement in Nauvoo, Illinois. Attempts to redistribute wealth and maintain equality were dismissed as unworkable. In 1841, the church instituted the law of tithing, which obligated members to donate 10 percent of their wealth at conversion and 10 percent of their income every year thereafter.

The kind of equality Mormons aspired to under the law of consecration and stewardship was distinctly that of the middling farmer or shopkeeper lauded by republican ideologues for his virtue. Each steward retained independent control over the use of his property, yet civic-mindedly surrendered his selfish private interests for the larger good of his society. The Saints sought neither to emulate the rich nor idealize the poor. As a movement of those on the marginal edge of economic subsistence, however, they held a clear bias against the affluent who scorned them. Revelations aimed at humbling the haughty rich into civic-mindedness came with great regularity from the prophet. In one such revelation, the Lord proclaimed, "Woe unto you rich men, that will not give your substance to the poor, for your riches will canker your souls! and this shall be your lamentation in the day of visitation, and of judgment, and of indignation: The harvest is past, the summer is ended, and my soul is not saved."[48] By contrast, Mormonism offered the poor not merely solace in their misery but nobility, power, and wealth. "Blessed be the poor," read one revelation, "whose spirits are contrite, for they shall see the kingdom of God in power and great glory unto their deliverance: For the fatness of the earth shall be theirs."[49] It cannot be overemphasized, however, that the Saints did not romanticize poverty. As poor people, they knew it to be no sin, but no great honor either. Mormon sympathies lay with the deserving poor, not loafers. "Let every man be diligent in all things," commanded the Lord, "the idler shall not have place in the church, except he repent and mend his ways."[50] Many gentiles, and some Mormons, thought that the church's attempt to enforce equality was coercive and therefore enslaving, but most Saints regarded it as a restoration of the virtue lost in the selfishness of larger society.

Under the law of consecration and stewardship, the insecurities of competition were abandoned. Yet despite their sympathy for the poor, the Mormons viewed the success or failure of a steward as a judgment of his character. Within their communal context, the Saints embraced the same code of personal behavior prized by republicans no less than other Jacksonians. The church demanded its members be industrious, self-disciplined, frugal, and sober, as well as righteous. In a revelation given to the prophet in 1832, the Lord enjoined His Saints,

> Cease from all your light speeches; from all laughter; from all your lustful desires: from all your pride and lightmindedness, and from all your wicked doings. Appoint among yourselves a teacher, and let not all be spokesmen at once; but let one speak at a time . . . that every man may have an equal privilege.
>
> See that ye love one another; cease to be covetous, learn to impart one to another as the gospel requires; cease to be idle, cease to be unclean; cease to find fault one with another; cease to sleep longer than is needful; retire to thy bed early, that ye may not be weary; arise early, that your bodies and your minds may be invigorated: and above all things clothe yourselves with the bonds of charity.[51]

Like their Puritan forefathers, the Mormons were sometimes tempted to look upon the material prosperity of their society as a sign of spiritual exaltation. Only by adopting republican ethics could they build a kingdom of both holiness and material plenty upon the ruins of the world's wickedness.[52]

All good Mormons attributed their success in building the kingdom to the Lord, not their good republican work habits. Still, as in the case of Jefferson's famous plowman, one cannot help noticing their pride in their yeoman virtues of simplicity, which gave them the advantage over their bookish, overcivilized opponents. In marveling at Joseph Smith's success, for instance, the editor of the Mormon *Gospel Reflector,* Benjamin Winchester, asked, "What but an almighty arm could take an obscure young man from the plough and raise him up to astonish the world, to lay a foundation of a work like this, and cause the wisdom of high minded priests of this generation to be confounded and the wisdom of the wise to perish."[53] Similarly, Parley Pratt praised God for the remarkable success of his tract, *A Voice of Warning*, but it was Pratt's simplicity and freedom from decadent abstraction that won him the understanding of God's ways. Pratt describes himself in third person as merely "a husbandman, inured to the plough—unpolished by education, untaught in the schools of modern Sectarianism—falsely called 'Divinity'—reared in the wilds of America, with a mind independent, untrammelled, and free." It was because of this background, he continued, that his writing "drank of the pure fountain of Truth . . . in all the simplicity of nature. As such it has flowed from his pen . . . not veiled in mystery; not dressed in the pomp of high sounding names, and titles, and learned terms."[54]

The great body of Americans in their allegiance to republican values balanced the dangers of raw nature against those of overrefined society, lauding a yeoman pastoralism suspended between the two extremes: The Mormons similarly had little use for the anarchy of unsubdued nature.[55] Most church members beheld nature with a farmer's eye, seeing through republican spectacles. Parley Pratt, for instance, imagined the earth at its creation as "probably one vast plain, or interspersed with gently rising hills, and sloping vales, well calculated for cultivation."[56] According to Mormon theology, when Adam fell, so did the earth, thus acquiring its rather unsatisfactory topography. Fortunately, when Christ returned, the world would regain its former beauty; or, in the cherished words of Isaiah: "Every valley shall be exalted, and every mountain and hill shall be made low: and the crooked shall be made straight, and the rough places plain."[57] What more could a farmer from the rocky hillsides of New England hope for? Control of the weather, perhaps. In a fantasy of the world to come, "One Hundred Years Hence," a Mormon writer betrayed the dreams of a farmer too long at the prey of the elements. In a futuristic newspaper, the author envisioned reading that "rain was expected in the beginning of the seventh month, according to the law of the Lord: for the promise is, it shall rain moderately in the first and seventh month, that the plowman may overtake the reaper."[58] Most interesting, Orson Pratt combined his great skill at mathematics with a guess as to

the physical appearance of the New Earth to determine that each righteous soul resurrected by the Lord at Christ's coming would receive
150 acres of arable land.[59]

It is no wonder that the Mormons longed for the millennium to
restore the earth to this proper form. The social, economic, and religious changes that had taken place since the American Revolution had
already destroyed the world as they had known it. Many had lost their
traditional economic roles as farmers and shopkeepers. Those of their
neighbors who had successfully adjusted to the new economic conditions exacerbated their plight by refusing to uphold their traditional
paternal role toward the poor. Even more painful, the clergy no longer
attempted to promote harmony between the rich and poor, but now
characterized the poor man's troubles as the fruit of his sin. Reared in
the religious republicanism of New England, the sense of oppression
felt by these displaced men and women led them to conclude that their
society had fallen irredeemably into corruption. Mormonism offered
converts an escape from this anguish. Both religious and social confusion were brought to an immediate end through the revelations of
God. In the guise of restoring the true religion of Christ and His
apostles, the Mormons breathed new life into the New England heritage of communal republicanism.

chapter 4

The Rise of Anti-Mormonism

Considering the violence that characterized the relationship of the Mormons to some of their later neighbors, the Saints and the gentiles of New York and Ohio lived in relative harmony. Yet from the start, the church had bitter opposition. The Mormons were continually harassed during their brief months in New York. Anti-Mormon mobs disrupted church services and intimidated individual Saints. Those opposed to the church singled out Joseph Smith and his family in particular for abuse, and the Smith family's creditors pressed Joseph to abandon his religious claims. Anti-Mormons twice succeeded in haling the prophet into court as a "disorderly person." All of these incidents drove the church into greater clannishness and secrecy and eventually helped spur the New York Saints' decision in January 1831 to join the converted followers of Sidney Rigdon in Kirtland, Ohio. The Saints originally viewed Kirtland only as a temporary resting place in anticipation of building a new Zion on the Missouri frontier, but their residence in Ohio stretched into seven years, and it was not restful. While no actual warfare broke out between Mormons and gentiles, the Saints often lived in fear of it and at times slept fully clothed with guns at their sides, ready for combat at a moment's notice. Anti-Mormon threats repeatedly placed Smith's life in danger. In March 1832, an angry mob of thirty to forty men moved from threat to action, tarring and feathering both the prophet and Rigdon. By the time the Saints left Ohio in late 1837, anti-Mormonism was fast maturing into a potent political force that augured widespread violence.

The Mormons stoutly maintained that all opposition to their church was religious persecution, pure and simple. They argued it was the rapid growth of their church that roused the anger of "hireling priests" who, seeing their "crafts endangered," incited mobs against them.[1] There is, in fact, an element of truth in this charge. After all, religious passion ran high in the Burned-over District in New York and in the Western Reserve in Ohio, and it was from ministers' flocks in these regions that the Saints had the greatest success in winning their first converts. Among the most prominent anti-Mormons in New York was a Presbyterian minister who once nearly stooped to kidnapping to prevent one of his parishioners from joining the Mormon church.[2] Another ardent Presbyterian frankly admitted in the *Evangelical Magazine and Gospel Advocate* that he secured the first warrant for Smith's arrest "to check the progress of the delusion, and open the eyes and understanding of those who blindly followed him."[3] In Ohio, the Mormons effected the conversions of a substantial number of Campbellites, thereby earning Alexander Campbell's blast against the Book of Mormon, "Delusion," and the enduring enmity of the Campbellites in the region.[4] That ministers wished to keep their congregations intact and faithful to their own particular creed is certainly understandable. Yet the pecuniary motive the Saints attributed to religious opposition seems highly questionable. If the same members of other churches had converted to Methodism rather than Mormonism, one doubts whether those who had remained faithful would have responded as vociferously as they did. On the other hand, sectarian opposition did intensify because neither the Saints nor their opponents recognized the other as a legitimate source of religious competition. As a vexed writer to the *Painesville Telegraph* complained, the Mormons declared that they "are the only persons on earth who are qualified to administer in [H]is name," and those who refuse to submit to their authority "must be forever miserable, let their life have been what it may."[5] Similarly, in denying Joseph Smith's spiritual authority many religiously motivated anti-Mormons felt free, not only to defend themselves from inroads upon their congregations, but to attack the Saints as beyond the boundaries of Protestant pluralism.

Obviously, persons need not be especially religious to take offense at being told they are members of prophetic Babylon, doomed to destruction upon Christ's return.[6] The majority of those who opposed the Mormon church did so for nonreligious reasons. The Saints struck out not only against other churches, but at the alleged corruption of society as well. In their rush to separate from the world, the Mormons deliberately placed themselves at odds with those outside the church. Non-Mormons well knew that the name "gentile" was not meant as a sobriquet of endearment. Some form of unfavorable reaction was inevitable. Those who came to oppose the Saints, however, dismissed Mormonism as a movement of genuine religious and social protest. Most anti-Mormons thought they were battling an aggressive fraud rather than defending society from subversion. In the light of later perceptions of the Saints as a revolutionary cultural force, the censure of the Mormons in New York and Ohio as an admixture of mere swindlers and fools might be considered the "immature" anti-Mormon critique. Yet this view persisted as the most characteristic form of anti-Mormonism throughout the nation even after citizens in Missouri and Illinois declared ideological war on the Saints.[7] This early anti-Mormonism, however, carried with it the seeds of the overt political judgments that later followed. Critics of the church spoke and wrote with an unconscious fidelity to republican ideas that only awaited the rising fear of Mormon power to transform their thoughts into an explicit ideological condemnation of the church.

Anti-Mormons made central in their attacks on the church an indictment of Joseph Smith's character. If they could succeed in discrediting the prophet, the whole edifice of Mormonism would quickly crumble. The fusion of republican and Christian ethics particular to the era mandated an individual deportment grounded upon the commitment to thrift, hard work, and temperate behavior. In the eyes of his critics, Joseph Smith could not lay an honest claim to any of these virtues, much less the more rigorous integrity expected of a clergyman. In September 1831, Ezra Booth, who had briefly belonged to the church, wrote a series of open letters in the *Ohio Star* denouncing the church. In one letter, Booth inquired of his former friend Bishop Edward Partridge, "Have you not frequently observed in Joseph, a want of that sobriety, prudence and stability, which are some of the most prominent traits in the Christian character? Have you not often discovered in him, a spirit of lightness and levity, a temper easily irritated, and a habitual proneness to jesting and joking?"[8] John Clark judged Smith still more harshly, but perhaps more typically of many opposed to the church, when he wrote, "The Mormons believe Joseph Smith to be a prophet of God, when there is not a man in our Penitentiary, that might not with just as much plausibility lay claim to that character."[9]

Anti-Mormons defamed Joseph Smith's character as a matter of course, but those who troubled to write sustained exposés paid special attention to the prophet's pre-Mormon life in New York, concentrating on the supposedly true nature of Smith and his family before the illusions of religiosity obscured their vileness. Pomeroy Tucker, who had casually known the Smiths in New York, recalled that their neighbors "popularly regarded [them] as an illiterate, whisky-drinking, shiftless, irreligious race of people"—Joseph Smith, Jr., "being unanimously voted the laziest and most worthless of the generation."[10] Newspaperman James Gordon Bennett in 1831 similarly reported that Joseph's former acquaintances judged him "a careless, indolent, idle, and shiftless fellow," able-bodied but unwilling to work.[11] This negative image of Joseph and his family's pre-Mormon life became indelibly imprinted on the public mind through the efforts of an angry excommunicated Mormon named "Doctor" Philastus Hurlburt. With the financial backing of some church opponents in Ohio, Hurlburt spent the winter of 1833–34 in New York investigating the background of the prophet and his family. He more than accomplished his mission. Hurlburt returned to Ohio bearing affidavits signed by over a hundred of the Smiths' former neighbors, all characterizing the family as "lazy," "intemperate," "lying," "in the habit of gambling," "destitute of moral character," and "addicted to vicious habits."[12] Many of the affidavits illustrated their charges with denigrating anecdotes. Most seriously, Hurlburt's research made generally known the prophet's career as a money digger. Those hostile to the church quickly saw a connection between money digging and Mormonism. Since the Smith family was unwilling to work for a living its members turned to fraud. The creation of Mormonism only increased the amount of "the take" while veiling the Smiths' crime under the cloak of religion. Upon his return, Hurlburt launched a lecture tour publicizing his discoveries. He succeeded in raising a brief, but intense, storm against the church, but lost his credibility when Mormon countercharges provoked him into threatening the prophet's life. The damage done by Hurlburt's work, however, proved enduring. The editor of the *Painesville Telegraph*, E. D. Howe, purchased Hurlburt's affidavits and incorporated them into his book *Mormonism Unvailed*, which became the major source book for nearly every anti-Mormon writer into the twentieth century.

How a man as lazy and illiterate as Joseph Smith could have written the Book of Mormon puzzled church opponents. They soon solved this mystery by concluding that Smith was not its real author. The Saints themselves inadvertently lent credence to this idea by continually highlighting Smith's ignorant farmboy image as proof of the Book

of Mormon's divine origin. Critics who agreed that Smith was ignorant, but inspired only by money, soon perceived a conspiracy afoot.
Anti-Mormons developed innumerable variations on the conspiracy
theme, but nearly all of them made the educated Sidney Rigdon not
only "the literary genius behind the screen," but "the *Iago*, the prime
mover of the whole consipiracy" of Mormonism.[13] Anti-Mormons regarded Rigdon's "conversion" to Mormonism through the instrumen-
tality of his supposed former associate, Parley Pratt, as a part of the
conspiracy. As J. B. Turner put it, "It may be hard to impeach men's
motives, but it is still harder for any man to believe that men, who can
write and speak with as much readiness as Rigdon and Pratt, ever did,
or ever could, honestly believe one word of Smith's stories, or of the
budget of lying, nonsensical gibberish, which he has the impudence to
call a revelation from God."[14]

The belief that Sidney Rigdon was the real power in Mormonism
and Joseph Smith merely his figurehead first appeared shortly after
Rigdon's conversion.[15] Yet to make their case convincing, anti-Mormons needed some sort of plausible evidence that Rigdon and Smith
had known each other prior to Rigdon's joining the church. Once
again, it was Philastus Hurlburt who unearthed the purported proof
necessary to substantiate anti-Mormon suspicions.[16] During his inves-
tigation of the prophet's background, Hurlburt learned of an unpub-
lished romance of pre-Columbian America by the late Reverend Solomon Spaulding entitled "Manuscript Found." According to Hurlburt's
theory, in 1823 or 1824, Spaulding's novel fell by chance into the hands
of Sidney Rigdon who, like Spaulding before his death, resided in
Pittsburgh. Over the next few years, Rigdon embellished Spaulding's
book with the aim of attracting followers to a new church he hoped to
lead. As a well-known minister, however, he decided his sponsorship
of the Book of Mormon would scarcely seem credible to the public, so
Rigdon began scouring the countryside for a front man. After hearing
of Joseph Smith's money-digging activities in Susquehanna County,
Pennsylvania, he sought to interest the young necromancer in the
scheme. As J. B. Turner argued, at first Smith's "aims rose no higher
than those of ordinary vagrants and jugglers" until his "fortunate
union with others of greater ability."[17] The two men thus secretly met
and agreed upon the plan. Smith returned to New York to announce
his discovery of the Book of Mormon and recruited "a dozen indolent
sots" to witness his golden plates.[18] In the meantime, Rigdon prepared

his Ohio followers for the advent of Mormonism. When they were ready, Smith sent Parley Pratt to Ohio to simulate Rigdon's fake conversion to the new church. Because Smith and his followers already had blackguard reputations in New York, "as soon as they had arranged their apparatus for deceiving weak unstable souls . . . the actors in the scene went off *en masse*" to join Rigdon in Ohio, "where their former character and standing were unknown."[19] Improbable as it is ingenious, the Spaulding-Rigdon theory of Mormonism's rise nevertheless remained the orthodox explanation among most non-Mormon writers until its definitive demolition by Fawn Brodie in 1945.[20] Curiously, however, most anti-Mormons forgot the idea that Rigdon secretly commanded the church and quickly returned to attacking Smith as its real leader as soon as they dropped their discussion of the Book of Mormon's origins.

It was an axiom of faith among church opponents that Mormon leaders created Mormonism solely "for the purpose of picking the pockets of the community."[21] Anti-Mormons charged Joseph Smith, in particular, with an insatiable lust for money, and they occasionally reported his candid "admission" of the fact. In an undoubtedly apocryphal story, one writer places a drunken Smith in a barroom sonorously intoning over and over, "I am a P. R. O. F. I. T. I am a P. R. O. F. I. T."[22] In a similar vein, one of the Smith family's New York neighbors quoted the prophet's father as boasting that upon the completion of the Book of Mormon, his family would be lifted "*on a level* above the generality of mankind."[23] Church critics found the elder Smith truly prophetic, if not his son. In their eyes, the poverty of the Smiths in New York made their comparative wealth in Ohio suspicious in and of itself, a telling point against the family. According to E. D. Howe, Ohio proved the Smiths' "promised land" where their "long cherished hopes and anticipations of 'living without work' were to be realized." From a condition of near beggary, they "were immediately well furnished with the 'fat of the land' by their fanatical followers, many of whom were wealthy."[24]

One need not be a republican ideologue to disapprove of swindling, but the common non-Mormon perception of Joseph Smith wallowing in his ill-gotten gain revealed a republican repugnance to the idea of decadent luxury. Although the prophet lived in only modest comfort in Ohio, polemicists described his life as opulent and decadent. Smith's adoring followers, wrote Pomeroy Tucker, lavished upon him enough tribute "to revel in whatever luxury or profligacy was most agreeable to his vulgar taste and ambition."[25] Republican theorists feared this love of luxury because it encouraged ambitious men to corrupt the virtue of other citizens and rob them of their independence. That Joseph Smith and fellow conspirators used religion to squeeze the last bit of wealth out of their impoverished followers left anti-Mormons sputtering with indignation. Adrian Orr, for example, denounced Mormonism as "a nefarious fraud" cynically perpetrated by "the Mormon *imposter* and his impious confederates" for the purpose of "robbing the poor of their hard-earned pittance, to keep up, as *gentlemen*, a set of *knaves*, who are too lazy to work, and yet too ignorant to be fit for anything else."[26] Critics perceived the fruits of this moral depravity when the church community in Kirtland broke up in 1837 amidst the failure of a Mormon wildcat bank, a proliferation of lawsuits, and an outbreak of violent apostasy. In the heat of this crisis, wrote one former church member, the prophet and his henchmen fled Ohio with "their boxes of silk and fine clothes" for Missouri. The trail of bad debts they left behind "brought destruction and misery on a great many respectable families, that are reduced to distress [while the church leadership] live in splendor and all kinds of extravagances."[27]

Smith's supposed method of robbing his "dupes" was at first quite primitive. The prophet simply informed his victim that God had need of his goods. In Smith's first New York trial, the prosecution accused him of trying to pressure one man into giving him a horse and another into giving him a yoke of oxen because an angel in one case and a revelation in the other dictated the transfer of property.[28] (The allegedly duped men denied that the sale of the animals took place under any extraordinary circumstances, and Smith was acquitted.) J. B. Turner saw the same principle involved in an early revelation: "The world is informed of what they very well knew before, that Joe Smith '*had no strength to work,*' though he is one of the best wrestlers in the county. Therefore, the churches are commanded to support him, with the usual benedictions and cursings."[29] According to critics, it was both too inefficient and too blatant to produce a revelation whenever Smith needed a draft animal or some money, so he soon developed a more sophisticated and orderly method of extracting funds from the faithful. He found his solution first in the law of consecration and stewardship, and later in tithing, which one critic labeled the "regular system of the appropriation of individual property for the support and aggrandizement of the prophet and his priesthood."[30] The mob that tarred and feathered Joseph Smith and Sidney Rigdon claimed they had discovered that the church leadership had conspired to expropriate their followers' property and place it under Smith's control. This, in fact, may have been their interpretation of the law of consecration.[31] Anti-Mormons believed the equality of property demanded in the law of consecration really meant equality of poverty for the great mass of Mormons and economic ease for Joseph Smith. E. D. Howe observed that after the prophet had promulgated the law of consecration, the indigent poured into Kirtland in excited expectation of possessing all things in common. To their great disappointment, however, they discovered after their arrival that "the revelation appeared to be that only the prophet and some of his relations should be supported by the church."[32]

Since church opponents believed Joseph Smith and his lieutenants fabricated Mormonism essentially for the purpose of fleecing the credulous, the image of rank-and-file members suffered slightly less than that of their supposed masters; it was only the church leadership that was unalloyedly evil. More dispassionate anti-Mormons conceded that within the church were a great many honest, industrious, pious, and even intelligent men and women. Observers of restrained anti-Mormon prejudices shared the sentiments of Illinois Governor Thomas Ford who, years later, found the majority of Saints "more objects of pity than persecution."[33] Some anti-Mormon writers even claimed they attacked the church for humanitarian reasons, thereby hoping to reclaim the good and honest from the evils of Mormonism.[34]

Most church opponents, however, dwelled on the basic goodness of the average convert to underscore the contrasting rapaciousness of their leaders. When anti-Mormon writers moved their discussion away from the hierarchy to a more general treatment of the church as a whole, the large body of Saints reappeared as the very dregs of humanity—a "low mean and dirty set, very poor and ignorant."[35] In this view, Smith did not so much corrupt the virtue of once good citizens as merely assemble those who had no civic virtue to begin with. Motives for joining the church were usually perceived as contemptible or knavish. Anti-Mormons believed the church's economic communalism virtually guaranteed that no men of quality would join. The *Niles' Weekly Register* assured its readers of as much, reporting that common stock principles gave the church "no want of recruits from the lazy and worthless classes of society."[36] Those not attracted by easy living were said to have taken up membership for vainglorious reasons. The church had attracted every "discontented dunce" ejected from respectable denominations and, no matter how "ignorant or worthless," anointed him with a fancy title and sent him out to recruit more of his kind.[37] One of the more sophisticated anti-Mormons, J. B. Turner, perhaps best summarized this negative view of conversion, noting that some joined the church

> from one motive, and some from another; men gaping for marvels, and women ready to swoon; some praying for an apostle's martyrdom, others for Smith's millennium; some thinking of their sins, and others of Ohio bank-stock and Missouri lands; some thinking the world was soon to be overturned, others hoping to overturn it; but all expecting prodigies of some sort, and to witness, if not to obtain, the gift of tongues, of prophecy, of healing, &c., in short a multitude of which everywhere abounds, who have been kindly gifted with all sorts of sense, except common sense.[38]

Turner's acid description of the motives that led people to become Mormons divides them into various categories of "fools" and "fanatics." Anti-Mormons often used these terms interchangeably when describing converts, but the tendency to use one of these words over another revealed basic differences in their camps. People who feared the church as a threat to the social order, like those living amidst the Mormon gathering in Missouri, tended to write of Mormon fanaticism, while those who lived far from the church or where the Mormons amounted to only a small proportion of the population, as in New York or Ohio, tended to write about Mormon delusion. This latter group feared the conversion of family members, or economic loss through fraudulent business practices, more than the prospect of their unwilling enslavement by a tyrannical Mormon majority. For them, the Saints were contemptible buffoons rather than zealous cutthroats. Only after 1835 did many Ohioans begin to fear Mormon numbers; but before serious violence could develop between the Saints and their neighbors, an apostasy crisis put an end to Kirtland as a major Mormon stronghold.

Both Ohioans and observers from afar saw the act of joining the church as a dethronement of reason. The wide publicity given to the camp meeting frenzy that followed the conversion of Sidney Rigdon's followers in Ohio fueled non-Mormon prejudices. Converts enacted gory imaginary Indian battles, preached to nonexistent congregations, baptized ghosts, chased fireballs across the hills, spoke in tongues, and engaged in other peculiar activities. Upon his arrival in Ohio, Joseph Smith did his best to quell the uninhibited behavior of his new followers, and cases of unrestrained enthusiasm cropped up rarely after that. Nevertheless, such stories lent credence to charges that converts had lost their senses.[39] Stories of Mormon delusion would have risen in any case; belief in "Joe Smith and his gold bible" seemed sufficient proof of insanity to most gentiles. According to his daughter, Emily, when Mormon Bishop Edward Partridge's parents discovered his conversion, they sent his brother after him, "thinking him deranged and not capable of taking care of himself."[40] In a similar case, William Holmes Walker believed with most people that the Mormons were the "most degraded people on earth," so upon first hearing of his father's conversion, he became seized with the fear that his father "had become suddenly deranged and entirely lost his reason."[41]

Like several other gentiles, an anonymous writer to the *Ohio Star* expressed surprise at how agreeable the Mormons seemed until he attempted to reason with them about their religion. In the end, he concluded that "the great mass of the [Mormon] disciples are men of perverted intellect and disordered piety, with no sound principles of religion, with minds unbalanced and unfurnished, but active and devout; inclined to the mystical and dreary, and ready to believe any extraordinary announcement as a revelation from God. None of them appear to be within reach of argument on the subject of religion."[42] E. D. Howe went further, claiming that the continued existence of Mormonism depended on a totally controlled environment to keep converts' minds unbalanced and out of reach of religious argument. Howe noted that when not all of the Mormons could afford to buy land in Kirtland, some were forced to live in gentile communities nearby and consequently "had their faith shaken by the influence of reason."[43] Joseph Smith, he argued, averted a major apostasy crisis by sending these people to Missouri where the availability of cheap land would allow them to live together and ensure their continuance as a "distinct people."

When seemingly normal, reasonable men became Mormons, church opponents sometimes sought a physical explanation for their conversion. Illness was frequently used half metaphorically and half literally as an explanation. Mormon elders spread a contagion to which good men fell victim. Converts, for instance, did not merely embrace Joseph Smith's teachings, but rather "inhaled the malaria of the impostor."[44] Ezra Booth, who briefly belonged to the church, called Mormonism "the pestilence which threatened my entire destruction," but he had "through the mercy of God recovered."[45] On a less metaphorical level, some anti-Mormons suspected that the church won its converts through an insidious method of mind control. John Whitmer observed in the Mormon newspaper, the *Latter Day Saints' Messenger and Advocate*, that it was "somewhat diverting, to see men of understanding afraid of being deluded," as if Mormons "must be in possession of some instinct that is not common to men."[46] Many gentiles feared not just some special "instinct" possessed by Mormons, but the Saints' widely supposed expertise in the necromantic arts. Daniel Tyler later recalled first coming across the Book of Mormon at the age of fifteen. He had barely begun to read the preface when his older brother discovered him and took the book away, informing Tyler "that good people said it carried the spirit of witchcraft, which caused those that read it to be bewitched and join the 'Mormon' church."[47] Perhaps only a few sentences were necessary for the Book of Mormon to cast its spell; Tyler later rose to prominence as a Saint. By the 1840s, anti-Mormons left black magic explanations behind in favor of those with a pseudoscientific ring. In 1842, for instance, James Gordon Bennett passed on to his readers the assurances of a "medical man" that "although [Joseph] Smith is not aware of the fact," the prophet produced his purported miracles through the use of animal magnetism on converts suffering from nervous disorders.[48] Bennett, as usual, quickly spotted a coming trend. A host of writers, continuing up into the twentieth century, "exposed" the capture of countless souls to Mormonism through the use of mesmerism.[49]

The Mormons had the audacity not only to deny their irrationality, but to charge their accusers with it. In what must have been a common experience, one visitor to the Saints who had hoped to enlighten them found himself instead denounced as "blind and ignorant and in the way to destruction."[50] From the Saints' perspective, the charges of delusion hurled at them appeared reckless and without merit. They frequently expressed a desire for better relations between themselves and those outside the church; but, as Gilbert Belnap explained, the Saints could not penetrate the climate of unreasoning hysteria whipped up against them.

> In the midst of those contending factions it was as impossible for
> the Saints to reason with the people as it was for Paul to declare glad
> tidings of a crucified redeemer, when the air was rent with the uni-
> versal cry of "Great is Diana of Ephesians." . . . As well might we at-
> tempt to converse with a drunkard while he reels to and fro under
> the influence of the intoxicating passion; or lift up your voice to the
> tumultuous waves of the ocean; or reason amidst the roar of ten
> thousand chariots rushing suddenly over the pavement, so great was
> the universal cry, delusion, Mormonism, fanaticism, and so
> forth. . . . [Such] were the solid arguments opposed to the
> prophet.[51]

Mormonism so fully answered the needs and hopes of its converts
that many Saints felt utterly mystified that other people did not see its
truth as clearly as they did. The Mormons did not lay down their
wealth and good reputation on mere faith, but had "actual knowledge"
of God's will.[52] Nearly all church members had revelations, visions,
spoke in tongues, or received visitations from God or His Angels.
Those who lacked spiritual gifts witnessed them in others or had the
testimony of those they trusted. These experiences convinced Benjamin Brown that "no power of sophistry or reason can possibly show
these proofs to be the effects of a fanatical or diseased imagination."
For the sake of argument, Brown noted that even if these proofs could
be overturned, "the Latter-day Saints have still stronger proofs found
in the evidences of glorious principles, never before discovered, har-
monizing with each other, and every known truth, and clearing up and
connecting Scripture statements from beginning to end, unlocking the
great science of life, shedding light on our existence, and discovering,
in the arrangement and combination of these truths, an infinite intelligence that none but a mind that knew the end from the beginning
could display!"[53] Anti-Mormons interpreted the faithful Saints' wonder at the harmony of church doctrine more as a set of blinkers rendering them impervious to reality. Ezra Booth observed that the Saints
"are generally inclined to consider their system so perfect, as to admit
of no suspicion." When their spiritual gifts failed to produce the expected miracles, the ensuing "confusion and disappointment are attributed to some other cause."[54]

If the Mormons marveled at the refusal of the unconverted to embrace the true gospel, their theology had nevertheless prepared them
for rejection. They, after all, were the righteous remnant of mankind.
The Saints carefully granted the honesty of many people outside the

church. Yet the perfection of Mormon doctrine made active opposition seem like willful error to them. Sidney Rigdon argued that those who defamed the Saints as crooks, fools, and fanatics simply threw up a smokescreen of base lies to cover up what they were really engaged in: religious persecution. "The very instant an individual . . . received the gospel," Rigdon charged, his former associates suddenly recalled that he "had always been enthusiastic, versatile, and unsteady minded"; his formerly blameless life was suddenly marred by various improprieties.[55] This persecution, however, reinforced the Mormon self-perception as God's chosen people. They found great consolation in the reflection that they shared the same trials with the righteous who preceded them. Had not the persecution of the Saints begun at Abel's death? If even Jesus suffered at the hands of the sects in his day, should the Latter-day Saints expect any better? This was the price of knowing God.[56]

Mormon hearts turned from satisfied consolation to joyous exultation when they contemplated their election as "the favorites of heaven" in the last days.[57] Unlike the suffering of past Saints, theirs would soon end. Throughout early church history, the Mormons erased the pain of persecution with flights of millenarian fantasy. If worldlings scorned and mocked them as the wretched of the earth, they did not despair. The Lord's swift judgment would soon draw the reign of the wicked to a close, "delivering his Saints out of the hands of their enemies" and "bear[ing] them off conquerors and more than conquerors in all things." It was only by this faith that the Mormons found the strength to steel themselves to "wade through all the tribulations and afflictions to which they are subjected by . . . them that know not God."[58] These sentiments rallied flagging spirits within the church. Today's troubles meant nothing if tomorrow they would rule with Christ. Ironically, however, even as these hopes built up church morale, they also served to fuel the hostility of those the Saints marked out for godly destruction.

Those whom God would soon sweep from the earth merited their fate, in no small measure, because they violated the Saints' republican rights. If anti-Mormons only slowly developed the use of overt republican rhetoric against the church, the Saints were correspondingly quick in adopting it against them. Republican sentiments permeated Mormon discussion from the beginning. Church leaders adopted political analogies to explain their situation as readily as religious ones.

William Phelps, for instance, perceived a similarity between the "insults and injuries" suffered by the Mormons and the "taxation and bondage" inflicted on their fathers by Great Britain. Political restraint had broken down, lamented Phelps, because "no preference is made to virtue more than vice, by men in high places." With the decline of civic virtue, the Saints had suffered at the hands of mobs engendered by unbridled political passions. Those who had maliciously harmed the church would soon receive their award upon the day of judgment. It was not too late for repentance, however. Phelps asked church opponents to "venerate the memory of our worthy forefathers" by making the love of liberty and sympathy for the oppressed their ideals once again, so that virtue might continue and their lives be saved.[59]

More than any other charge, church spokesmen consistently accused their opponents of not really believing in republicanism. "All, or nearly all [of our opponents]," wrote Oliver Cowdery, "profess to be republican in principle, to allow every man to think as he pleases in matters of religion," but this republicanism extended only as far as their self-interest. The rise of the Mormon church had endangered priestcraft, and sectarians responded with "the state cry of false prophet, false teacher, away with him," hoping to maintain their position by denying the Saints their political rights.[60] In an article appearing in the *Messenger and Advocate* in January 1837, Sidney Rigdon wrote that God had granted the "unalienable right" of religious freedom to man. Although the United States boasted of its religious liberty and free institutions more than any other nation, it did not live up to its pretensions. The sad experience of the Saints, declared Rigdon, revealed "that there is not a State in this UNION, where a man is at liberty to worship God according to the dictates of his conscience."[61] Rigdon, as usual, took a more hysterical and bellicose view of relations between Mormons and gentiles than did most of his brethren. In time, the great body of Saints would decide their country had fallen into irretrievable political corruption; but in 1837, most Mormons believed republican virtue was menaced, not ruined. Oliver Cowdery displayed an opinion nearly the reverse of Rigdon's in the very next issue of the *Messenger and Advocate*. Cowdery celebrated the nation's commitment to free speech and press as the means of the Saints' triumph. The sects had strained every nerve to malign the Mormons as a deluded people; and yet they had failed. Invoking "the immortal Jefferson," Cowdery exclaimed "that there is little danger from the propagation of error while reason is left free to combat it." The church had now been successfully battling error for more than six years, he claimed, and had won many hearts to the truth.[62]

By loudly protesting the injury to their republican rights, the Mormons won sympathy from many otherwise indifferent to their church and succeeded in embarrassing their opponents. Yet just as the Saints denied the republicanism of their critics, anti-Mormons accused the church of trying to hide criminal activity behind claims for liberty of conscience. In their eyes, the Mormons merely embraced republicanism as a handy weapon with which to beat their critics. Yet however much the Saints deviated from the canons of republican ideology in actual practice, they sincerely believed themselves to be staunch republicans. Unquestionably, the church did actively seek an image of hostility to American culture. After all, they aimed their appeal at those looking for an escape from the corruptions of the world. Still, Mormons felt no sense of alienation from American political ideals even if other aspects of American life disgusted them. Their rebellion contained political implications from the beginning, but the Saints naively missed their import. This curious bifurcation in the Mormon mind is starkly revealed in an article appearing in the *Evening and Morning Star* written by Oliver Cowdery in 1834 to commemorate the Fourth of July. As Cowdery drew his essay to a close, he lauded American freedom and prayed for the long life of the government, but then, without any awareness of inconsistency, abruptly concluded with an announcement of the coming destruction and his hope that many Americans would number among the saved:

> Believing as we verily do, that our privileges are superior to any others, we are bound to offer up our feeble petitions for the long continuance of this Government and the increasing prosperity of its citizens. We cannot but wish that it may long continue, a sample for others, and a resting place for all—and when destructions and desolations come upon all nations, and the indignation is poured upon all who are unprepared, as assuredly will be the case, we sincerely pray that God may here have a people, yea many thousands redeemed from the corruptions of the world, taught in the mysteries of the kingdom, and prepared to rise and meet him when he comes to reign on earth with his elect! Then the earthly kingdoms governed by the wicked will be no more![63]

Given their sharp demarcation between politics and society, the Mormons thus felt no contradiction in expressing republican outrage at opponents who denied the church's right to equal participation within a society the Saints themselves deemed illegitimate. Even after persecution and the internal dynamics of church doctrine brought them to the brink of Mormon nationalism, their efforts to formulate an alternative political ideology to republicanism never fully cohered. When the Saints finally left the United States in 1846 for a wilderness refuge beyond the Rocky Mountains, they posed not only as Israel fleeing doomed Babylon, but as the exiled defenders of American political virtue.

Mormon political ideas throughout the 1830s, in fact, differed little from those of their fellow citizens. The Saints did not cease to be nationalists upon joining the church. When they raised their eyes above local conflicts to look upon the nation, they praised their country with an ardor equal to that of the most enthusiastic Whig or Democrat. They rejoiced with other freemen in the same conventional rhetoric of the era in the liberty and equality unknown to the tyrant's degraded subjects and held sacred the memory of the Founding Fathers who had bequeathed them their happy form of government. God, Himself, told Joseph Smith that He had "established the Constitution of this land, by the hands of wise men."[64] Even when the Saints declared they would revolt against the government should their religious liberty ever be denied, they were merely claiming the right of revolution against tyranny publicly expressed by all Americans.[65]

The Mormons shared most of the civil-religious views of Protestants as well. Both groups argued that God had kept America hidden before Columbus's voyages so it might one day provide a sanctuary for His oppressed people. The Mormons believed the American republic was part of God's plan for the restoration of the true gospel. Oliver Cowdery confessed that the idea that the Lord had created the United States exclusively to give birth to Mormonism might seem "foreign to the minds of most men," but they should soon learn the truth.[66] As Parley Pratt later reflected in 1855, Christ's church needed "a land of free institutions, where such an organization could be legally developed, and claim constitutional protection until sufficiently matured to defend itself against the convulsions, the death struggles, the agonizing throes, which precede the dissolution of the long reign of mystical tyranny."[67] Similarly, Protestants agreed the United States would become a new Zion, destined to redeem the world, even if they would have balked at the idea that Mormonism was to be the vehicle for redemption. Both groups looked forward to the millennium if Americans were faithful (although their criteria of faith differed), and warned of God's wrath if the elect should stray from the path of virtue.[68]

The nature of Mormon political ambitions in the 1830s has been a subject of lively debate among historians. Did the Mormon intent to build a kingdom fit for Christ mean only a church composed of those obedient to the true gospel, or did it necessitate the creation of a church political kingdom outside the traditional American political system? To put it another way, would the Saints present Christ with a kingdom to rule, or would the church rule with Christ only after His return? There is some evidence that the Mormons envisioned their own assumption of political power as early as 1830. The church was born in the white heat of millennial enthusiasm, and this led to some extravagant expectations of the Saints' coming glory. Sidney Rigdon recalled the high spirits of the new church when in 1830 the entire membership could be easily accommodated in a twenty-square-foot log cabin: "We began to talk about the kingdom of God as if we had the whole world at our command, we talked with great confidence, and talked big things . . . we talked about people coming as doves to the windows; and that nations should flock unto it; that they should come bending to the standard of Jesus . . . and of whole nations being born in one day."[69] Martin Harris frequently gave way to dramatic outbursts that often embarrassed the prophet, but he, too, declared the Saints should soon govern the earth:

> Within four years from September 1832, there will not be one wicked person left in the United States; . . . the righteous will be gathered to Zion . . . and . . . there will be no President over these United States after that time.

> I do hereby assert and declare that in four years from the date hereof, every sectarian and religious denomination in the United States, shall be broken down, and every Christian shall be gathered unto the Mormonites, and the rest of the human race shall perish. If these things do not take place, I will hereby consent to have my hand separated from my body.[70]

Unmistakably, these sentiments display Mormon confidence that they should one day have sovereignty over the earth. Nevertheless, it should not be inferred from this that the Saints envisioned an independent political kingdom of God at such an early date. Unlike other contemporary religious radicals, such as the Shakers, the Mormons neither scorned nor felt it necessary to remove themselves from political involvement along conventional lines. They felt a deep allegiance to republican principles in the abstract. Republican rights gave them a means of protection from their enemies. Locally, republican practices of voting and officeholding offered them power. Furthermore, why should they abandon a system of government they believed divinely inspired? It might be suggested that the Saints hoped to acquire power through established political methods. Clearly there are indications that the church cherished the hope of electoral victories in Ohio as early as 1834. Yet would the sinful majority ever vote the righteous remnant into power, or would the approaching millennium wait until Mormon converts made up the majority? Ironically, the Mormons' exercise of their political rights brought them not protection but persecution from their politically insecure neighbors. It is a lamentable truth that had the Saints abdicated their right to political involvement, the course of early Mormon history would have been a good deal less bloody. Mormon belief in the political system, however, was the last tie with American society to be broken.[71] In 1844, continuing hostility finally spurred the Mormons to organize a formally structured political kingdom outside the boundaries of traditional American politics. In the 1830s, the Saints placed their hopes for rule upon God's destruction of the wicked, not on their own abilities to acquire power.[72]

Mormon political activities in Ohio were wholly conventional. Converts brought into their church the prejudices of small farmers and shopkeepers who felt a keen sense of injury at the hands of the well-to-do. Such sentiments made them a natural constituency of the Democratic party and staunch supporters of Andrew Jackson's administration. On December 5, 1833, Joseph Smith wrote Edward Partridge that the Saints "expect shortly to publish a political paper, weekly, in favor of the present administration . . . [and] thereby we can show the public the purity of our intention in supporting the government under which we live."[73] The newspaper Joseph Smith envisioned, the *Democrat*, did not appear until February 1835, reincarnated as the *Northern Times*. The content of the *Northern Times* was perfectly indistinguishable from other Democratically controlled papers. The Whigs received routine abuse as the reembodiment of Federalist "aristocrats" ever ready "to enslave the poor and rivet firmer and firmer the fetters of despotism upon all" until they finally "rode over us in gilded coaches, bought with money thus filched from the pockets of farmers and mechanics."[74] Local Whigs expressed understandable irritation over what they termed Mormon "parroting" of the Kitchen Cabinet line. In an unsigned letter to the *Painesville Telegraph*, one Kirtland Whig even fumed that the Saints had not obeyed their vow to shun involvement with the world: "When the fooleries of Mormonism were first brought to this town by Smith & Co., their proselytes were commanded to hold the least possible intercourse with 'the world'—to avoid and abstain from all concerns of a public nature. But now they have entered *pell mell* into the arena of political controversies and strife, started a Jackson paper without the least prospect of support or patronage, and are pratering about church and state, Bank, Democracy, Federalism, &c. &c."[75] In the presidential election of 1836, the Saints enthusiastically supported the candidacy of Martin Van Buren, and he carried Kirtland, if not Ohio. Ironically, a few years later, Van Buren would temporarily shake the church's Democratic loyalties, becoming the Mormons' second most hated politician (after Missouri Governor Lilburn Boggs) for his refusal to redress their grievances after the "Mormon War" in Missouri.

The year 1835 marked a heightening of Mormon political activity in Ohio, reflecting the church's growing awareness of its numerical strength. Previous to that year, the Saints had voted for non-Mormon Democrats in Kirtland and shared in some of the "spoils" of victory.[76] In the 1835 township elections, the church broke with "regular" Democrats and attempted to "smuggle in" an all-Mormon ticket "independent of the '*democrats*' not under the orders of the prophet."[77] The prospect of Mormon town rule, however, frightened non-Mormon Democrats and Whigs into each others' arms and they narrowly defeated the church ticket. The continuing surge of Saints "gathered" to Kirtland from other areas of the country nevertheless guaranteed the Mormons eventual control of the town. In the following year, the Saints swept all local offices and did not relinquish them until their removal from the state two years later. Mormon political independence in Kirtland, of course, did not mean a disavowal of Democratic party ties. Their efforts to win control of Kirtland corresponded with their increased efforts on behalf of the Democratic party on the state and national level. The Mormons simply preferred their Democrats also to be Mormons when possible.

Political anti-Mormonism in Ohio grew with church membership in the region. Although sectarianism waned as conversions among Ohioans slowed in the early 1830s, the steady influx of Saints from other parts of the country gave rise to a new set of fears. Non-Mormons in Geauga County did not need pythonic powers to foresee that they would soon make up a minority of the population. In 1834, Sidney Rigdon bragged that the Saints would elect their own congressman in five years and capture control of Kirtland within three.[78] Many non-Mormons suddenly felt as if their lives were slipping beyond their control. While revulsion against Joseph Smith as a confidence man and contempt for his followers as credulous dupes continued to typify gentile hostility to the church, by the mid 1830s their distaste for Mormonism was gradually changing into a fear of tyranny.

Actually, these apprehensions had formed a minor current in anti-Mormon thought from the beginning. As early as 1830, when harassment of the church had driven the membership into secret meetings, rumors arose among New Yorkers that the Mormons were plotting to overthrow the government.[79] Early critics also charged the church with ties to the subversive designs of Masonry. The crusade against the fraternal society still raged as a potent force in the Western Reserve of Ohio, and only weeks after Joseph Smith's arrival in Kirtland, E. D. Howe attempted to associate Mormonism with Masonry.[80] Too many Mormons, however, had been conspicuous in the anti-Masonry movement to make Howe's charges plausible. Ezra Booth, on the other hand, more closely anticipated the political anti-Mormonism of later years when, in 1831, he warned of the antirepublican spirit within the church. Booth derided Mormon claims that the "voice of the people" decided any important matters within the church. "It is like this," he wrote, "a sovereign issues his decrees, and then says to his subjects, hold up your right hands, in favor of my decrees being carried into effect. Should any refuse, they are sure to be hung for rebellion."[81]

Republican theorists argued that in order to prevent tyranny, each citizen must have the ability to exercise his own free judgment to decide political questions. Church critics expressed concern that Mormon converts had lost that ability. The Mormon rank-and-file, they charged, had prostrated their political will to that of their prophet, who, if unchallenged, would soon hold despotic sway over Mormon and gentile alike. Analogies comparing Mormon rule to the old Protestant image of papal tyranny over the Catholic masses came readily to mind. E. D. Howe, for example, commenting on Rigdon's boast about church electoral expectations, sarcastically wrote that the Mormons "say that when they get the secular power into their hands everything will be performed by revelation. Then we shall have Pope Joseph *the First* and his hierarchy."[82] By 1835, gentiles in Kirtland claimed, at long last, to have seen Mormon ambition. The Saints possessed an unbridled lust for power and would obtain it by any means at their disposal: "The people of this township who are not governed by the pretended revelations of Jo Smith [now] think they can fully comprehend the design of these religious impostors. Their object is to acquire political power as fast as they can, without any regard to the means made use of. They are willing to harness in with any party that is willing to degrade themselves by asking their assistance. They now carry nearly a majority in this township, and every man votes as directed by the prophet."[83] These fears succeeded in submerging old political differences between the gentiles in the town to stave off Mormon rule in 1835. When the church captured the township in 1836, Ashael Howe angrily charged ballot fraud and exhorted gentiles to rise up and save their liberties from Mormon tyranny.[84] Howe's exhortations, however, were never heeded, nor did they prove necessary. By late 1837, most Saints had left Ohio or were leaving. That year a vicious apostasy crisis broke out that sent the prophet and his loyal followers fleeing to Missouri.

As serious as anti-Mormonism was in New York and Ohio, relations between gentiles and Saints remained relatively peaceful, if less than cordial. Never did Ohioans make the transition from exposé to political violence. The most significant violence, in fact, stemmed not from anti-Mormon hostility, but from factional division within the church. Angry apostates instigated and led the mob that tarred and feathered Joseph Smith and Sidney Rigdon and precipitated the furious schism that destroyed the church settlement in Kirtland. In light of the bloody clashes between the Saints and their neighbors in Missouri and Illinois, the pertinent question seems not why the Mormons met with hostility in Ohio, but why it was not worse. Even a hardened anti-Mormon like E. D. Howe denounced Missourians for infringing upon the Saints' rights when they razed the office of the church newspaper in the summer of 1833 and again when they expelled the Mormons from Jackson County.[85] Undoubtedly, the New England cultural background the Ohioans shared with the Saints was one important reason for their comparative restraint. Mormons spoke in terms easily understood by Ohioans, and the church made a great number of conversions in the region they settled. Most Missourians, by contrast, had migrated to the state from the South; and conversions among them, as in the South, were rare. Equally important, the church posed no threat to the social structure in Ohio, unlike later in Illinois, where the Saints' great numbers made their stronghold in Nauvoo appear so menacing to outsiders. Only in the small town of Kirtland did the Saints threaten to overwhelm nonchurch members, and many of these people happily sold their land to incoming Mormons at inflated prices and moved on.[86] At the precise moment potentially dangerous political opposition to the church began to arise, the Saints left the state. The Mormons left Ohio bitter against their gentile opponents, but it would be many years before they found greater peace with their neighbors.

chapter 5

Anti-Mormonism Becomes Violent

In 1831 the Saints began migrating to Missouri, where they planned to build their "New Jerusalem." The Mormons originally intended "Zion" to be their avenue of escape during the "last days," for God had declared that in the coming holocaust only those gathered into His holy city would find safety. In one of the crueler ironies of Mormon history, Zion did not become "a land of peace, a city of refuge, a place of safety for the Saints of the most high" as promised in revelation, but a perilous land of armed struggle between Mormons and gentiles.[1] On the eve of his first journey to Missouri in the summer of 1831, Joseph Smith received a more prescient revelation warning that "the land of Missouri which is the land of your inheritance . . . is now in the hands of your enemies."[2] Within two years of the arrival of the first Saints in the state, political violence erupted that would eventually drive them from their divinely chosen settlement.

Although opposition to the church in Missouri arose simultaneously with the advent of anti-Mormonism in Ohio, the fears the Saints aroused and the tactics gentiles used against them differed fundamentally from one state to the other. While Ohioans viewed the church mainly as a contemptible nuisance, the "old settlers" on the Missouri frontier felt only counterrevolutionary violence could save their way of life from Mormon domination. The deep enmity the Missourians and the Saints quickly developed for each other sprang from well-grounded disagreements over concrete, specific issues; but both sides instinctively sought to articulate their grievances and justify their conduct in the language of classical republicanism. Each side sought to portray themselves as the embodiment of republican tradition, while casting the other as its un-American oppressor. The two groups, however, stressed different aspects of the republican ideal to complain of their injury: the Missourians invoked "the spirit of '76" to put down Mormon tyranny, while the Mormons bewailed the loss of republican rights to lawless "mobocracy." But whether by tyranny or anarchy, both sides firmly believed that the other meant to drag society from civic virtue into corruption.

The Book of Mormon revealed that the Saints of the last days would build a New Jerusalem in anticipation of Christ's return, yet it designated no specific location for the holy city. The millennial enthusiasm among Joseph Smith's converts in the wake of the church's organization in 1830 made them anxious to begin building Zion. The prophet's hesitation to name a gathering place, however, fostered speculation among his less cautious brethren, who threatened to take the matter out of his hands. This pressure finally brought forth Smith's revelation in 1830 announcing that Zion "shall be on the borders of the Lamanites."[3] The Lord would reveal an exact location later. "On the borders of the Lamanites" meant rather vaguely the area anywhere on the far western frontier near the Indian reservations established just outside the organized territory of the United States. In the minds of the Saints, the advent of the millennium depended in no small measure upon the Indians' "reembracing" their ancient faith as chronicled in the Book of Mormon. Happily, the Jackson administration, unaware of its role in this divine plan, was uprooting eastern tribes and congregating them in the West to facilitate their conversion. Accordingly, Smith sent Oliver Cowdery, Parley Pratt, and two other missionaries to take the message of the restored gospel to the Indians and scout the region for a suitable place of gathering. It was, in fact, during the course of this mission that Pratt visited his old mentor, Sidney Rigdon, and effected his conversion to the new religion. Thus, as tempting as it must have been, when Joseph Smith led his New York followers to Ohio a few months later, the church's permanent settlement in Kirtland had already been ruled out.

By the spring of 1831, the millennial fervor for finding a permanent home for the church took on a practical urgency as well. In expectation of a revelation announcing their removal to Zion, Saints emigrating to Ohio felt reluctant to commit their resources to establish homesteads in the Kirtland area. More important, church members from Colesville, New York, had settled on a large tract of land belonging to a wealthy convert named Leman Copely. In June, Copely apostasized and demanded the immediate removal of all Mormons who lived on his land. At about this same time, both Pratt and Cowdery reported favorably on the area surrounding the village of Independence in Jackson County, Missouri, as a possible site for Zion. Smith soon received a revelation sending the Colesville Saints to Missouri; and on June 19, he and about thirty elders left Kirtland to inspect the region. Upon their arrival, the Lord affirmed, "This is the land of promise, and the place for the city of Zion," and on August 3, the prophet dedicated the temple site.[4] Shortly thereafter, Smith returned to Kirtland; but he left behind about three hundred settlers to commence the building of the New Jerusalem.

In abstract religious terms, the settlement in Missouri made a great deal of sense because of its situation between the Indians whom the Mormons hoped to win to their faith and the heavily populated areas of doomed Babylon in the East, from which the righteous would flee. Unfortunately, the location of Zion made little sense in any other way. Smith had scant knowledge of Missouri before he irrevocably committed the church to permanent settlement in the state. Even upon his first visit, the questionable suitability of the location became apparent, causing considerable murmuring among the brethren. In 1831, Independence was the westernmost outpost of American civilization, developed primarily as a point of departure for traders journeying down the Santa Fe trail and trappers bound for the Rocky Mountains. Reaching Independence itself, however, was an exercise in pioneering, necessitating travel down bad or nonexistent roads and on dangerous and expensive waterways. Zion lay eight hundred miles from Kirtland and even farther from the fertile fields of potential converts in the East waiting for harvest by church missionaries. Furthermore, the mass conversion of the Indians, a notion so dear to Mormon millennial expectations, had no realistic basis, as years of effort by Spanish missionaries proved. Many antebellum Protestants, of course, similarly hoped to Christianize the Indians, but their churches had firm establishment in the East. The Saints, by contrast (albeit with divine assurance), gambled the success of their holy city in an unknown region on the receptivity of the Indians to their proselytizing efforts.[5]

Overshadowing all of these problems, however, were the cultural differences between the Mormons and their intended neighbors. Although Jackson County was sparsely settled by eastern standards, it had 5,071 inhabitants in 1832. The overwhelming majority of these settlers had come originally from Tennessee, Kentucky, and states further south. These new Missourians made up a rough-and-ready lot, just developing the rudiments of a stable community. Fights marked their elections and often their conduct of business. Many of them were poor and had come to squat on public land prior to its official sale on the open market. Joseph Smith later recalled his first impression of these people, noting that he and his brethren having come "from a highly cultivated society in the east" could only naturally observe "the degradations, leanness of intellect, ferocity, and jealousy of a people that were nearly a century behind the times, and . . . roamed about without the benefit of civilization, refinement and religion."[6] While Smith exaggerated the rudeness of an admittedly primitive society, he accurately conveyed Mormon opinion. The Saints found the Missourians' personal behavior repugnant. "Puritan" in their own habits, the Mormons recoiled from the old settlers' addiction to horse racing, gambling, drinking, and swearing.[7] The Saints could perceive the potential for conflict right from the start. W. W. Phelps published an account of the brethren's first journey to Zion in the Canadaigua (New York) *Ontario Phoenix* on September 7, 1831. Phelps observed that the southerners who had settled the area held to "customs, manners, modes of living and a climate entirely different from the northerners, and they hate Yankees worse than snakes, because they have cheated them or speculated on their credulity with so many Connecticut clocks and New England notions. The people are proverbially idle or lazy, and mostly ignorant; reckoning nobody equal to themselves in many respects, and as it is a slave holding state, Japheth will make Canaan serve him, while he dwells in the tents of Shem."[8]

Phelps rightly understood the Missourians' distaste for Yankees, and their original prejudice against northerners became exacerbated as the character of the Mormon immigrants among them became clear. Many Saints in Ohio were reluctant to abandon their property and established way of life for the hardships of a pioneer's life on the frontier. Consequently, the first Mormons to arrive in Jackson County tended to be either the poor, who had little to keep them in Kirtland, or the more zealous converts caught up in the rapture of building Zion. Often they were both. The Saints had planned an orderly immigration. Church leaders instructed those headed for Zion to send money ahead to the bishop, who would buy land and prepare a place for the newcomers. Few immigrants, however, had either the money to send ahead or the means to support themselves once they arrived.[9] Many Saints naively believed that God would make all things available to them in their New Jerusalem. Despite the efforts of church leaders in Jackson County to stem the flow of their brethren without means, Zion soon became the sanctuary of the Mormon poor.[10]

Both the poverty and the zeal of the Mormon immigrants stirred the anger and resentment of the old settlers. From these elements, they began forging their antirepublican indictment against the Saints. In 1833, one anti-Mormon spokesman declared that "each successive autumn and spring pours forth its swarm [of Mormons] among us, with a gradual falling of the character of those who compose them."[11] Samuel D. Lucas, a rabid Mormon hater who would hound the church throughout the decade, was more rhetorically violent, terming the Saints a "mass of human corruption" and a "tribe of human locusts," who "from their pestilent hive in Ohio and New York" threatened "to scorch and wither a goodly portion of Missouri."[12] The Mormons, the old settlers claimed, lacked those personal qualities that would make them worthy members of the community. Some Missourians considered them little more elevated than blacks, which in the eyes of a slave society meant that they had no legitimate right to participate in community affairs. One anti-Mormon manifesto claimed that if the Saints

> had been respectable citizens in society and thus [religiously] deluded, they would have been entitled to our pity rather than to our contempt and hatred; but from their appearance, from their manners, and from their conduct since coming among us, we have every reason to fear that, with but very few exceptions, they were the very dregs of that society from which they came, lazy, idle, and vicious. This we conceive is not an idle assertion, but a fact susceptible to proof, for with these few exceptions above named, they brought into our country little or no property with them and left less behind them.[13]

The old settlers feared that the continuing influx of Mormon settlers would soon corrupt their society.

The obvious attribute that set the Mormons apart from the old settlers was, of course, religion. The Saints believed that religion should dominate every meaningful aspect of life; and perhaps in this wide sense, the old settlers opposed the church on religious grounds. Yet despite heated Mormon protests to the contrary, the Missourians displayed a relative indifference to the actual content of Mormon theology. It is true that a few clergymen either encouraged or abetted the anti-Mormon movement in Jackson County, but there is no evidence that the growth of anti-Mormonism depended upon this encouragement.[14] In an anti-Mormon manifesto listing their grievances against the Saints, the old settlers declared that on the subject of religion "we have nothing to say," observing that in such matters "vengence belongs to God alone."[15] The Mormons responded that the Missourians simply disguised their true motivation. But, unlike in Ohio, the Saints made very few conversions among the old settlers, and church opponents did not perceive Mormonism as a threat to their own religious views. The Missourians typically reacted to Mormon religious claims with satire devoid of any sense of moral outrage.

The aggressive zealotry of the Saints, however, excited the deepest hatred of the old settlers. Far from attempting to assuage the fears of their new neighbors, many Mormons displayed a haughty and clannish self-righteousness. Revelation had told them that the land of their inheritance was in the hands of their enemies, and they knew Jackson County belonged to them by divine right. In February 1831, the Lord had promised to "consecrate the riches of the Gentiles, unto my people" in the last days; and the Mormons considered it merely a matter of time before gentile land became theirs.[16] In a subsequent revelation given to Joseph Smith in Missouri in August 1831, the Lord declared "The land of Zion shall not be obtained but by purchase, or by blood, otherwise there is none inheritance for you." The revelation continued that if they purchased the land, they should be blessed; but because the shedding of blood was forbidden, any attempt to win Zion by violence would cause them to "be scourged from city to city."[17] Apparently a number of Saints either forgot or dismissed the Lord's injunction against the use of arms and boasted that they would claim Jackson County by force if necessary. As the storm clouds of civil war gathered, church leaders attempted to silence such talk as both "setting at naught the law of the glorious Gospel" and as "reproaching to this great republic."[18] Unfortunately, the damage could not be undone. "We are daily told," wrote an anti-Mormon spokesman, "and not by the ignorant alone, but by all classes of them, that we [the gentiles] of this county are to be cut off, and our lands appropriated by them for inheritances. Whether this is to be accomplished by the hand of the destroying angel, the judgment of God, or the arm of power, they are not fully agreed upon among themselves."[19]

Most Missourians believed the Mormons would, in fact, use the arm of power. In their opinion, the Saints would stop at nothing short of violent revolution, if necessary, to deprive them of their land and rights. The old settlers, however, suspected that the "arm" used might not be Mormon. The edgy frontiersmen took a dim view of the Saints' contact with the Indians. In 1831, the Mormon apostate Ezra Booth had warned that the Mormons planned to imitate the sixteenth-century Jesuits in Latin America, who "by gaining an entire ascendancy over the hearts and consciences of the natives . . . became their masters."[20] If the Mormons succeeded in winning the loyalty of the Indians all other whites fell into danger. However, the notion that the Mormons, in the words of Isaac McCoy, were "secretly tampering with the neighbouring Indians to aid them in event of hostilities" is highly unlikely.[21] Nevertheless, anti-Mormon suspicions were not totally groundless. The Book of Mormon promised that if the gentiles did not repent their wickedness, the Lord would send the Indians to slaughter them "as a young lion among flocks of sheep."[22] Some Saints, no doubt, did indulge in injudicious speculation upon the prospect of Indian aid in their troubles with the old settlers. At the height of the crisis in Jackson County, church president Frederick G. Williams sent a letter rebuking the Missouri Mormons for openly declaring that brethren speaking in tongues had revealed that "the Indians will fight for us."[23]

The old settlers' fears of an Indian uprising paled before their anxiety that the Mormons might incite a slave revolt to secure their lands. Statistically, the number of slaves in Jackson County was small. In 1832, 62 slaveholders owned only 360 slaves. Most Missourians, however, clung to the proslavery sentiments of their southern homeland and its endemic paranoia of slave rebellion. The Mormons had emigrated from New England, New York, and the Ohio Valley; and the old settlers rightly suspected them of antislavery attitudes, if wrongly fearing they would act upon them. The old settlers detected a conspiracy on the part of the Mormons to import free blacks from the eastern states. This policy would be tantamount to a direct instigation of a slave uprising because, as every slaveholder "knew," free blacks, by example or design, spread the hope of freedom among those in bondage. "With the corrupting influence of these [free blacks] on our slaves," declared an anti-Mormon manifesto, "and the stench, both physical and moral, that their introduction would set afloat in our social atmosphere, and the vexation that would attend the civil role of these [Mormon] fanatics, it would require neither a visit from the destroying angel, nor the judgments of an offended God, to render our situation here insupportable."[24]

By July 1833, rumors accusing the Mormons of inviting free blacks into Missouri reached such a magnitude as to compel an official church denial. In that month's issue of the *Evening and Morning Star*, newspaper editor William Phelps published an article entitled "Free People of Color" reprinting the Missouri law forbidding free blacks from either entering or settling in the state.[25] The old settlers, however, took this as merely a part of a strategy to show blacks how to evade the law. In a second attempt to assuage gentile opinion, Phelps hastily issued an "extra" on July 16, unequivocally stating, "We are opposed to having free people of color admitted into the state and we may say, that none will be admitted into the Church." With an attentive eye to the rapidly escalating anti-Mormon sentiment, Phelps emphasized, "We are determined to obey the laws and constitution of our country, that we may have that protection which the sons of liberty inherit from the legacy of Washington, through the favorable auspices of a Jefferson and Jackson." Yet Phelps undermined his own attempt to assure the old settlers about Mormon attitudes by proclaiming in the same article, "As to slaves we have nothing to say: in connection with the wonderful events of this age much is doing towards abolishing slavery, and colonizing the blacks in Africa."[26] These words, penned not long after Nat Turner's rebellion, the Nullification Crisis, and the rise of "immediatism" in the antislavery movement, were hardly designed to soothe the fears of hypersensitive southerners. It probably did not matter anyway. By the summer of 1833, the old settlers were beyond the reach of argument. They simply dismissed Mormon protestations on the issue as base hypocrisy that "paid a poor compliment to our understanding."[27] Suspicious of the North in general, the Missourians viewed the Saints as the worst element in a culture increasingly hostile to their way of life.

Even if the Mormons incited neither an Indian uprising nor a slave revolt, their continued immigration into Jackson County would lead to the subversion of the old settlers' society. This immigration, probably more than any fantasy of armed struggle, underlay anti-Mormon fears. By mid-1833, the swelling Mormon community numbered 1,200 souls. This, in turn, generated a fierce competition for land between the old settlers, who wished either to acquire homesteads or engage in land speculation, and the Mormons, who purchased land communally. No one person could match the collective resources of the church, no matter how poor its individual converts. Ezra Booth observed in the fall of 1831, "It is conjectured by the inhabitants of Jackson county, that the Mormonites, as a body are wealthy, and many of them entertain fears, that next December, when the list of lands is exposed for sale, they [the Mormons] will out-bid others, and establish themselves as the most powerful body in the county."[28] Within two years, the Missourians felt that their very livelihood was at stake. Non-Mormon immigrants to Missouri shunned settlement in Jackson County to avoid the Saints. If gentiles did not wish to live among the Mormons, they would be forced to sell out to them and most likely at a loss. "Some [of the old settlers]," explained Isaac McCoy, "had considerable possessions[;] should they be compelled to leave, the Mormons alone would be purchasers of their property, and consequently at their own prices, as they often boasted would be the case."[29]

On the other hand, if the gentiles attempted to remain in Jackson County, Mormon immigration ensured the Saints would soon make up the majority of the population, which would thereby permit them to oust the old settlers through ostensibly legal methods. The Missourians felt sure their republican institutions would soon fall prey to the corrupt private will of the church. Unlike other citizens, the fanatical Saints gave their primary loyalty to the church, not to the larger community, and their growing power would attract others with selfish motives willing to cooperate with them. "It requires no gift of prophecy," declared anti-Mormons, "to tell that the day is not far distant when the civil government of the county will be in their hands; when the sheriff, the justices, and county judges will be Mormons, or persons wishing to court their favor from motives of interest or ambition."[30] The result would be a perfect disaster. If the Saints had no civic virtue, they did have an unquenchable lust for gentile lands. "What would be the fate of our lives and property," said the old settlers, "in the hands of jurors and witnesses, who do not blush to declare, and would not hesitate to swear, that they have wrought miracles, and have been the subject of miraculous and supernatural cures, have converse with God and His angels, and possess and exercise the gifts of divination and of unknown tongues, and fired with the prospect of obtaining inheritances without money and without price—may be better imagined than described."[31] Thomas Pitcher noted that by the summer of 1833, the gentiles had become desperate "to devise some means to put a stop to [the Saints'] seditious boasts as to what they intended to do."[32]

Unorganized anti-Mormon acts had begun as early as the spring of 1832, when night-riding gentiles stoned Mormon homes, broke windows, set hay stacks afire, and discharged random shots into church settlements. The following spring, anti-Mormons made their first attempt to organize those opposed to the church, but opinion among the old settlers had not yet crystallized against the Saints. By July, however, the majority of Missourians had become sufficiently fearful of Mormon domination to make unified action possible. On the twentieth, the old settlers met in Independence to discuss methods of thwarting the impending Mormon revolution.

Yet the old settlers faced a dilemma. On the one hand, the Mormons had done nothing manifestly illegal. In spite of the serious accusations and petty crimes charged against them, no individual Saint had ever been accused, much less convicted, of violating the law. On the other hand, the Missourians firmly believed that the church imperiled their society. The old settlers expressed their frustration at the situation, observing that they faced an evil "that no one could have forseen, and is therefore unprovided for by the laws."[33] Because they could not appeal to written law, they reluctantly fell back upon the less tangible "higher laws" of "nature" and "self-preservation" to justify their anti-Mormon activities.[34] More importantly, the Missourians labored assiduously to buttress their position by cultivating the image of respectable republicans putting down the threat of tyranny. They based their common effort on a "constitution," published a manifesto describing their injuries to the public, held mass meetings open to the community, elected officers, and set up committees. Their phrases similarly echoed the popular patriotic rhetoric of the day. "Peaceably if we can, forcibly if we must," the Missourians vowed to repel the Mormon invaders of their society. In a final republican flourish, imitative of the Declaration of Independence, the old settlers pledged "our bodily powers, our lives, fortunes, and sacred honors."[35]

The writer and trader Josiah Gregg, who happened to be in Independence during the Mormon crisis, characterized the old settlers as patient and long-suffering until the Saints' impudence finally "roused the spirit of the honest backwoodsmen."[36] Appealing as this democratic cliché might be, those who banded together to oppose the Mormons were not a collection of rustic Natty Bumpos fighting for democratic freedom on the frontier. The anti-Mormons in Jackson County came from all classes of society, but those conspicuous as leaders came from the ranks of so-called "gentlemen of property and standing." One anti-Mormon manifesto that listed the major organizers of the movement contained the names of nearly all the men who held county offices, along with those whose wealth gave them eminence in the community.[37] Poorer men displayed their anti-Mormon zeal by taking on the brunt of the violence that ensued; but obviously those having the most to lose, should Mormon power grow, were foremost in instigating a defense of the old settlers' "rights."

The anti-Mormon meeting resulted in the unanimous adoption of four demands to be presented to the Saints. First, all Mormon immigration into Jackson County was to halt immediately. Second, those Mormons already living in the county were to leave as soon as possible without material sacrifice. Third, the Mormon newspaper, the *Evening and Morning Star*, was to cease publication. Fourth, the old settlers would hold church leaders personally responsible for overseeing compliance with these orders. (Because the Missourians believed the Saints blindly followed their leaders, this would insure the church's removal.) Finally, the old settlers, with grim humor, resolved that "those who fail to comply with these requisitions, [should] be referred to those of their brethren who have gifts of divination, and of unknown tongues, to inform them of the lot that awaits them."[38] The assembled anti-Mormons then authorized a small delegation to present their ultimatum to the Saints and adjourned for two hours to await a reply.

Mormon leaders did not reject the Missourians' demands out of hand, but pleaded for time to consult with their brethren in Ohio. When the old settlers reassembled, they rejected the Mormon response as a delaying tactic. They then marched into the church settlement, razed the newspaper office, destroyed the press, and scattered its type. Anti-Mormons thought of these actions as extralegal rather than illegal. While they passed silently over the issue of freedom of the press, they labored to portray themselves as embodying the will of the community. To win respect for their republican claims, the Missourians did their best to pose as men of cool deliberation and discrimination who shunned even the hint of mob anarchy. Writing for the public, the old settlers' secretary noted that the destruction of the Mormon printing press took place "with the utmost order, and the least noise and disturbance possible, forthwith carried into execution, as also some steps of a similar tendency; but no blood spilled, nor any blows inflicted."[39] The secretary did not explain that those "other steps of a similar tendency" included the tarring and feathering of Bishop Edward Partridge and Charles Allen; but, no doubt, this would have undermined their image of enraged republican virtue. After waiting in vain three days for a reply, the mob returned to the Mormon community and threatened each church leader with fifty to five hundred lashes if he did not agree to anti-Mormon demands. Under these circumstances, the Saints dared not refuse. The Mormons, however, felt no obligation to carry out an agreement made under duress and resolved to remain in the county. No less than the Missourians did they feel the sting of their injured republican rights. Their minority status in Jackson County, in fact, encouraged Mormon allegiance to republicanism as the only safeguard against losing their divinely chosen settlement. Upon learning of his brethren's difficulties in Zion, Joseph Smith received a revelation on August 6 counseling the Missouri Saints to bear their troubles in meekness and to seek protection for their constitutional rights.[40] On September 28, the Mormons petitioned Missouri Governor Daniel Dunklin for troops to help them defend their lives and property. While the Saints admitted their honest poverty, they assured the governor that all of the charges against them were untrue. Through their actions the old settlers, not they, had revolted against republican government. A storm of lawless anarchy swirled across the frontier which, they claimed, only the governor could becalm. In a passionate appeal to Dunklin's principles, they pleaded for his aid, not so much for their church, but to maintain republican government:

> Believing with all honorable men, that whenever that fatal hour shall arrive that the poorest citizen's person, property, or rights and privileges, shall be trampled on by a lawless mob with impunity, that moment a dagger is plunged into the heart of the Constitution, and the union must tremble! Assuring ourselves that no republican will suffer the liberty of press, the freedom of speech, and the liberty of conscience, to be silenced by a mob, without raising a helping hand to save his country from disgrace, we solicit assistance to obtain our rights, holding ourselves amenable to the laws of our county whenever we transgress them.[41]

On October 19, Governor Dunklin wrote to the Mormons expressing his sympathy, but he refused to act on their behalf until they could thoroughly prove their inability to obtain relief through the local courts.[42] The Saints certainly doubted that the courts would redress their grievances. Nearly all of the local officials in Jackson County had played a prominent role in organizing the anti-Mormon forces; but to satisfy form, on October 30, they retained four attorneys. The news that the Saints planned to initiate legal proceedings against the old settlers touched off an explosion of violence in Jackson County. What little sense of restraint remained among the Missourians disappeared. On November 4, a pitched battle between the old settlers and the Saints left two Missourians and one Mormon dead and several wounded on both sides.

When the Saints had at last organized to fight their tormentors, Lieutenant Governor Lilburn Boggs, a resident of Independence, called out the militia to restore order. A merchant and one of the region's largest and most ambitious landowners, Boggs, no less than the other old settlers, feared the mass invasion of land-hungry Mormon settlers. While it is uncertain if he played any role in the original agitation against the Saints, he clearly harbored deep anti-Mormon prejudices. In calling out the militia, Boggs only made the slightest pretense to impartiality. Most blatantly, he appointed Thomas Pitcher, a conspicuous anti-Mormon, to its head. After mustering the troops, Boggs and Pitcher demanded the surrender of Mormon arms, promising they would likewise disarm the old settlers. The Saints reluctantly obeyed the order, but Pitcher failed to carry out his pledge to disarm their enemies. This injustice emboldened the Missourians to greater fury. By November 7, the old settlers had driven the Mormon people from their homes. Many families left Jackson County with nothing more than their lives. Zion had become the land of empty promise.

The Saints never doubted that the gentiles had expelled them from Jackson County for any other reason than their religious beliefs. They had not committed a single demonstrable crime. They had not interfered with anyone's peaceable enjoyment of rights or property. They had only asked that they be accorded this same treatment. Therefore, they reasoned, their only possible offense could be their religion.[43] The series of charges the Missourians had manufactured against them were a tissue of lies from beginning to end. These were created merely as part of a conspiracy to cover up the real reason for their persecution. The Saints did not deny that some of the old settlers actually believed the accusations against them, but these were the duped rabble. The local men of wealth and position knew better. Mormonism troubled them, but they could not refute its doctrine through reason. Because of their inability, they whipped up the ignorant classes, "men . . . never troubling about religion," into a frenzy "by instilling into their minds a belief that something was materially wrong, that their personal liberty as freemen was about to be infringed, or was already trampled upon, and only one course remained to rid themselves of those evils and secure to themselves permanent peace and safety, which was to rise *enmass*, and do by *force* what they could not by flattery nor threats."[44]

The Saints, having exposed the true motivation of the mob, intended to cast its members into ignominy as antirepublicans. Success in this endeavor depended in great measure on their own ability to claim the mantle of republicanism for themselves. Regaining their homeland would necessitate the aid of others who probably cared little about the fate of their church, but cherished republican principles. The Mormons thus no longer posed as religious revolutionaries, alone obeying the word of God amidst their iniquitous fellow citizens, but simply as "many hundreds of American citizens . . . deprived of their land and rights." "We are citizens of the republic," insisted a Mormon appeal to their countrymen, "and we ask for our rights as republicans."[45]

Republican rhetoric, in fact, flowed easily and sincerely from Mormon pens into an endless stream of newspaper articles and appeals intended to sway the emotions of patriots to their cause. With great pathos, the Saints recounted how their forefathers had fled to America to escape persecution and had given their lives to create a land of liberty. That the blessings of liberty should continue until Christ's return "was, no doubt the wish, the fervent prayer, of the framers of our Constitution."[46] Now this prayer might go unanswered. The Mormons, no less than other Americans, had imbibed from their youth the belief that republican government was easily destroyed without constant vigilance. Patriots warily eyed the usurpation of any right as the first telltale sign of the republic's decline. Quite naturally, the Saints perceived this evidence in their expulsion from Jackson County, which they labeled as "one of the most shocking scenes, which has disgraced the character of any citizen of the United States, since her freedom was purchased by the shedding of blood."[47]

The Mormons decried their persecution in Missouri as no less than "high handed treason against the government," "inflicting one vital stab to the Constitution and laws of our country."[48] The civil order had collapsed under the onslaught of "lawless banditti" as vicious as "the most abandoned savage." The Saints admonished Americans that all liberties would disappear if the government could not, or would not, protect the people against those who called vice virtue and tyranny democracy:

> When ever a government is found to be insufficient to protect its subjects from lawless depredators, and to ensure peace and safety of its citizens against the assaults of men whose principles may differ from their neighbors, and when any part of a community can rise up and subvert civil authority, and turn their whole proceedings into a *mock*, *mob* legislature, where crimes are considered a virtue, and open rebellion against the laws, a responsible recommend to a seat in that body, that country is hastening toward ruin, and the day is not far distant when every one who may be bold enough to oppose such proceedings, will find they do it at the hazard of property and the imminent risk of life![49]

The Mormons had begun their movement in protest against America's religious pluralism; but now, in the face of persecution, they became its most ardent defenders. When Christ returns, they said, He will restore religious harmony; but until that time, there will always exist religious division. The American form of government and the equilibrium of influence among denominations had up to that time guaranteed religious freedom. Should this precarious equilibrium become upset, history taught that their happy form of government would soon change, and the weaker sect would tremble for its safety. For when not all groups could "enjoy the liberties of the constitution, then the day is near when the most powerful *party* will obtain the ascendancy over our government; and if we take the Jackson country *mob* for a pattern, we may unhesitatingly conclude, that the rack and the *fagot* are the consequent remedies which will be immediately resorted to, to bring men to their senses."[50]

The Saints thus warned other Americans that it was in their self-interest to put down all encroachments on liberty, as well as to give justice to those whose rights had been injured. If they, feeling secure in their numbers, remained indifferent to the persecution of others, their implicit countenance of such acts would encourage the growth and ambitions of unscrupulous men. "The fate of our church now," they cautioned, "might become the fate of the Methodists next week, the Catholics next month, and the overthrow of all societies next year." The Saints' line of logic, of course, led to its inevitable conclusion: if patriotic men wished to "help perpetuate the great legacy of freedom, which came unimpaired from the hands of our venerable fathers, they will also protect us from insult and injury" and thereby save their own liberty and earn the favor of God.[51]

The Mormons had scurried out of Jackson County without any idea of where to go. Those who chose neighboring Van Buren County received a ruthless reception from residents who feared they would inherit Jackson County's problems. Nevertheless, the brutalities of the mob won sympathy for the Saints throughout most of the state. The citizens of nearby Clay County, shocked by recent events, accepted the refugees with warmth and helped relieve immediate needs. The Saints soon looked upon Clay County as a temporary asylum from which to fight for their right to return to their property in Jackson County.

On December 16, 1833, Joseph Smith received a revelation from God commanding the church to remain firm in its efforts to reclaim Zion and to press the government to come to their aid. If a judge should not help them, said the Lord, they must appeal to the governor. If the governor turned a deaf ear to their troubles, they should plead before the president. If a government be devoid of all virtues, religious-minded republicans knew God's wrath was sure to fall upon it. The Lord of the Saints behaved no differently. If neither judge, nor governor, nor president helped the Mormons in their distress, God promised His "fury would vex the nation."[52]

Unfortunately, efforts to compel officials at any level of government to aid the Mormons' return to Jackson County brought little result. At one point, Governor Dunklin did authorize a military guard to protect Mormon witnesses in legal proceedings against the mob; but no sooner had they arrived in Independence than the old settlers intimidated the court into dismissing both the guard and the witnesses. Failing in this, the governor held out some hope that he might help the church help itself by offering the Saints a military escort back to their land in Jackson County. Dunklin gave notice, however, that the troops could not remain in the county to protect them after their arrival.

As meager as this pledge was, it fired the Mormons with new hope of resettlement in Zion. On February 24, 1834, Smith received a revelation ordering the Saints in the East to raise a military force to help protect their brethren in Missouri after the militia had withdrawn.[53] Finally, on May 5, a little less than two hundred men began marching toward Missouri. Although the church meant to keep the existence of

"Zion's Camp" a secret, the old settlers soon learned of its coming. They quickly reacted by burning nearly all Mormon property in Jackson County (about 170 buildings) and began preparing for battle. The fear of impending civil war frightened the governor into reneging on his promise to the Saints to provide troops. Without official support, the Mormons realized they could not reasonably continue their efforts, and they reluctantly abandoned their plans to march into Jackson County. To make matters worse, the pointless trek turned tragic when cholera broke out among the Saints, killing fourteen and afflicting fifty-four others. In sadness, the prophet disbanded Zion's Camp and told his disarrayed followers to return to Ohio the best way they could.

The march of Zion's Camp left two legacies, both of them bitter. The mission's failure seriously demoralized many of Smith's followers, thus contributing to a major apostasy crisis a few years later. Zion's Camp also began the erosion of public sympathy away from the Saints in their struggle with Jackson County. Since their expulsion from their lands, the Mormons had bewailed the loss of their republican rights and trumpeted their pacifism with great effect. To a great many Missourians, however, and not only those in Jackson County, Zion's Camp looked like a military invasion. This seemed to substantiate the old settlers' charge that the Saints intended to possess Jackson County by blood if necessary. False rumors added to this impression by wildly overestimating the size of the Mormon force and its intention. The *Niles' Weekly Register*, for example, reported that the Saints had been "assured by their prophet, *Smith*, that he would raise from the dead all that should be killed in fighting the battles of the Lord!"[54] Another report had circulated that the Saints had recruited a mercenary army from among the unemployed manufacturing laborers of the East, thus playing on regional prejudices and old republican fears of an army that fought only for fortune. Still another rumor claimed that bloodthirsty Mormons planned to cross into Jackson County and slay women and children.[55] As preposterous as this gossip may have been, it raised the fears of the gentile population. Many non-Mormons no longer viewed the Saints as injured republicans, but as crazed fanatics.

Just before the arrival of Zion's Camp, moderate politicians in Clay County made an effort to head off bloodshed by inviting a deputation of old settlers from Jackson County to Clay to try to negotiate a settlement with the Mormons. Not only did these talks fail to end the crisis, but a number of hotheaded anti-Mormons from Jackson attempted to exacerbate the situation by inciting the citizens of Clay against the Saints. These men found some willing listeners, but sympathy among the citizens of Clay for the Mormons still remained firm. The meetings' moderator, a man named Turnham, answered the agitation by calling on his fellow citizens to "be republicans; let us honor our country; and not disgrace it like Jackson County. For God's sake don't disenfranchise or drive away the Mormons. They are better citizens than many of the old inhabitants."[56]

In June 1834, Turnham's sense of republican restraint, and those who shared it, carried the day; but during the course of the next two years, the once sympathetic citizens of Clay grew to despise the Mormons. On August 16, 1834, Joseph Smith had instructed the High Council of Zion to begin settling the region surrounding Jackson County in anticipation of reoccupying Zion.[57] As Mormon numbers in Clay County mounted, so did complaints similar to those lodged against the Saints by the citizens of Jackson County. By the early summer of 1836, rumors of a new civil war spread through the region.

The letters of a new Missouri settler named Anderson Wilson provide a convenient window on the troubles in Clay. On July 4, 1836, at the height of the crisis, Wilson noted that the Saints were "flocking here faster than ever" and planned to keep coming until they outnumbered the old inhabitants. Wilson repeated the Mormon boast that they should have the region by blood or money; but, so far, they had been content to buy. Sometimes they offered fabulous sums. Wilson claimed, for example, that the Saints gave $1,000 for land that had sold for only $250 the year before. The Mormons, he said, considered this only a temporary extravagance, believing that once they moved in the other old settlers would sell out at any price. At the same time the Saints squeezed the Missourians out of their land, they would also squeeze them out of their political rights. Swelling Mormon numbers meant they would soon "elect all their own officers from among the Brethren & even remove the postmaster by petition." This quiet move toward Mormon domination left Missourians like Wilson keenly aware of a dilemma they found difficult to resolve. "Now you may See Just where we are," he lamented, "we must either submit to a Mormon government or trample under foot the laws of our Contry. To go away was to Just give up all for if emigration once Begun none would buy our land but mormons and they would have it at their own price. . . . We thought of petitioning the governor but He was Sworn [to uphold the law?] We thought of fleeing. Their was no place to flee to. We thought of fiting. This was Cruel to fight a people who had not Broke the law & in this way we became excited."[58]

On June 28, the non-Mormon citizens of Clay County met at Liberty to devise a strategy for ridding themselves of the Saints. Like those who opposed the church in Jackson County, they believed that their intent was patriotic, if not obedient to the letter of the law. As Wilson explained, "[A]ltho we are trampling on our law and Constitution we can't Help it in no way while we possessed the Spirit of 76."[59] In their common struggle, the old settlers felt an exhilarating sense of solidarity and union. Wilson rejoiced that the entire community had joined the cause; the preachers and elders of the churches, gray-headed fathers, and beardless boys all linked arms in mystical union with their revolutionary forefathers. Only preliminary discussion took place at the meeting with the exception of a resolution to put an immediate halt to all Mormon immigration into the country. That evening, a band of old settlers rode out and successfully turned back a party of three hundred Saints intending to settle in Clay. By doing so, Wilson exulted, "we obeyed the Call of our Contry, the Call of liberty & freedom."[60]

On the following day, the old settlers remet to discuss more long-range action. Although the citizens of Clay expressed an unswerving hostility toward the Saints, men of more moderate temperament than those of Jackson County controlled the anti-Mormon movement. Both Alexander W. Doniphan and David Atchison, who had represented the Saints as lawyers in their troubles in Jackson County and would help them again, played prominent roles in drawing up the meeting's report. In their account, the old settlers reminded the Saints how they had taken them in when they were friendless and without means. At that time, the Mormons had assured them that they looked upon Clay only as "a temporary asylum; and that, whenever, a respectable portion of the citizens of this county should request it, they would promptly leave us in peace as they found us. That period," said the old inhabitants, "has now arrived." In apologetic but firm tones, they rehearsed the Mormons' by now familiar faults: the Saints' immigration threatened to overwhelm them; they were buying up all of the good land; their more fanatical members provoked them by claiming the whole region as their inheritance; they opposed slavery; they foolishly or maliciously communicated with the Indians; and, finally, as eastern men they possessed customs and manners so different from their neighbors as to make them incompatible. For these reasons, declared the old settlers, the Mormons had become the "objects of the deepest hatred and detestation to many of our citizens." The Missourians suggested the church might find Wisconsin more to their liking. There slavery was forbidden, the region had little population, and the few people already there had emigrated from the North and East. Without the republican bravado of the anti-Mormons in Jackson County, the report concluded with a realistic assessment of the situation in Clay and a frank admission that their request that the Mormons leave had no legal merit:

> We do not contend that we have the least right, under the Constitution and laws of the country, to expel them [the Mormons] by force. But we would indeed be blind, if we did not foresee that the first blow that is struck, at this moment of deep excitement, must and will speedily involve every individual in a war, bearing ruin, woe, and desolation in its course. It matters but little how, where, or by whom, the war may begin, when the work of destruction commences, we must all be borne onward by the storm, or crushed beneath its fury. In a civil war, when our homes are the theatre on which it is fought, there can be no neutrals; let our opinions be what they may, we must fight in self-defense.[61]

Two days later, the church elders met to consider the old settlers' demand for their removal. The Mormons, of course, resented the accusations against them as unjust. As to the charge that they intended to drive gentiles out of the land market and then the county, they replied they wanted no land other than that legally purchased, nor "more than the Constitution allows us as free American citizens." Further, while the church had no stand on slavery, it disapproved of abolitionism. Finally, the Saints argued that they had no communication with the Indians; and, in event of attack, they would defend their country like good patriots.[62] The Mormons, however, were not ready to repeat their experience in Jackson County, and a certain amount of good will remained for the earlier kindness of Clay residents. The church, therefore, voted to relocate and accepted the Missourians' subsequent efforts to help facilitate their departure.

Even as they were leaving, the Mormons once again appealed to Governor Dunklin concerning their plight. But the governor had lost whatever feeling of obligation toward this troublesome sect that he may once have held. To his mind, "the people," had spoken concerning their case and whether they had done so wrongly or rightly, the Saints must acquiesce. "The time was," he wrote them, "when the people (except those in Jackson County) were divided, and the major part in your favor: that does not now seem to be the case . . . all I can say to you is that in this Republic the *vox populi* is the *vox Dei*."[63] When the Saints lost their political base of support, the governor lost his sympathy for them. Democratic majoritarianism had triumphed over republican rights.

Although the Mormons willingly left Clay, they remained unwilling to venture from the vicinity of their divinely chosen homeland. At this critical juncture, the church received aid from Alexander Doniphan, a Democratic member of the state House of Representatives. During the winter of 1836–37, Doniphan guided a bill through the legislature incorporating Caldwell County in sparsely settled northwestern Missouri as a Mormon refuge. The new year found the Saints building their third Missouri settlement in six years. Their travail in the state, however, had not yet come to an end. During the course of the next two years, the church grew at a phenomenal rate until it seemed on the verge of dominating all of western Missouri. The political violence that rose in response to this challenge would quickly dwarf the comparatively timid warfare of Jackson County.

chapter **6**

Republican Dissent in the Kingdom of God

Scarcely had the Mormons quit fighting the gentiles in Jackson County than they began quarreling among themselves. Apostasy and dissent had been a problem in the church since its founding in 1830. Flamboyant conversions were often matched with equally flamboyant renunciations of the faith. Some former church members were content to melt silently away, but others became converted to rabid anti-Mormonism. For instance, it was disillusioned ex-Mormons who tarred and feathered Joseph Smith and Sidney Rigdon in March 1832; and as mentioned previously, the excommunicated Mormon Philastus Hurlburt seriously damaged the prophet's reputation in early 1834 with his investigations into Smith's pre-Mormon career as a money digger. These incidents and lesser ones, while harmful, did not fundamentally damage the Mormon movement. Beginning around 1834, however, a breach within the ranks of the church began to appear and grew bit by bit until a cultural crisis transformed internal bickering into dissent, and finally into schism and mass apostasy. The quarrel within the church centered on the identity of Mormonism itself and, implicitly, its relationship with American culture. By and large, the dissenters retained a deep affinity for mainstream American values, particularly those of republican individualism. Their dissent was triggered by specific actions on the part of the church leadership, especially those of Joseph Smith, that they perceived as a departure from the democratic elements inspired by the Christian primitivism of early Mormonism, and the subsequent growth of the church's tyranny over its membership. The prophet, and the majority of Mormons, completely rejected this charge of antirepublicanism. The dissenters had mistaken libertarianism for republicanism, and libertarianism would not help build the kingdom of God. Obedience to the Lord through His prophet was necessary for that. Dissenters who challenged church authority were not principled opponents but morally flawed men, weak in faith, whose efforts threatened to subvert the kingdom. The split between these two factions could not be healed through compromise. Peace only came finally when, in the summer of 1838, the last leading dissenters were sent, in Sidney Rigdon's words, "bounding over the prairies" of Missouri; and the doubters who remained were intimidated into silence with strong-arm tactics.[1]

In retrospect, dissenters would trace the origins of their opposition to the prophet right to the day the church was formally organized in 1830, but the first significant outburst of discontent appeared in the wake of the failure of Zion's Camp to redeem Zion in the late summer of 1834. The camp had been born of a revelation, and it began with great excitement, mixing the exhilaration of a crusade to redeem the holy land from the infidels with righteous indignation over infringement of the Saints' republican rights. However, the spirited enthusiasm of the brethren wore thin along with their shoes as the long hard march from Ohio to Missouri progressed. The irritation of many camp members turned to outrage when Joseph Smith called off the return to Jackson County in the face of the Missouri governor's opposition. Although Smith attempted to mollify his followers by declaring that God had accepted their journey as an acceptable sacrifice, the whole adventure seemed a tragic farce when a deadly epidemic of cholera swept through the camp. Even recalling these events many years later, the prophet's brother, William Smith, could find nothing redeeming in them, describing his experience as "a very fatiguing, dangerous and difficult journey, without having accomplished the object for which we undertook the task; except to visit the brethren in Missouri, suffer a great deal of trial and trouble, and come back penniless once more."[2]

Many felt a great deal angrier than the prophet's brother. Some loudly proclaimed their disbelief in the Book of Mormon, while others simply left the church.[3] In *Mormonism Unvailed*, E. D. Howe compared Zion's Camp with the escapades of Cervantes' Knight of La Mancha, gloating that the misadventure "came well nigh loosening the scales from the eyes of most of the dupes to the imposition—and the whole camp [i.e., the Mormon settlement in Ohio] came near breaking up, after the return of the Prophet to Kirtland."[4] Smith, himself, confirmed the impression, writing on August 16 to the elders in Missouri, "I was met in the face and eyes, as soon as I got home, with a catalogue of charges as black as the author of lies himself; and the cry was Tyrant—Pope—King—Usurper—Abuser of Men—Angel—False

Prophet—Prophesying lies in the name of the Lord—Taking consecrated monies—and every other lie to fill up and complete the catalogue."[5] While most discontented spirits merely groused, Sylvester
Smith succeeded in subjecting the prophet to a church trial for prophesying lies and misappropriating the camp's funds. After lengthy debate, however, the prophet succeeded in justifying his actions to the
council's content and Sylvester Smith was forced to ask forgiveness for
his accusations. While many Mormons lacked Sylvester Smith's effron-
tery, they too wondered if they had placed too much confidence in one
man. In 1834, these people reined in their suspicions; but as Marvin
Hill has demonstrated, those who became leading dissenters two years
later, such as Frederick G. Williams, Parley Pratt, Luke and Lyman
Johnson, John Boynton, and Martin Harris, had participated in Zion's
Camp and felt a certain amount of disillusionment over its conduct
and failure.[6]

The debacle of Zion's Camp, coupled with economic difficulties,
made the remaining months of 1834 a gloomy time in the church. But
when faced with a crisis, Joseph Smith usually found the means to
divert his followers from their disappointment. Shortly after the advent of the new year, the prophet announced that the time had come
to select the members of the Quorum of the Twelve Apostles and the
First Quorum of the Seventies. The Quorum of the Twelve Apostles
was designed to be equal in rank to the First Presidency and would
direct the missionary activities of the church. The Quorum of the
Seventies was to be the church's elite missionary body, and coveted
places within this Quorum were reserved for those men who had
"proved" themselves in Zion's Camp. This new missionary effort
helped spark a spirit of rededication among the Saints and, at last,
dispelled the church's frustration with its failure to redeem Zion.

During 1835 and 1836, in fact, the Mormons were optimistic, and
harmony reigned over their Ohio settlement. There were seemingly
good reasons for this cheer. On March 26, 1836, after great economic
and physical sacrifice, the Saints finally dedicated the Kirtland Temple.
Joseph Smith, as a rule, disapproved of excessive display of religious
enthusiasm, but on this occasion, he whipped it into a frenzy. As
Benjamin Brown observed, on that day "the Spirit of the Lord, as on
the day of Pentecost was profusely poured out."[7] Many Saints beheld
angels, the chariots of Israel, and other heavenly visions. Smith, himself, beheld the Savior, and hundreds of elders spoke in tongues. Most

Mormons would recall this day as one of the greatest religious experiences of their lives.

If the Saints believed the dawn of the anxiously awaited millennium was drawing near, they seemed to think it would arrive amidst temporal power and economic plenty. The Mormons in the Kirtland vicinity had numbered only 175 in 1833, but by 1835 the figure reached 1,000 and by 1836, 1,900. This growth in population allowed the Saints to sweep all Kirtland township offices in 1836 and led them to expect that they would dominate all Geauga County and, eventually, northeastern Ohio. The influx of immigrants also swelled land values, and the ceaseless construction of new homes and businesses gave the town an air of prosperity. On October 26, 1836, Joseph Young wrote with feverish excitement to Phineas Richards about the rising tide of prosperity sweeping through the Mormon settlement, declaring, "There is not a Town in the United States to my Knowledge that will increase for Some Years Equal to Kirtland."[8] Young was scarcely alone in his opinion of Kirtland's prospects. The prophet himself not only reflected the Saints' general optimism but encouraged it. On January 6, Smith announced he had heard the audible voice of God guarantee the success of the Saints' ambitious Kirtland Safety Society Anti-Banking Company if the brethren would remain faithful to the Lord's commandments. Wilford Woodruff added in his diary his prayer that the new bank should "become the greatest of all institutions on EARTH."[9] Even more extravagantly, Woodruff recorded that the prophet declared to the assembled church on April 6, 1837, that God had permitted him a vision of Kirtland's coming glory. "The city," Smith claimed, "extended to the east, west, north & south, steam boats will come puffing into the city our goods will be conveyed upon railroads from Kirtland to many places & probably to Zion. Houses of worship would be reared unto the most high beautiful streets was to made for the Saints to walk in kings of the earth would come to behold the glory thereof & many glorious things not now to be names would be bestowed upon the saints, but all these things are better imagined than spoken by the Children of Jacob."[10]

This general expectation of economic boom eventually whetted the Saints' appetite for the finer things they had previously believed they could not afford. As Benjamin Johnson noted, "Goods were sold upon credit with great hope of better times; and 'Why be deprived of luxury and fashion today' seemed to be the spirit of the hour."[11]

If the Mormons did not really indulge themselves in an orgy of spending, they nevertheless let themselves fall into economic imprudence. The successes and hopes of 1836 and early 1837 would all come back to haunt them. The prophet's multiplication of church offices offended many of Smith's earliest followers who believed he was deserting the purity of original Mormonism. The political power won through the growth of Mormon membership frightened many gentiles into anti-Mormonism. But most important, the Saints had built their house of prosperity upon the sand of credit, and a storm of economic misfortune would soon bring it down.

The building of the Saints' beloved temple, the enormous purchase of land, the provision for the poor, and the construction and stocking of church businesses had over the years left the Mormon community in awkward economic circumstances.[12] In the fall of 1836, the Saints determined to rationalize their economic situation by pooling their resources in a bank. The Saints' primary assets were tied up in land, which created a serious lack of liquidity in the Kirtland economy. But by using mostly land to back notes the bank intended to issue, the Mormons hoped to ease their cash flow problems. On November 2, church leaders accordingly drew up a constitution for the Kirtland Safety Society Bank that named Sidney Rigdon president and Joseph Smith treasurer. Oliver Cowdery was then dispatched to Philadelphia to purchase plates to print the currency, while Orson Hyde left for Columbus to obtain a state charter for the Society. Unfortunately, the legislature had become alarmed at the sharp increase in the number of private banks in recent years and denied the Saints' petition. Although the Mormons interpreted this refusal as religious persecution, their request for a charter was only one of many denied by the legislature that year. To make matters worse for the Saints, however, Oliver Cowdery had succeeded in purchasing the expensive plates in Philadelphia. With the plates in hand, and perhaps with the encouragement of bad legal advice, the temptation to proceed with the plans without a charter proved too strong. On January 2, 1837, the Saints attempted to disguise their wildcat bank with an appeal to the prevalent prejudices against banks by retitling their association the Kirtland Safety Society Anti-Banking Company. Four days later, they began circulating currency with the apparent blessing of the Lord, if not the state of Ohio.

The Mormon bank quickly fell into trouble. Poorly capitalized from the outset, the bank offices suspended specie payments after little more than two weeks. In February, Joseph Smith was indicted for illegal banking and, on March 24, found guilty and fined $1,000 plus court costs. In June, Sidney Rigdon was indicted for counterfeiting, but he left the state before his case came to trial. In spite of these legal difficulties, the Saints allowed the bank to limp along until its final collapse on July 2. Even before legal charges had been pressed, the failure to obtain a state charter had probably doomed the bank. The unreliability of so many banks during this era made people reluctant to invest in the charterless Society stock or accept its notes. To the great annoyance of the prophet, many Mormons as well as gentiles refused the bank's currency. This lack of confidence, in fact, ensured that the bank would fail. In addition to the obvious economic loss to Society stock and currency holders (which may not have been great), the bank's failure had the most serious effect of damaging Smith's reputation among some of his creditors, who started calling for immediate payment. The church might have succeeded in weathering these problems, but by May the Panic of 1837 reached Ohio and more church creditors responded by retrenching and demanding immediate payment for debts. The overall effect of these events was to destroy the Kirtland economy. The remainder of the year would see a flurry of lawsuits and forced sales among the brethren.

The Kirtland bank fiasco and the subsequent collapse of the economy triggered sharp and bitter dissent within the church. What drove seemingly exemplary church members into opposition against the prophet, however, was not their economic losses per se. As Marvin Hill has shown, many dissenters lost small or negligible amounts, especially in comparison to the losses sustained by many of those who remained loyal to the prophet.[13] Rather, what troubled the dissenters, Hill argues, was the fear that the bank's fall merely symbolized deeper wrongs within the church. As the controversy between Smith and his critics evolved over time, it gradually became clear that the two factions within the church held different and irreconcilable conceptions of what the Mormon kingdom should be: the dissenters wanted, in Hill's words, "a more open society, closer to the values and traditions of evangelical Protestantism, while those who supported Smith tolerated a more closed society based on higher law, where the Saints were of one mind and one heart, ready to do battle against the ungodly."[14] Yet while Hill rightly perceived this controversy as focusing upon the degree of "openness" of the Mormon kingdom, his basic insight may be further refined. Sometimes consciously, sometimes not, Joseph Smith's opponents leveled their attack from the perspective of republican ideology.

Mormons had always insisted that the kingdom of God be built upon the republican virtues of hard work, self-denial, and the shunning of luxury, but the economic collapse in 1837 revealed to dissenters just how mired in worldly ambition the church had become. The Saints had let the temptation of luxury lead them into sinful pride and into mortgaging the fate of the church to men of wealth. John Corrill, for instance, charged that the church leadership had "suffered pride to arise in their hearts, and became desirous of fine houses, and fine clothes, and indulged too much in these things, supposing for a few months that they were very rich" until, to their sorrow, they learned otherwise.[15] Yet even before the economic crisis broke, there had come a few jeremiads warning against the spirit of Mammon in the church. President David Whitmer thought he perceived in the brethren the same spirit of grasping after luxury that had proved the undoing of the Nephites in the Book of Mormon. In a sermon Whitmer delivered on January 17, 1837, Wilford Woodruff recorded that he exhorted the Saints "to humble ourselves before God lest his hand rest upon us in anger for our pride & many sins that we were running into our days of prosperity as the ancient Nephites did & it does not appear evident that a scourge awates this stake of Zion if their is not great repentance immediately & almost every countenance indicates the above expectation especially the heads of the church."[16] The apostle Parley Pratt echoed Whitmer's words five days later calling on his brethren "to humble ourselves before God & feed the poor & clothe the needy & put away our sins lest judgment overtake us speedily."[17]

To the thinking of men like David Whitmer, the taste for luxury was neither the first nor necessarily the worst of the corruptions that had crept into the church. Equally ominous, the church leadership had gradually developed an obsession with earthly power and station that undercut the original purity of Mormonism. The Mormon religion originally arose out of the Christian primitivist movement. That movement had fused religion with a belief in republican equality to attack learned ministers as power-hungry, money-grubbing tyrants whose priestcraft kept their flocks servile. If each person read the self-evident truths contained in the Bible, the people would have no need for ministers, but in a communal spirit minister to each other. When private interpretation of scripture led to chaos, Joseph Smith came to the rescue of many confused primitivists. Mormonism had the virtue of providing definitive clarification of religious issues through the Book of Mormon as well as an egalitarian church structure. The Mormon church thus began in this democratic spirit simply as a society of elders: Smith was exalted only as "first elder" and Oliver Cowdery as "second elder."

The church, however, did not long retain this pattern of organization. Although the Saints officially retained a commitment to lay leadership, between 1830 and 1835 ecclesiastical offices proliferated, increasingly transferring power from the general membership to a developing hierarchy of church officials. To the embarrassment of the leadership, however, some of the changes in church government contradicted earlier revelations. To clear up these inconsistencies, in August 1835 the church published a new scriptural work entitled Doctrine and Covenants, which, through a bit of unpublicized editing, tidied up earlier revelations and ratified the centralization of authority in the church. The result of these changes in ecclesiastical government was to send the original congregational authority of the church into eclipse. At the scheduled biennial conferences of the church, where the general membership supposedly exercised its sovereignty, voting became a rubber stamp for decisions already made by the leadership.[18]

The small but influential group of Saints who felt uneasy with these organizational innovations still held dear the spirit of ecclesiastical equality within Christian primitivism and mourned the loss of the membership's authority over church policy. Mormonism, after all, had in part come into existence to put down priestcraft and its worldly striving. While they granted Smith the right to receive revelations for the whole church, they nevertheless regarded him as a fallible man whom the membership could depose should his actions become objectionable. God's primary relationship, they stressed, lay with the body of believers, not with any man or set of men. The Lord would accordingly give His revelations to His people through any member the church appointed as its prophet.

Some of Joseph Smith's earliest and most trusted disciples eventually followed this line of thought into rebellion against his leadership. Smith, they concluded, had abandoned his role as God's servant in favor of using his religious influence to gratify his own desires. Among those taking this point of view was Oliver Cowdery, to whom Smith had dictated much of the Book of Mormon. On one occasion, the Lord Himself appeared to Cowdery and denounced Smith, who He said had

> given revelations from his own heart and from a defiled conscience as coming from my mouth and hath corrupted and altered words [in the Doctrine and Covenants] which I had spoken. He hath brought in high priests, apostles and officers, which in these days, when the written Word sufficeth, are not in my church, and some of his deeds have brought shame to my heritage by the shedding of blood. He walketh in the vain imaginations of his heart, and my spirit is hold and does not dwell in an unholy temple, nor are my angels sent to reveal the great works of God to hypocrites.[19]

Oliver Cowdery would dramatically leave the church in Far West, Missouri, about a year after the apostasy crisis began in Kirtland. He would at that time be joined by David Whitmer, but it was around Whitmer that many of the dissenters in Kirtland first coalesced. Whitmer had been one of the witnesses to the Book of Mormon plates and had subsequently played an important role as one of the presidents of the church. In 1834, Smith retained such confidence in Whitmer that he appointed him as his successor as prophet should he die in the attempt to retake Zion. Yet even while Whitmer personally benefited from the growing power of the church leadership, he had always looked askance upon the growing institutionalization of Mormonism, and well before the economic crisis in Kirtland swelled the ranks of dissenters, he began opposing the drift of the church. When the "woe" he had pronounced upon the Saints came to pass in 1837, Whitmer finally found willing listeners for his doubts and concerns, and he became the head of a revolt against the prophet's leadership.

More than any other leading dissenter, David Whitmer clung to the original Christian primitivist vision in Mormonism of a democratic priesthood of all believers. Whitmer gloried in the memory of the early days of the church, even before its formal organization. "We were a humble happy people," he wrote, "and we loved each other as brethren should love." But just as the church was being organized "some of the brethren began to think that the church should have a leader, just like the children of Israel wanting a king." This led to Smith's ordination as "Prophet, Seer and Revelator" of the church. Whitmer regarded this as the first of the errors that would transform Smith from a humble seeker of God into a man hungry for power and rule. "A true and humble follower of Christ," he explained, "will never have any desire to lead or be first, or to seek the praise of men or brethren. Discussing any prominence whatever is not humility, but it is pride; it is seeking the praise of mortals instead of the praise of God." Whitmer noted, however, that none saw this as an error at the time because of their innocent belief that since "God had given so great a gift [to Smith] as to translate the Book of Mormon, that everything he would do must be right."[20] Whitmer claimed that, even after this, Smith remained humble for a time, but the prophet's corruption deepened quickly after he met Sidney Rigdon. An ambitious man, Rigdon turned Smith's head with his education and eloquence. "Through the influence of Sydney Rigdon," Whitmer lamented, "Brother Joseph was led on and on receiving revelations every year, to establish offices and doctrines which are not even mentioned in the teaching of Christ in the written word."[21] The two men soon "drifted into error and spiritual blindness" giving revelations that came from their hearts rather than God and thereby polluting the original purity of Mormonism.[22] The turning point in Whitmer's feeling about the church came with the publication of the doctored revelations in Doctrine and Covenants in 1835. Although these textual changes were published quietly and downplayed as corrections or printing errors, the truth soon slipped out. Yet even though "many of the brethren objected seriously to it, . . . they did not want to say much for the sake of peace, as it was *Brother Joseph* and the *leaders* who did it. The majority of members— poor weak souls—thought anything Brother Joseph would do, must be all right; so in their blindness of heart, trusting in the arm of flesh, they looked over it, and were led into error, and finally talk about it ceased."[23] In Whitmer's eyes, the striving after wealth and power among the leadership and unquestioning obedience of the faithful had drawn the Saints into the snares of a priestcraft as vile as any gentile church. Whitmer claimed he labored with Smith after 1835 to recall him from his errors, but the prophet "was blinded and . . . ensnared by proud, ambitious men" beyond redemption.[24]

While dissenters like David Whitmer denounced the removal of power in the church from the general membership, others, no less disturbed over this institutional change, concentrated on how that power was used. A revelation given to Joseph Smith in September 1830 read, "I say unto you, that all things unto me are spiritual, and not at any time have I given unto you a law which was temporal, neither any man nor the children of men."[25] During the next seven years, some Saints came to view with dismay the implications that developed out of this revelation. Steadily, the church subsumed more and more aspects of its members' lives. Converts surrendered their own private interests to serve as missionaries, to build the temple, or serve the church in some other capacity. The church leadership also dictated a strict social code, regulated marriages and diet, and subjected transgressors to ecclesiastical trial. More importantly, the church controlled almost all significant economic relationships, and by 1835 effectively guided the political opinions of the general membership.

Most Mormons welcomed this direction. A great many Saints had suffered from social or economic displacement in "the world" and happily exchanged their former insecurity for the discipline of the kingdom. By contrast, most dissenters felt less need for the social, economic, and psychological props of the church. Many of these men had already possessed a measure of affluence or social prestige when they joined the church or had acquired it in the intervening years.[26] While they gratefully accepted Mormonism's resolution of their inner religious turmoil, they deeply resented the church's authoritatian and, after 1836, bungling intrusion into their personal independence. The shock and disappointment these Saints felt over the collapse of the bank led them to believe that the church had surrendered too much power to one man.

Yet had not *God* told Smith that the Kirtland bank would thrive beyond all expectation? The dissenting apostle John F. Boynton had thought so, claiming that he had understood that "the bank was instituted by the will of God, and . . . it should never fail, let men do what they would."[27] If the prophet could talk to God, and tell men how to save their souls, why could he not manage lesser matters like running a bank? The dissenters were forced to conclude that, despite the prophet's claim, there had been nothing of God in the running of the bank at all. Smith, they claimed, had deserted his true calling as a servant of God and now used the cloak of religion to disguise his selfish temporal ambitions. Warren Parrish, the prophet's disillusioned former scribe, charged that Smith and Rigdon "lie by revelation, swindle by revelation, cheat and defraud by revelation, run away by revelation, and if they do not mend their ways, I fear they will be damned by revelation."[28] While more moderate dissenters demanded that Smith restrict his leadership to an explicitly religious sphere, others, like Parrish, sought to depose him as a fallen prophet.

These charges against the prophet went beyond the mere question of personal corruption. Some feared, more seriously, that Smith was creating a tyranny within the church, uniting ecclesiastical and temporal power to rob the members of their republican rights. The best and most explicit defense of this sense of menaced republicanism came in July 1837 from the pen of Warren Cowdery, the editor of the *Messenger and Advocate*. Without denouncing Smith by name, Cowdery sought to reawaken the Saints to the danger to their liberty posed by the ambitious man:

> If we give all our privileges to one man, we virtually give him our money and our liberties, and make him a monarch, absolute and despotic, and ourselves abject slaves or fawning sycophants. If we grant privileges and monopolies to a few, they always continue to undermine the fundamental principles of freedom, and sooner or later, convert, the purest and most liberal form of Government, into the rankest aristocracy. These we conceive, are matters of history, matters of fact that cannot be controverted. Well may it be said, if we thus barter away our liberties, we are unworthy of them. The syren song of liberty and he who does not allow himself to think, to speak, to reason and act only as his wealthy landlord shall dictate, has virtually resigned the dignity of an independent citizen and is as much a slave, as if the manacles were upon his hands. His boasted liberty is a deception, and his independance a phantom. We will here remark . . . that whenever a people have unlimited confidence in a civil or ecclesiastical ruler or rulers, who are but men like themselves, and begin to think they can do no wrong, they increase their tyranny and oppression, establish a principle that man, poor lump of mortality like themselves, is infallible. Who does not see a principle of popery and religious tyranny involved in such an order of things? Who is worthy the name of a freeman, who thus tamely surrenders, the rights the priveleges, and immunities of an independant citizen? . . .
>
> Intelligence of the people is the only guarantee against encroachments upon their liberties, whether those encroachments are from the civil or ecclesiastical power. All chartered companies privileged orders, or monopolies are more or less dangerous to liberty, and destructive to a free Government. Intelligence then, that such is the fact necessary, that the people may appreciate their rights and guard them with that vigilance that prudence dictates to prevent any infraction of them. The great object of all privileged classes is money and power, and the universal undeviating course of all who possess both, is to add both at the expense of the liberties and best interests of their fellow citizens.[29]

Unlike Cowdery, the partisans of the prophet rejected the idea that their liberties had been endangered in the least. They regarded themselves as being republicans as staunch as those who challenged them, but it was a republicanism with a difference. They clung to an older conception of republicanism that emphasized communal obligation within a socially hierarchical society. Loyalists gave Smith and their other chosen leaders free obedience in exchange for moral guidance and a benevolent concern for their physical well-being. They conceived their task as preparing for Christ's return, and the church offices and doctrines revealed by the prophet were means to that end. In their eyes, the prophet was no ordinary mortal. While for the dissenters, God's special relationship was with the great body of believers, the prophet's backers thought His covenant was with Joseph Smith, whom they revered as an irreplaceable man chosen by the Lord to lead them. To oppose the prophet was to oppose God. What the dissenters viewed as their surrender of individual liberties to church authority, those loyal to the prophet understood as the abandonment of selfish personal desires for the greater civic needs of the kingdom. Thus, loyalists turned the charges of luxury seeking back upon the dissenters, accusing them of letting materialism override ultimate religious concerns. Benjamin Johnson epitomized this view, writing that after the fall of the bank, the "spirit of charity was not invoked, and brethren who had borne the highest priesthood and who had for years labored, traveled, ministered and suffered together, and even placed their lives upon the same alter now were governed by a feeling of hate and a spirit to accurse each other, and all for the love of *Accursed Mammon*. All their former companionship in the holy anointing in Temple of the Lord . . . was forgotten by many, who were like Judas, ready to sell or destroy the Prophet Joseph and his followers."[30] To most Saints, then, the dissenters were not men of principled differences, but moral defectives, and even worse than the gentiles because, while knowing the truth, they permitted their temporal lust to overcome their faith. More importantly, God had warned the Saints, "If ye are not one, ye are not mine."[31] The dissenters by the mere fact of dissent imperiled the salvation of all. Consequently, it was often not enough for faithful Mormons to castigate dissenters for loving money more than God; they needed to vilify them as "liars," "drunkards," "adulterers," "thieves," "swearers," "blacklegs," and "debauchers."[32]

These two irreconcilable ideological divisions within the church soon led to active conflict. During the late spring and summer of 1837, the church swirled in a vortex of anarchy that neither Smith nor his enemies could master. In May, when the prophet was absent from Kirtland, the dissenters called a meeting in the temple to discuss replacing Joseph Smith with David Whitmer as head of the church. This nascent coup abruptly ended, however, amidst threats of violence when Smith loyalists, led by Brigham Young, hotly defended the conduct of the prophet. In June, again without Smith, the prophet's father, Joseph, Sr., attempted to rebuke the dissenters in the temple and was dragged from the pulpit by Warren Parrish without any effective opposition from the congregation. Shortly thereafter, the dissenters began meeting weekly to organize a purification movement within the church. According to the prophet's mother, Lucy, they then circulated a paper among the Saints "to ascertain how many would follow them, and it was found that a great portion of the church were decidedly in favor of the new party."[33]

Joseph Smith had other problems that summer in addition to the organized dissent of disgruntled Saints. In June, a rabid anti-Mormon named Grandison Newell attempted to make the most of the confusion in Kirtland by charging the prophet with conspiring to murder him. The charge was dismissed by a state court, but it succeeded in further blackening Smith's reputation. The prophet also fell prey to countless suits for debt (some of them maliciously instigated) by gentile merchants and disillusioned followers. Much of his absence from Kirtland that year can be explained as an attempt to avoid "vexatious lawsuits." Almost as trying was the infestation of cranks who attempted to take advantage of the chaos in the church. One man walked barefoot from New York to Kirtland to announce Smith's fall because he permitted women to wear caps and men to wear shoulder pads in their coats. On another occasion, a small band of Saints declared their loyalty to a young boy to whom they claimed the Angel Moroni had appeared. Yet another group founded a totally communitarian society. More serious, however, was a prophetess who derived illumination from a black stone and briefly attracted the notice of David Whitmer, Frederick G. Williams, and Martin Harris.[34]

The prophet by no means remained passive in face of these threats, but a ready means to heal the schism within the church eluded him. On May 29, the Smith-controlled Kirtland High Council attempted to try dissenting Presidents David Whitmer and Frederick G. Williams,

Apostles Lyman E. Johnson and Parley Pratt, and Warren Parrish for misconduct, but instead it broke up in confusion. Several days later the prophet endeavored to elevate the Saints above their troubles by announcing God's command for the church to begin its foreign mission. This distraction tactic had worked well when Smith used it to relieve the gloom following the failure of Zion's Camp, but hard feelings now ran too deep to recapture the dissenters' imagination with new excitement. Finally, in mid-July when dissent had reached menacing proportions, Smith conceived a master stroke. On July 23, the prophet received a revelation sharply exhorting the apostles to humble themselves and go out on a preaching mission. For the dissenting apostles to disobey the revelation would have put them in an attitude of apostasy rather than dissent, and that was a step they were not yet prepared to make. Smith thus effectively deprived the dissenters of much of their leadership. During August, Smith continued to strengthen his position, and on September 3, he called for a general reorganization of the church. Brigham Young, determined to leave nothing to chance, packed the conference with Smith partisans and discouraged dissenters from attending. Each of the General Authorities of the church was then subjected to reappointment. Smith treated his opponents generously. To retain their positions, dissenters needed only to acknowledge the prophet's right to the leadership of the church. Most did so, but Apostles Luke and Lyman Johnson and John Boynton, along with Book of Mormon witness Martin Harris and several other lesser officials, were excommunicated. Presidents David Whitmer and Oliver Cowdery received only a warning to humble themselves and end their transgression. A week later, the crisis seemed over when the three dissenting apostles made their confessions and regained their offices.[35]

With the situation in Kirtland apparently well in hand, Smith and Rigdon left Ohio on September 27 to continue the reorganization in the Mormon settlement in Caldwell County, Missouri. The schism in the church, however, had been only superficially healed. When the prophet returned to Ohio on December 10, a fresh outbreak of dissent was tearing the church apart. Dissenters led by Warren Parrish now termed themselves "the old standard," called upon the Saints to reembrace their original membership in the "Church of Christ," and declared those loyal to Smith heretics. The prophet attempted to put an end to the turmoil by having forty to fifty dissenters excommunicated, but to no avail. The continuing foreclosure of property had sent a steady stream of Mormons migrating to Missouri. By December, the exchange of violent threats and lawsuits between the two church factions dramatically swelled this group. On January 12, 1838, Joseph Smith, facing death threats and criminal proceedings, found it necessary to flee Kirtland under the cover of night for the relative safety of Missouri. The temple, the printing press (until torched by an arsonist), and other church property that remained fell into the hands of dissenters. Although many poor Mormons lacked the means to follow the prophet immediately, Kirtland as a stronghold for the kingdom of God was finished.

Smith loyalists, however, did not leave dissent behind when they fled west. Prominent dissenters, such as Oliver Cowdery, David and John Whitmer, Lyman Johnson, Frederick Williams, and William Phelps, had left for Missouri in the fall of 1837. Not only did these men maintain contact with the Kirtland dissenters who remained behind, they organized themselves along similar lines. Like those calling themselves "the old standard," the Missouri dissenters saw themselves as conservatives remaining faithful to the early spirit of the church. Oliver Cowdery hoped, for instance, that their resistance to "those disorganizing doctrines lately introduced into the church" would prove "instrumental in preserving the Church of Christ on earth."[36]

Yet even as Cowdery and men like him agreed with David Whitmer that the recent innovations in the church had corrupted Mormonism's original purity, he fought these innovations in practice more in the name of republicanism than for the standard of the true faith. The prophet and certain other church leaders, Cowdery charged, were "desperate, and hot-headed, power-seeking ignorant men," who, to conceal their tyrannical ambitions, equated "not being friendly to Joseph" with not being friendly to God.[37] It was to foil these tyrannical designs that the Missouri dissenters met at Cowdery's home on January 30, 1838, and set up a committee on resolutions and declarations to determine their course of action. According to Cowdery, this committee intended to investigate "the manner in which some authorities of the [church] . . . have, for some time past and are still, endeavoring to unite ecclesiastical and civil authority, and force men, under the pretense of heaven to use their earthy substance contrary to their own interest and privilege; and also how said authorities are endeavoring to make it a rule of faith for said church to uphold a man or men right or wrong."[38] Cowdery conceded that he did "not expect the great body of the church here to unite in our views." Republican government, whether in society or in the church, depended upon individuals able to exercise their own free judgment, and in Cowdery's opinion, too many Mormons had already weakly prostrated theirs before the prophet. "We want none but independent men," he wrote, "not the ragamuffins who believe in man more than God."[39]

Cowdery was particularly nettled over the church's presuming to dictate how he used his property. When the High Council later charged him, in April, with selling his land contrary to revelation, Cowdery responded with an outburst of defiant republicanism, declaring that since feudalism did not exist in America, he had a perfect right to dispose of his property without the permission of a superior. One of his ancestors, he observed, had been among the small band of Plymouth pilgrims who had brought with them the rights of personal security, personal liberty, and property upon which rested America's happy form of government. These rights, Cowdery explained, "are so woven in my nature, have so long been inculcated into my mind by a liberal and intelligent ancestry that I am wholly unwilling to exchange them for anything less liberal, less benevolent, or less free." Unfortunately, it was exactly the surrender of these rights that the church demanded of him. The Mormon leadership, he continued, had created its own "petty government, controlled and dictated by ecclesiastical influence" within the more benevolent forms of American state and national government. He granted that the church leadership would deny any conflict between Mormon institutions and the political institutions of the country; but, he went on, "the bare notice of these charges [against me], over which you preserve a right to decide is, in my opinion, a direct attempt to make the secular power subservient to church direction."[40]

The dissenters' avowal that their individual freedom should take precedence over the judgment of church authorities made active conflict inevitable. Nor was it long in coming. In January, against church policy, William Phelps, Oliver Cowdery, and David Whitmer sold their land in Jackson County. The Saints had never abandoned hope of one day returning to their God-ordained Zion, and revelation specifically forbade the Mormons to sell their "inheritance" in the county. The dissenters' disobedience of this command struck many Saints as tantamount to denying the faith. In reaction, Smith loyalists called church conferences in February throughout the various Mormon settlements in Missouri and stripped dissenting presidents David Whitmer, John Whitmer, and William Phelps of their offices. The dissenters, however, believed themselves "illegally" tried and refused to acknowledge their suspension. Here matters rested until the early spring when Joseph Smith and other church leaders from Ohio began trickling into Far West, the main Mormon settlement in Missouri. The Kirtland apostasy crisis had left them deeply embittered. Smith characterized the Ohio period of the church as "seven years of servitude, persecution, and affliction in the midst of our enemies," and he, and those loyal to him, were in no mood to reason with men who challenged their leadership.[41] Accordingly, on April 12, the Missouri High Council charged David and John Whitmer, Oliver Cowdery, and Lyman Johnson with various counts of dereliction of duty, violation of church policy, and disrespect for the church leadership and cut them off from the church.

Even after the excommunication of the leading dissenters, however, Joseph Smith and Sidney Rigdon harbored a deep fear of the disruptive presence of their former brethren. In past years, disaffected Mormons had tarred and feathered the two leaders, repeatedly threatened them with death, and driven them from Ohio. In Missouri, despite their loss of church membership, the dissenters continued to agitate against the prophet, and Oliver Cowdery promised to take the church to court if Smith carried out his plans to reinstate the law of consecration. It was in this context that Dr. Sampson Avard approached the prophet with a plan to protect the First Presidency from physical violence through the creation of a bodyguard composed of members of a secret brotherhood. This brotherhood first appeared in June under a variety of names, but soon earned notoriety as "the Danites."

If the Danites began merely as a defensive bodyguard for the Presidency, they evolved quickly into an aggressive, malicious secret police force, and eventually into a nineteenth-century version of storm troopers. Unfortunately, Sampson Avard was, in John Corrill's words, "as grand a villain as his wit and ability would admit of."[42] The achingly ambitious Avard soon set out to make himself a power in the church. Toward this end, he hammered home the single principle of blind obedience to the prophet. According to Reed Peck, who attended several Danite meetings, initiates were informed that a command from Smith was a command from the Lord; therefore, they would not have "the privilege of judging whether it would be right or wrong, but [should] engage in its accomplishment and trust God for the result."[43]

Avard went so far as to say that this included murder. Should any member of the brotherhood, he forcefully added, reveal its secrets or designs, he would face execution. Avard's words had the desired effect. John Corrill reported that "some individuals went so far as to state, that they would kill any person, if the presidency would say it was the will of God; for these things were necessary sometimes to save the church from corruption and destruction."[44] Reed Peck, who related similar declarations, expressed only modest relief in believing Smith feared the consequences of such acts more than did his energumenical followers.[45] Not surprisingly, John Whitmer and other dissenters soon saw the Danites as a "secret combination," like the "Gadianton Robbers" who subverted the liberty of the Nephites in the Book of Mormon.[46]

The Danites' first task was the forcible removal of the excommunicated dissenters from Caldwell County. On June 17, Sidney Rigdon preached a rabble-rousing discourse, popularly known as "the salt sermon," derived from his exegesis of Matthew 5:13: "Ye are the salt of the earth: but if the salt have lost his savor, wherewith it be salted? It is thenceforth good for nothing, but to be cast out, and to be trodden under the foot of men." From this text, Rigdon reasoned that the Saints had not only a right but an obligation to suppress the dissenters who had lost their savor by abandoning the faith. The dissenters, he claimed, were guilty of heinous crimes and gross immoralities and were worthy of hanging. Joseph Smith then seconded Rigdon's remarks and, while cautioning the brethren against illegal action, asserted that Judas did not hang himself but was, in fact, hanged by Peter.[47] Rigdon and Smith probably wished only to scare the dissenters out of the county, but to make their message unmistakably clear, Rigdon quickly followed up his sermon with "A Note of Warning," signed by eighty-three elders, threatening the Whitmers, Oliver Cowdery, and Lyman Johnson with violent removal if they did not leave the county within three days. Upon receiving this ultimatum, the dissenters rode to Clay County to secure legal aid against the church. In their absence, however, the Danites turned their wives out of their homes, and Mormon-controlled courts confiscated their property through writs of attachment.[48]

The high-handed tactics employed against the dissenters offended the republican instincts of other Saints and eventually drove them into dissent. The most prominent of these men, John Corrill, Thomas

Marsh, Reed Peck, and John Clemison, had been in Missouri during
the Kirtland crisis and shared none of its bitterness. The most articulate, and perhaps the most important, was John Corrill. Unlike the
Ohio dissenters, Corrill never opposed the new church institutions,
but, on the contrary, welcomed them. In his view, they emulated the
republican principles of checks and balances while reserving ultimate
authority in the people.

> The first presidency, the high council, the twelve, and each of the
> seventies, were equal in power, that is to say, each had a right to dis-
> cipline their own members, and transact other business of the
> church within their calling, and a decision of either one of these
> bodies, when in regular session, could not be appealed from to any
> other, for one had no right or power to reverse or overthrow the
> judgment or decision of the other, but they could all be called to-
> gether and form a conference, consisting of all the authorities, to
> which an appeal could be taken from either one and the decision re-
> versed. These were the regular constituted authorities of the church;
> but, besides this, Smith and Rigdon taught the church that these au-
> thorities, in ruling or watching over the church, were nothing more
> than servants to the church, and that the church, as a body, had the
> power in themselves to do anything that either or all of these au-
> thorities could do, and that if either or all of these constituted au-
> thorities became deranged or broken down, or did not perform their
> duty to the satisfaction of the church, the church had a right to rise
> up in a body and put them out of office, make another selection and
> re-organize them, and thus keep in order, for the power was in the
> people and not in the servants.[49]

While Corrill subsequently found the system of checks and balances
within the church government inadequate to the challenge of prophetic infallibility, Sidney Rigdon heaped scorn on him and others like
Peck and Marsh who denounced the treatment of the dissenters as
antirepublican. Peck quoted Rigdon as arguing that the expulsion of
the dissenters was actually republicanism in action: "When a country,
or body of people have individuals among them with whom they do
not wish to associate and a public expression is taken against their
remaining among them and such individuals do not remove it is the
principle of republicanism itself that gives that community a right to
expel them forcibly and no law will prevent it."[50] Surely an argument
extolling democratic majoritarianism was a curious one from a leader
of a people so recently expelled from Jackson County upon that very
principle. Yet Rigdon and other church leaders were beyond abstract

discussions of republican rights. The dissenters had threatened to overthrow both them and the kingdom of God (which they regarded as synonymous). A minority when in Kirtland, they now had the whip hand and intended to use it.

The banishment of the dissenters initiated a veritable reign of terror against those who might doubt the wisdom of church policy. Men who had spoken out against the expulsion of the dissenters now found themselves, in turn, suspected of disloyalty. "We found that events of a few days," wrote Peck, "had placed Caldwell County under a despotic government where even liberty of speech was denied to those not willing to support the New Order."[51] Part of the campaign for conformity included an effort to ferret out malcontents by church-appointed secret agents who denounced church actions as unrepublican in hopes of soliciting agreement from likely suspects. Those found deviating from official opinion were castigated from the pulpit and often privately threatened with violence.[52] These tactics succeeded in forcing some Saints into confessing error while effectively frightening others into silence.[53]

The effort to enforce compliance with church policy reached its apogee when Joseph Smith received a revelation reinstituting a modified version of the law of consecration on July 8. Much to the chagrin of the leadership, many Saints chafed at the prospect of turning over their property to the church. Sidney Rigdon, accordingly, warned the Saints that any man resisting the revelation would be turned over to the "Brother of Gideon" (a code name for the Danites),[54] and Avard soon began an assiduous effort to insure submission to church direction. To those from whom he expected trouble, Avard minced no words, at one point warning Peck and Corrill that those attempting to evade the law would "meet with the fate of Ananias and Sophia who were killed by Peter."[55]

Despite the threats of retribution, promulgation of the law of consecration drove Corrill, Peck, and a handful of others into irrevocable opposition to the church leadership. Like the dissenters before them, they regarded as a menace to their liberties the union of ecclesiastical and temporal power that the revelation symbolized. Peck compared Saints obeying the law to slaves willingly submitting to a driver. Even worse, the Danites' attempt to compel acceptance of this union was nothing less, in Corrill's words, than an effort "to set up a monarchical government, in which the presidency should tyrannize and rule over all things."[56] Corrill's public opposition to the law of consecration finally provoked an angry confrontation with the prophet, who angrily told Corrill, "If you tell about the streets again that you do not believe this or that revelation, I will walk on your neck, sir!"[57] In a heated exchange of words, recorded by Smith, Corrill informed the prophet that

> he would not yield his judgment to anything proposed by the Church, or any individuals of the Church, or even the Great I Am, given through the appointed organ [i.e., the prophet] as revelation . . . for he was a Republican, and as such would do, say, act, and believe what he pleased.
>
> Mark such republicanism as this! A man to oppose his own judgment to the judgment of God, and at the same time to profess to believe in that same God, who has said: "The foolishness of God is wiser than man; and the weakness of God is stronger, than man."[58]

With these words, Smith summed up the irreconcilable differences that had separated the two factions of the church since the outbreak of dissent in Kirtland. Over the first seven years of the Mormon church's existence it grew to dominate larger and larger aspects of the convert's life. The dissenters, still attached to the belief in individual rights and liberties affirmed by republican culture, came to fear these developments as a growing tyranny within the church. To the main body of Saints, this particular application of republican principles to the kingdom of God seemed irrelevant. For them, church direction was God's direction, and to oppose the prophet's authority was to rebel against God.

Yet because the Mormon leadership crisis of 1837–38 pitted more theocratically minded Saints against more libertarian-minded dissenters, it is easy to forget that even the most fanatical devotees of the kingdom of God counted themselves firm republicans. Sometimes, however, defending the kingdom of God seemed to demand of loyalists a certain intellectual schizophrenia. The repressive measures taken against the dissenters were not republican in spirit. But Joseph Smith and his followers did espouse an unfeigned allegiance to republicanism. It was simply a republicanism of a more communal nature, in which the virtuous Saint transcended his own selfish interest for the benefit of the kingdom. In a sense, this style of republicanism was out of date; well before the late 1830s, most Americans had pressed their religious beliefs into the service of their political ideals. The Saints reversed this pattern. The Mormon's New England forefathers would have more readily appreciated the Saints' views than most of their contemporaries. These anachronistic ways made conflict inevitable both within the church and between the church and society. Those Mormons who insisted on resolving this conflict in favor of republican liberty at the expense of republican duty either left the church or were forced out. The purging of the dissenters, however, had the serious effect of moving the church even farther away from the mainstream of American society.

chapter 7

Republican Virtue
"Exterminated" in Missouri

When the Missouri legislature created Caldwell County in 1836–37 to provide a haven for the Mormons recently expelled from Clay County, it hoped to put an end to the persistent conflict between the Saints and their neighbors. The dispossessed Mormons eagerly accepted this offer of sanctuary, and Caldwell County filled up rapidly. The transplanted Saints from Clay were soon joined by church members fleeing schism-torn Kirtland and by a steady influx of new converts. In less than eighteen months, the number of Mormons in the area swelled to over 10,000 persons. Far West, the largest Mormon town, claimed 3,000 residents. Nearly 2,000 farms encompassed over 250,000 acres of land bought from the federal government. When one considers that only 1,200 Saints had been expelled from Jackson County in 1833, the magnitude of Mormon immigration becomes apparent.

The Saints' territorial ambitions, however, did not stop at the Caldwell County line. The church leadership soon envisioned a whole string of Mormon settlements stretched across several counties. It took little imagination for them to perceive that the immigrants would soon settle the best farm land in Caldwell and that more land for newcomers would be required. The Saints were grateful for the legislature's actions on their behalf, but as equal citizens of the state, they felt no legal or moral obligation to restrict themselves to one county and soon planted a number of small communities beyond the borders of Caldwell. This alarmed old settlers living near the new church settlements. These Missourians angrily denounced the church's expansionism as a violation of its agreement with the state and predicted the resumption of civil discord should the Mormons persist in settling outside of

129

Caldwell County. Nevertheless, the old citizens made no effort to halt Mormon settlement, and the initially circumspect manner of the Saints partially quelled gentile fears.

Although well-entrenched in their Caldwell County stronghold by the late spring of 1838, the Mormons possessed little sense of repose. Twice hounded from their Missouri homes, they remained fearful of being persecuted again. The bitter struggle between Joseph Smith's loyal followers and the dissidents had enhanced this sense of precariousness and left them yearning for greater security. Increasingly, the Mormons found this security in millenarian fantasies. In the May issue of the *Elders' Journal*, Alanson Ripely expressed the hopes of many of his brethren when he pronounced the day of their redemption to be near at hand. The Saints, he said, should comfort their hearts with reflection upon "the grand events which will transpire at the morn of the millennium; when there shall be no mobs to rise up against you; no weapon formed against you by lawless marauders; and no tongue to scandalize your character, by vain and groundless reports."[1]

Millenarian beliefs, of course, had always been central to Mormon thought. From the beginning, the Saints had viewed their gathering as a flight from the iniquity of Babylon. In the safety of their refuge, they would purify themselves and thus escape the awful judgment of God upon the wicked. The enthusiasm with which the Saints embraced millenarianism, however, ebbed and flowed according to changing circumstances. As the spring of 1838 turned into summer, the millenarian mood of the church deepened and altered in tone. Traditionally, the Mormons believed that they would play no role in the coming apocalyptic violence; vengeance belonged to the Lord alone. Yet from their perspective, the history of the church up to 1838 had been a long tale of religious persecution, and they were sorely tired of it. Instead of continuing to suffer passively the evils of the world, the Saints grew increasingly militant and ready to inflict God's vengeance upon any enemy—even a potential enemy.[2]

The Danites were the most extreme embodiment of this new Mormon militancy. When the leadership crisis faded, Avard, with the Presidency's blessing, transformed his three-hundred-member band into an antimob force. Already distinguished by their zealotry, the Danites proved ready to wage holy war against the gentiles if so commanded. Danite Alexander McRae even went so far as to swear, "[I]f Joseph should tell me to kill Van Buren in his presidential chair I would immediately start and do my best to assassinate him."[3] No one, of course, anticipated the need to assassinate Van Buren, but they were reasonably certain that war would come. When Avard presented the Danites for Smith's inspection, he and Rigdon prophesied that "great military glory and conquest" awaited them as one of the Lord's instruments in the last days.[4]

The great body of Danites were honest enough, if fanatical in their zeal. Unfortunately for the church, Sampson Avard was neither. A cynical opportunist, hungry for wealth and power, Avard pursued his goals single-mindedly. If many Mormons viewed war with the neighboring Missourians as likely, they nevertheless believed they would not be its instigators. Avard, on the other hand, informed his brethren that they would not merely defend the church in the event of mob attack, but carry out a religious duty to rob and plunder the old citizens, telling his captains:

> Know ye not, brethren, that it soon will be your privilege to . . .
> take to yourselves spoils of the goods of the ungodly Gentiles? for it
> is written, the riches of the Gentiles shall be consecrated to my peo-
> ple, the house of Israel; and thus you will waste away the Gentiles by
> robbing and plundering them of their property; and in this way we
> will build up the kingdom of God, and roll forth the little stone that
> Daniel saw cut out of the mountain without hands, and roll forth
> until it filled the whole earth. For this is the very way that God
> destines to build up His kingdom in the last days. If any of us
> should be recognized, who can harm us? for we will stand by each
> other and defend one another in all things. If our enemies swear
> against us, we can swear also. . . . As the Lord liveth, I would swear
> to a lie to clear any of you; and if this would not do, I would put
> them or him under the sand as Moses did the Egyptian; and in this
> way we will consecrate much unto the Lord, and build up His king-
> dom; and who can stand against us?[5]

Although the existence and purpose of the Danites was a carefully guarded secret, the old settlers soon learned of the brotherhood, which they nicknamed "the Damnites."[6] The specter of bloodthirsty fanatics moving secretly among them struck terror in their hearts, and they readily ascribed crimes both real and imaginary to the band. While the Danite organization would last only for about five months, for the next half century the church would be plagued with rumors of its continued existence.

Mormon belligerence was sounded more publically at the 1838

Fourth of July celebrations at Far West. Joseph Smith proclaimed the day's theme to be a "Declaration of Independence from all mobs." Sidney Rigdon's keynote address consisted largely of the conventional republican pieties expected upon the occasion.[7] Rigdon praised the nation's founders, extolled the constitution's guarantee of rights and liberties, and warned Americans that the maintenance of freedom depended upon their virtue rather than their legislators. Rigdon went on, however, to express Mormon anger at the past treatment of the church. Coupling Biblical and republican rhetoric, he declared,

> We have not only when smitten on one cheek turned the other, but we have done it, again and again, until we are weary of being smitten, and tired of being trampled upon. . . . But from this day and this hour, we will suffer it no more.

> We take God and all of the holy angels to witness this day, that we warn all men in the name of Jesus Christ, to come on us no more forever; for . . . the man or set of men, who attempts it, does it at the expense of their lives. And that mob that comes on us to disturb us, it shall be between us and them a war of extermination, for we will follow them, till the last drop of their blood is spilled, or else they will have to exterminate us: for we will carry the seat of war to their own houses, and their families, and one party or the other shall be utterly destroyed. . . .

> We therefore . . . proclaim our liberty on this day as did our fathers. And we pledge . . . to one another, our fortunes, our lives, and our sacred honors, to be delivered from the persecutions which we have had to endure for the last nine years.[8]

At the conclusion of Rigdon's speech, the largely Mormon audience burst into loud cries of "Hosanna," symbolically "sealing" his words.

An angry man by nature, Sidney Ridgon emerged as the foremost of a number of advocates of a hard line against the Mormons' enemies. Similarly, the influence of the hot-headed Lyman Wight, whom Joseph Smith (genuinely pacifistic at heart) had previously held in low regard, rose significantly. Wight positively itched for combat. As the leader of a settlement called Adam-ondi-Ahmam in Daviess County, Wight continually pushed his followers toward violence. On June 24, a Mormon named William Swartznell wrote in his diary that he could no longer "listen with ease to the preaching of Lyman White [*sic*] [and] his exhorting war upon the peaceful citizens of Missouri. . . . In one of his sermons he denounced [them] . . . as 'hypocrites, long faced dupes, devils, infernal hobgoblins, and ghosts, and that they ought to be damned and sent to hell, where they properly belonged.'"9 Two weeks later, Wight told his brethren "that Peter's having cut off the ear of the High Priest's (Caiphus) servant, was a strong argument for war."10

Similar speeches soon echoed throughout the Mormon settlements. John Corrill noted some months later that "this kind of preaching was the chief topic of conversation all last summer, until many of the church became inspired with the belief that God would enable them to stand against anything, even the state of Missouri, or the United States, if they should come in a mob."11 Yet beneath the swagger of the more boastful members of the church lay a deeper fear that they would again lose their homes and their rights, a fear revealed by a curious incident after Rigdon's Independence Day address. A few days after the Fourth, when the Mormons had raised a liberty pole, lightning blasted it into a thousand fragments. So deep was the impression on all the settlers in Far West that few Mormon diarists or memorialists failed to mention the event. To most, it symbolized, in Parley Pratt's words, "an end to liberty and law in . . . [Missouri], and that our little city strove in vain to maintain the liberties of a country that was ruled by wickedness and rebellion."12 Ebenezer Robinson recalled that when Joseph Smith perceived the panic among the Saints, he rushed to where the pole had stood, "walked over the splinters, and prophesied that as he 'walked over these splinters, so we will trample our enemies under our feet.' This," said Robinson, "gave encouragement to the fearful and timid."13

Whether the Mormons would inevitably have come into conflict with their neighbors must remain an open question, but there can be no doubt that their bellicose defense of their rights did much to ensure its likelihood. As John Corrill pointed out, Lyman Wight's verbal assaults upon his gentile neighbors caused them to fear for their own security and to band together against the Saints. Sidney Rigdon's Fourth of July address was even more influential in this regard. Many local Missourians of standing had attended his speech, and others could read it in either the gentile paper, *Far West*, or in a pamphlet published by the Mormons themselves. Ironically, rather than forcing the old settlers into a new respect for the Saints' rights, Rigdon's words, as Ebenezer Robinson observed, "exerted a powerful influence in arousing the people of the whole upper Missouri."14

On August 6, an election riot at Gallatin in Daviess County opened a three-month death struggle between the Mormons and the old settlers. Before the election, a Whig office seeker named William P. Penniston attempted to court the new Mormon voters in the county. Previously, the county had been evenly divided between Whigs and Democrats, and the Mormons could now provide the winning margin. Most Mormons, however, were Democrats and spurned Penniston's advances. Their rejection made the ambitious Penniston the Saints' implacable foe. On election day, he railed against the church leadership, calling them lying thieves and their followers degraded fanatics. Their depravity, Penniston claimed, made them unfit for the rights of citizenship. Their political participation would make a mockery of the citizenship of others. He warned that the old settlers were in danger of losing their suffrage altogether if they did not immediately halt Mormon immigration. Penniston boasted that he had led anti-Mormon forces in Clay County and would not oppose Mormons' being mobbed at the polls. At these words, an old settler shouted that the Mormons had no more right to vote than "niggers" and then struck a Mormon voter.[15] It quickly became apparent that this was not a spontaneous outburst of anti-Mormonism; the Missourians had planned the attack. The Saints, however, were not caught off guard. Two weeks earlier, a Democratic judge named Morin had disclosed the conspiracy to the Mormons. While the Saints later claimed to have ignored the warning, a cadre of Danites had spent election day lounging around the polls.[16] When the first Mormon voter was struck, John L. Butler, a Danite leader, gave a secret signal to his brethren; and in the general melee, the Saints routed their enemies.

If, for their part, the Missourians had attacked the Mormons to preserve the civic virtue of the community, the Saints, likewise, counterattacked in defense of republican rights. After the victory, Butler declared from the top of a pile of timber that his ancestors had fought the Revolution for an independent government of equal rights and he would willingly die before he surrendered the right to vote.[17] In high spirits, the Mormons proceeded to the polls; but before they had finished voting, the mob, now armed, returned and forced the Saints to flee for their lives.

The first report of the election riot that reached Joseph Smith in Caldwell County claimed that two Saints had died in the skirmish and that the old settlers had forbidden their burial. Outraged, Smith,

Sampson Avard, and a large group of followers set off for Daviess to recover their dead and defend their brethren. In Adam-ondi-Ahmam, however, Smith learned the true circumstances of the fight and found the Mormons there no longer in immediate peril. The prophet nevertheless remained indignant at the rising hostility against the Saints in the county. When Smith discovered that a local justice of the peace, Adam Black, had organized the anti-Mormons, the prophet and perhaps 125 to 150 men rode to Black's farm and extracted from him a pledge to uphold the constitution and divorce himself from further anti-Mormon activities: "I, Adam Black, a Justice of the Peace of Daviess County, do hereby Sertify to the people coled Mormin, that he is bound to support the Constitution of this State, and of the United States, and his is not attached to any mob, nor will he attach himself to any such people, and so long as they will not molest me, I will not molest them."[18]

The Mormons' call upon Judge Black proved to be a major error. Not surprisingly, the Missourians considered the Saints' attempt to insure Black's judicial independence a shameless attack upon it. Anti-Mormons easily worked the incident to great advantage, eventually galvanizing the old settlers of the entire region into unified action. Two days after the Saints' visit to Black's farm, the untiring William Penniston submitted an affidavit to Judge Austin King claiming that an insurrectionary band of 500 Mormons had invaded Daviess County. The Saints, Penniston charged, came "to take revenge for some injuries, or imaginary injuries, done to some of their friends," and he himself was targeted for death. Revenge, however, was said not to be their primary motive. Ultimately, the Mormons intended "to intimidate and drive from the county all old citizens, and possess their lands, or force such as do not have, to . . . submit to their dictation." This intimidation, Penniston observed, had begun with Judge Black, whom the Saints had forced "under threats of immediate death, to sign a paper of a very disgraceful nature."[19] Eighteen days later, Black affirmed Penniston's version of the incident and added that the Mormons had openly declared "they could not submit to the laws."[20]

Judge King was ready to listen to Mormon atrocity stories. The Saints had killed few gentiles in Jackson County, but King's brother-in-law was one of them. On the strength of Penniston's affidavit, King issued arrest warrants for Joseph Smith and Lyman Wight. By this time, however, Smith had returned to Caldwell County, and he pointed out to the Daviess County sheriff that his jurisdiction ended at the county line. On the other hand, Lyman Wight, a citizen of Daviess, angrily vowed he would never submit to arrest "despite the whole state of Missouri." According to Swartznell, Wight informed a group of peacemakers from Clay County "that he owed nothing to the laws—the laws had not protected him—he had been on the rack for seven years—he had suffered enough—God did not require him to endure more—and that he would not yield to the laws of Missouri— he would sooner die and be buried."[21] Unfortunately for the Saints, the newspapers soon broadcast Wight's injudicious words across north-western Missouri.

The inability to bring Smith and Wight to trial seemed to confirm that the Mormons would not "submit to the laws." Soon men from eleven counties began planning their capture. Smith saw the demand for his extradition to Daviess as a prelude to his lynching. Yet he feared the onset of open warfare between the Saints and anti-Mormons if he refused. As tension rose, this fear overrode his concern for his own safety. Although consenting to his arrest, Smith demanded and obtained as a price for his cooperation an agreement from Judge King to hold his trial just inside Daviess County. The prophet then stationed a Mormon company on the Caldwell County line in the event of trouble. In the end, the trial proved anticlimactic. King merely required Smith and Wight to post a $500 bond to keep the peace, and both returned safely to their homes.

Smith had hoped to pacify anti-Mormons by submitting to trial, but hostilities had gone too far, and appeasement was impossible. The Black affair and its aftermath consolidated gentile opinion that they could no longer live in peace with the Saints.[22] Mormonism seemed a kind of insanity separating church members from the rest of humanity. Take, for instance, the case of one perplexed mobber who, after the onset of general warfare, threatened Lucy Smith with death. Mother Smith replied that she would then "be at rest." "There it is again," exclaimed the frustrated Missourian. "You tell a Mormon that you will kill him, and they will always tell you, 'that is nothing—if you kill us we will be happy.'"[23]

By harnessing this diseased religious imagination, Joseph Smith seemed to have corrupted the Saints' civic independence and made their will an extension of his own. "As old Joe Smith votes," grumbled one old settler, "so will every Mormon in the county vote."[24] In the nineteenth century, Americans believed that neither the "degraded" black nor the "savage" Indian had the necessary republican character to participate in civic affairs. With remarkable ease, the Missourians lumped the Mormons together with these disenfranchised people. This debasement left Parley Pratt sputtering with indignation. For while the old citizens, rather than the Saints, painted themselves for war like Indians and committed all manner of crimes, they "were denominated citizens, whites, etc., in most of the journals of the state. While those who stood firm for the laws, were denominated 'Mormons' [still a hated nickname], in contradistinction to the appellation of 'citizens,' 'whites,' etc., as if we had been some savage tribe, or some colored race of foreigners."[25] But the mobber who shouted that Mormons had no more right to vote than "niggers" at the start of the Gallatin election riot was, at least in his own mind, defending the republican basis of the franchise. Allowing the Saints to vote would make a mockery of republicanism.

If the Mormons voluntarily surrendered their freedom to a man they worshipped as God, the gentiles feared that Joseph Smith would compel them to do the same. They regarded the Mormon prophet as an aspiring tyrant, who dreamed of ruling an empire stretching across northwestern Missouri. Smith's original plan of domination had hinged upon filling up the region with his fanatical followers until he could effortlessly subvert the Missourians' liberties. The old citizens in Daviess, explained John Corrill, feared that the growing Mormon colony at Adam-ondi-Aham would surpass "their" county seat at Gallatin, that the whole county would fall to Saints soon afterwards, and that they themselves would be forced "to live under the laws and administration of 'Joe Smith.'"[26] Those who initially doubted the prophet's evil intent were certain of it after the Black affair exposed his hidden ambition in all of its stark hideousness. Clearly if the old citizens did not quietly submit to his tyrannical sway, Smith would impose his will by the sword. The pivotal moment for the survival of republican freedom, what J. G. A. Pocock calls the "Machiavellian moment," had thus arrived.[27] If the Missourians were to save their homes and liberties, they had to expel the Mormons immediately. "If we would not do so now," declared an old Daviess resident, "they will be so strong that we cannot compel them to go," and "they will rule the country as they please."[28]

During August, both antagonists prepared for battle. While anti-

Mormon volunteers began gathering from the countryside, the Saints mustered every able-bodied male into the "Army of Israel." On the thirtieth of that month, Governor Lilburn Boggs called out the militia to preserve the peace. Before long, over three thousand men took to the field, with, as one newspaper quipped, "no scarcity of Generals."[29] The militia, however, was hardly an ideal peacekeeping force. Composed of old settlers from northwestern Missouri, most militiamen hated the Mormons as intensely as the most antagonistic old settlers, and they made little effort to disguise their prejudices.

After weeks of bluster, the old settlers finally initiated operations at a little Mormon town called DeWitt, located in the southeast corner of Carroll County. A group of recent Canadian converts had settled in DeWitt to provide the Saints with a port on the Grand River. Because of its remoteness from the heavily Mormon areas in Caldwell and Daviess counties, DeWitt made an ideal point at which to begin rolling back the Mormon empire. On September 20, emissaries from the mob approached the townspeople with a warning to leave the county by October 1 or face destruction. When the Saints rejected the ultimatum, the old settlers laid siege to the town, denying its inhabitants food and firing upon any person attempting to aid them from the outside.

The state militia made no attempt to interfere with the siege. Its commander in Carroll County, General H. G. Parks, declared his troops too few and too mutinous to disperse the mob. Thus, when the old settlers briefly attacked the townspeople on October 4, the militia stood idly by. If General Parks was unable or unwilling to help the Saints, however, General Samuel Lucas, another commander in the area, clearly desired to see the Mormons massacred. Five years earlier, Lucas had helped drive the Saints from Jackson County. Upon learning of the skirmish between the Missourians and Mormons at DeWitt, he wrote Governor Boggs: "If a fight has taken place, of which I have no doubt, it will create excitement in the whole upper Missouri, and those base and degraded beings will be exterminated from the face of the earth. If one of the citizens of Carroll County should be killed, before five days I believe there will be from four to five thousand volunteers in the field against the Mormons, and nothing but their blood will satisfy them."[30]

Although no one in fact died in the exchange of fire, Lucas accurately predicted the effect of the fight. Anti-Mormonism now spread across the state. Even in relatively distant Howard County, recruiters beat the drum for volunteers, exhorting the citizenry to rise up in its sovereignty and crush the Mormon rebellion before it could gather strength. By firing upon the old settlers at DeWitt, they charged, the Saints had become "guilty of high treason; they have violated the laws of the land and shed blood of our citizens; and we think this is one of the cases of emergency in which the people ought to take the execution of justice in their own hands. Speedy action is necessary; the progress of their imposition, insult, and oppression must be checked in the beginning. . . . We must be enemies to the common enemies of our laws, religion, and country."[31]

As the anti-Mormon forces grew larger and bolder, DeWitt's fall became inevitable unless outside aid was immediately forthcoming. In a desperate attempt to secure that support, Joseph Smith sent a sympathetic gentile named Caldwell to plead the Saints' cause before the governor. Unfortunately, his appeal fell upon deaf ears. On October 9, Caldwell returned to Far West and reported Boggs as saying that "the quarrell was between the Mormons and the mob," and that "they might fight it out."[32] With no prospect of relief from either the governor or the militia, on October 11 the half-starved residents finally agreed to abandon the town and marched to Caldwell County under a white flag.

The success in driving the Mormons from Carroll County scuttled an attempt to negotiate a peaceful settlement between the two belligerents in Daviess County. There, General Alexander Doniphan, the Saints' former lawyer, had succeeded in persuading many Missourians to sell out to incoming church members. Some settlers needed little convincing. Feeling helpless before the Mormon juggernaut, they offered to part with their homes and farms, many for less than the cash value of their crops already in the ground. The timid were emboldened to stay, however, by the expulsion of the Saints from Carroll County. Anti-Mormon forces now came pouring into Daviess County to reenact their triumph at DeWitt.

Despite the old settlers' patriotic crusade to destroy the Mormon empire, the Saints themselves also rallied to the defense of God and country. Many church members expected the Lord to unleash his anger at those who had violated their rights. And at first it appeared that he had. Albert Rockwood, a young Mormon, discerned divine punishment in the gentiles' earlier flight from the county after their attempt

to deny the Saints' right to vote at the Gallatin election riot.[33] However, when the old settlers returned to the attack, heavily reinforced by
anti-Mormons from other counties, God's ways once again became
inscrutable. Still, a warming sense of solidarity enveloped the Saints,
knowing as they did that they fought for something larger than themselves. Rockwood reported that in Adam-ondi-Aham, the brethren
met and decided, "Our lives, honors and fortunes are now pledged to
defend the Consitution of the U. States our individual rights and our
Holy Religion. The strongest cords of Union appear to be writhed
around the heart of every man . . . here the hoary headed Sire and the
striplen youth gird on their armor to the field prepare. Death appears
to have lost its terrors among the armies of Israel."[34]

The Mormons in Daviess County were not alone in welcoming the
coming battle. The Saints had wallowed in frustration during the siege
of DeWitt. It was hard to resist the urge to rescue their brethren and
to rely instead on the legal authority of the militia and the governor.
Ironically, when the militia displayed its sympathy with the mob and
Governor Boggs callously ignored their plight, the Mormons were
simply freed from their debilitating anxiety. The situation now at least
seemed clear. They could depend only upon themselves to protect
their rights.

On October 15, Joseph Smith delivered a highly emotional address
to his followers.[35] Smith believed the political corruption festering in
the state had finally extinguished its republican form of government.
"The Governor," he declared, "is mob, the militia are mob, and the
whole state is mob."[36] Ever since the Saints arrived in Missouri, they
had repeatedly pleaded for their rights before judges, the governor,
and even the president of the United States, but none of them cared
for the law except as a weapon against the church. The Saints had
looked to the legal system long enough, and Smith swore they would
do so no longer. If the Missourians did not cease making war upon the
church, the prophet warned that "he would be a second Mahomet to
this generation, and he would make it one gore of blood from the
Rocky Mountains to the Atlantic Ocean; that like Mahomet, whose
motto in treating for peace was 'the Alcoran, or the Sword,' so should
it be eventually with us, 'Joseph Smith or the Sword.'"[37] Changing the
metaphor, the prophet went on to compare the church to the little
stone Daniel had foreseen that crushed the kingdoms of the world.[38]
Those seeking to destroy the church would find themselves destroyed

instead. If neither the militia nor the governor would help the Saints, Smith assured the brethren, they would have angels fighting by their side. One Mormon would put a thousand mobbers to flight, two Mormons ten thousand mobbers.

Once the Saints decided to take the offensive, the martial spirit waxed strong. Lyman Wight bragged that the church would take St. Louis before the winter's end.[39] On October 18, the Mormons opened their military campaign in Daviess County, sacking and burning gentile homes in Gallatin, Millport, and Grindstone Fork. The prophet had told the Saints he did not expect them to go to war at their own expense, but the Mormons' passion for plunder shocked even Danite John D. Lee. From "the first moment when the restrictions of the church were withdrawn," said Lee, "the most devout men in our community acted like they had served a lifetime in evil and were natural born thieves."[40] Yet while some Saints undoubtedly did steal for private gain, the church commanded that all booty be consecrated to the bishop's storehouse for distribution to the needy. In any case, the old settlers had already pillaged all but the largest church settlements and had burned most of the Mormons' crops. Thus, from the Saints' point of view, they waged war for their lives, homes, food, and sacred liberty; looting the gentiles was not only honorable, but virtuous. As Benjamin Johnson explained, "It should not be supposed . . . that we were common robbers because we took by reprisal that with which to keep from starvation our women and children. Ours was a struggle for our lives and homes, and a more conscientious, noble, and patriotic spirit never enthused man than that which animated our leaders in this just defense of our rights."[41]

Although the Mormons and their enemies continued to despoil each other's property, both sides studiously avoided any more direct challenges to the other. On October 22, however, the former mob leader Captain Samuel Bogart led a detachment of the Ray County militia into Caldwell and captured three Mormons who had been spying on its movements. On the following day, the Saints decided to liberate their brethren by a surprise raid upon the militia's encampment on Crooked River. Shouting "God and liberty," the Mormons stormed into the camp and successfully routed Bogart's men. With grim humor, Hosea Stout boasted that thirty or forty of the mobbers fleeing across the river were "there baptised without faith or repentance under the messingers of lead sent by the brethren."[42] Stout's exultation over the Saints' victory was misplaced. The Mormons had in fact killed only one militiaman—the sole gentile to die in the so-called "Mormon War." The Saints, on the other hand, lost three men, including their beloved apostle, David Patten.

More important, the Battle of Crooked River marked the beginning of the end of the Mormon church in Missouri. At first, after the Saints' attack scattered Bogart's men, it appeared that nearly the whole company of fifty to sixty men had been slaughtered. Hysterical officials in nearby Richmond quickly wrote Governor Boggs of the presumed bloodbath and warned that Mormons were marching toward Richmond promising to burn it to the ground.[43] Boggs also received a copy of an affidavit sworn to by dissenting apostle Thomas Marsh that reported Joseph Smith's threat to become "a second Mahomet to this generation." Accepting both of these accounts as accurate, the governor wrote General John B. Clark on October 27, declaring the Saints in rebellion against the laws and in open warfare against the people of Missouri. "The Mormons," he ordered, "must be treated as enemies, and must be exterminated or driven from the state, if necessary for the public good."[44]

The real massacre did not take place at Crooked River, but in a small Mormon community called Haun's Mills. Even without knowledge of the governor's "exterminating order," a number of locally prominent men led a mob of 240 into the church settlement on October 30 and shot every Mormon male they could catch. Out of the 38 men living in the community, 18 were murdered and 13 wounded. No mobber was injured.

Anti-Mormon violence now raged unrestrained. Boggs's exterminating order made anti-Mormonism official. Militiamen from neighboring counties swarmed into Caldwell to lay siege to Far West. The inhabitants of the town feared that they would soon share the fate of their Haun's Mills brethren, but the elders boldly declared they would honor their country and constitution by fighting to the last man for their rights.[45] Publically, Joseph Smith encouraged this bravado to sustain the church's morale, but privately he felt no yearning for a bloodbath, however noble its cause. Acting in secrecy, the prophet sent dissenters John Corrill and Reed Peck to find General Doniphan and "beg like a dog for peace"; later adding that he would "rather go to States-prison for twenty years, or . . . die himself than have the people exterminated."[46]

Unfortunately for the Saints, General Samuel Lucas had assumed command of the combined militia. Lucas refused to accept Far West's surrender except under the harshest of terms: all Mormons were to sign over their property to those who suffered losses in the "war" against them; the church leaders were to deliver themselves up for trial; and all of the Saints not under arrest were to leave the state. Seeing no realistic alternative to compliance, the prophet and his lieutenants turned themselves over to their enemies and the militia triumphantly entered Far West. With the church leaders now at his mercy, Lucas decided to make an example of them to the rest of the Mormons, and after a hasty court-martial he ordered General Doniphan to shoot them. Doniphan not only refused to obey the order, but promised Lucas he would see him tried for murder if he executed the Mormons, thus narrowly saving their lives.

The conflict between the Saints and the Missourians occurred within a growing tangle of accusations; each side saw the other as perpetrating such manifest violations of the principles of republican government as interference with the rights of conscience, free speech and assembly; forcible exclusion from the franchise; intimidation of judicial authority; vigilantism; armed resistance to an authorized militia; confiscation of property; and imprisonment without due process. Seriously outnumbered, the Mormons lost the debate over who had infringed upon the other's republican rights.

In the gentile view, the Mormons had violated the spirit of republicanism as interpreted by antebellum America. In an age that extolled individualism as a cardinal republican virtue, the clannish Saints, who submitted their lives to the total control of their prophet, appeared the very antithesis of good republicans. This theme was heavily underscored by General John B. Clark, who succeeded Lucas as the occupational commander of Far West on November 4. Two days after his arrival, Clark assembled the Mormons and lectured them on their civic sins, informing them that all of their troubles stemmed from their disaffection from society and their refusal to submit to its governance. While many Saints struck him as intelligent people, he only wished he could somehow "invoke *that Great Spirit, the Unknown God,* to rest upon you, and make you sufficiently intelligent to break that chain of superstition, and liberate you from the fetters of fanaticism with which you are now bound—that you no longer worship a man." Clark not only believed that the Mormons had lost their civic virtue in their slavish obedience to their prophet; he also thought they forfeited the right to toleration by causing their neighbors to fear their own forced subjugation to the church. If they wished to save themselves from irretrievable ruin, Clark advised the Saints to "scatter abroad" and "become as other citizens," shunning the control of their bishops and presidents lest they once again "excite the jealousies of the people."[47] Furthermore, if General Clark implicitly conceded that the great body of Mormons were probably a decent, if deluded, people, he also saw them as the foot soldiers of an evil conspiracy that aimed at no less than the overthrow of the state government and eventually the national government. In his "Full Report" to Governor Boggs, Clark called the supposed Mormon revolt "an insurrection of no ordinary character. It had for its object *Dominion*, and the ultimate subjugation of this State and the Union to the laws of a few men called the Presidency."[48] On November 9, Austin King, acting as a committing judge, began gathering evidence for the state to prove these charges of treason, as well as murder, arson, and other crimes, against fifty-six leading Mormons. In the end, the state's case hung almost exclusively upon the testimony of a handful of church dissenters. Sampson Avard, who now exchanged his opportunistic Mormonism for opportunistic anti-Mormonism, did his best to incriminate the church Presidency by producing a previously unknown Danite constitution which, for all its plebeian bluster, was quickly heralded as a blueprint for monarchy. The most serious evidence against the church emerged from dissenters' accounts of the heated speech Joseph Smith delivered after Governor Boggs refused to aid the besieged Saints at DeWitt. The prophet's claim that the church was the little stone destined to crush the kingdoms of the world, as foretold in the prophecy of Daniel, was construed as proof of the Mormons' seditious intent, and Smith's condemnation of the governor, the militia, and the laws was considered a Mormon declaration of war. Largely on the basis of this testimony and the subsequent attack on Bogart's militiamen, Judge King ruled that there was sufficient evidence to try the prophet and nine of his closest associates.[49]

As fear of the Mormons subsided with their surrender, a new wind of public opinion more favorable to the Saints began to blow. On closer inspection, the evidence of Mormon revolutionary designs dissolved into rumor. More important, the largely abstract case against the church's intentions paled against the brutal facts of anti-Mormon violence. The looting and burning of Gallatin and Millsport seemed a trifle compared to the ruthless slaughter at Haun's Mills. During the entire course of the conflict, the old settlers lost only one man: at least forty Saints died. Furthermore, the quick resettlement of Mormon lands by their conquerors suggested that the latter had gone to war only for the spoils. Most shameful of all, Governor Boggs's order to expel or exterminate the Mormons seemed to many Missourians the act of a tyrant.

The Mormons derived little benefit from this new-found sympathy. An appeal to the Missouri legislature for the restitution of their property brought no result, nor was the governor's explusion order rescinded. Between November 1, 1838, and May 1, 1839, ten thousand Mormons made their exodus from Missouri to a safer home in Illinois. The changed political climate did work, however, to the advantage of the imprisoned church leaders. During the spring of 1839, their captors either gradually released them or permitted their escape. Such was the case of Joseph Smith, when, once on the verge of execution, his captors connived at his bolt for freedom during a change of venue on April 15.

If Missouri officials wished to forget the Mormon War, the Saints did not. The death of their brethren, the loss of their homes and farms, and their expulsion from the state under the color of law left them with wounds that would not heal. For the next five years, the Mormons tirelessly petitioned the governors and legislatures of other states; President Van Buren; presidential aspirants, such as Henry Clay and John C. Calhoun; Congress; and the American public to bring pressure upon Missouri to indemnify them for their losses. Although their pleas achieved nothing tangible, the Saints won considerable sympathy by portraying the Missouri citizenry as half-lettered barbarians.

The Mormon effort to secure the support of the rest of the country in their contentions with Missouri usually began with an almost storybook description of their fidelity to the American republican tradition. The Saints were well aware of the common belief that they were alienated from this heritage, "native-born foreigners," as it were. Consequently, they usually strove to shed Mormon peculiarity by tracing their Americanism back through American revolutionary and Pilgrim ancestors.[50]

However republican their pedigree, the Saints still had to prove themselves faithful heirs of their forefathers' legacy. In that attempt, they relied heavily upon the popular sentimental republicanism of the day, which celebrated the industrious worker who devoted his blessed freedom to creating a civilization of comfortable homes, productive farms, and benevolent government. With great pathos, one such church writer related how the Saints, after their brutal expulsion from Jackson County, had migrated to Caldwell in hope of finding

> a place of refuge, an abode of comfort, a residence of safety and an asylum of repose; where they might, for a time, shun the turbulence of oppression's tide, and enjoy the blessings of Freedom and privileges of American Liberty. For a time, all was peace, harmony and contentment—industry prevailed, homes of comfort were erected, prosperity shed its enlivening radiance around, and the aspect of comfort, happiness and domestic enjoyment, soon reared its concolating [*sic*] ensign to gladden the heart and cheer the low depression of spirit, that reigned in the bosom of each afflicted saint. A county, embracing a considerable extent of territory, was soon densely populated. Farms began to be opened up in all directions, dwellings to spring up as if by magic, and where once the solitude of the forest reigned supreme, and naught was heard but the appalling scream of beasts of rage or fear, or the gentle cooing of the timid dove and merry chant of birds of song, now resounded the pleasing echo of the forester's axe. The rude tones of nature began to recede before the swelling tide of emigration and give way to the more cheering tones of civilization. They settled in peace, purchased lands of the Government, and began to exercise all of those political rights so dear to Americans—guaranteed to them by every endearing tie of patriotism, of philanthropy, and by the Constitution of our country.[51]

In the Mormon view of things, it was precisely this good republican character that got them into trouble with their neighbors. As the result of the Saints' "laudable industry and blessings of heaven," said Noah Packard, old settlers and Mormons alike expected Caldwell to become the wealthiest and most populous county in the state within five years. Unfortunately, this growing prosperity "awakened a covetous spirit in the hearts" of these old citizens, who did not share the Saints' virtues.[52] The Mormons as an "intelligent, industrious and enterprising people," noted Sidney Rigdon, provided a stark "contrast to the general idleness and lazy habits" of the Missourians who, as Packard pointed out to the Massachusetts legislature, "depended mostly upon the labor of their slaves for their prosperity," rather than their own exertions.[53]

Thus, fearing the loss of their economic and social position in the state, and jealous of the Saints' success, the old settlers set to scheming against the church until finally "a regular system of mobocracy was entered into, to rid the state of their rivals in prosperity."[54]

In response to the mob's first threats, the Mormons at the July 4 celebrations had put the old settlers on notice that they would no longer passively submit to persecution. Rigdon said that, for a time, this seemed to have curbed the Missourians' appetite for the Saints' lands, but in reality, they had merely decided to wait until the Mormons had more worth taking away.[55] If Rigdon was correct, the gentiles must have thought the Mormons were prospering quickly—they attacked the Mormons at the Gallatin election only one month later. The old settlers argued that the Saints had lost their right to vote because they acted in the unthinking service of their prophet's private ambitions rather than for the good of the whole community. But the Mormons would have none of this argument, which they saw as a cover-up for avarice. Elias Higbee, speaking on behalf of a Mormon petition before a U.S. Senate committee, implicitly conceded that the Missourians might have been justified in their actions if their charges were true. But, he said, the Saints acted just as independently as other citizens; each member "exercised the right of suffrage according to his better judgment, and without any ecclesiastical restraint being put upon him." Higbee granted that it was true the Mormons had voted overwhelmingly for Democratic candidates, yet most church members had been Democrats before their conversion. More important, the church did not have to tell the brethren for whom to vote. In the light of past persecutions, they would naturally support those who promised to protect them from their enemies. Unfortunately, Higbee concluded, in the troubles that followed, the Democrats proved as willing to mob the Mormons as the Whigs.[56]

The Saints found the subsequent charges of treason against them for resisting the mob's attack particularly nettling when they obviously held American institutions in greater reverence than did their oppressors. Parley Pratt, the foremost Mormon commentator on the war, claimed that the Mormons had behaved peacefully until the old settlers attempted to deny them their rights and drive them from their homes. When the Saints finally resisted these attacks, a coalition of priests, bigots, and a corrupt press successfully obscured reality by branding the whole affair "the Mormon insurrection." "A deceived public," Pratt complained, soon viewed "all of our acts of defense precisely as they would look upon the same acts performed, without cause or provocation, upon a peaceable citizenry." Even more galling, the Missourians pointed to the Mormons' opposition to the militia as prima facie proof of their treason. The Saints, however, could perceive no difference between the mob and, in Pratt's words, the "murderous gangs" assembled in the state's service. The Mormons were thus faced with a dilemma; if they had respected the militia's official status, they would have lost their homes without even endeavoring to save them, yet in fighting the militia, they had brought down upon their heads the wrath of the state as if they were revolutionaries.[57]

The supposed Mormon ambition to build a temporal kingdom, independent of the state and national government, was, they said, a preposterous lie, originating with their enemies, not the church. Parley Pratt wrote of his astonishment when the Missourians not only accused the Saints of creating an independent nation, but treated them as one. Pratt lampooned the old citizens, saying that they converted the various church settlements into "Mormonia" and transformed George Hinkle, the Mormon colonel who negotiated Far West's surrender,

> into a foreign minister, an envoy extraordinary, in behalf of the mormon empire, to enter into treaty stipulations with his Majesty's forces, under Generals Lucas, Wilson, and Clark. The city of Far West, the capital of Mormonia, is the Ghent where this treaty of peace is ratified. After which the standing army of Mormonia stack their arms, which are carried into triumph to Richmond. The royal family and other nobles are surrendered in the treaty to be tried by court martial and punished, and the inhabitants of the fallen empire, like those of Poland, are to be banished to Illinois instead of Siberia. . . . And at the same time a deed of trust is drawn up, and all the Mormons are compelled, on pain of death, to sign away their houses, lands, and property, for the disposal of their conquerors.[58]

Pratt argued that treason had, indeed, been committed during the Mormon War, but by the state of Missouri rather than the hapless Saints. Missouri's fall from civic virtue had began six years earlier when Lilburn Boggs, then lieutenant governor, secretly conspired to expel the Mormons from Jackson County. "These crimes," wrote Pratt, "which in a country of laws would have hanged them or imprisoned them for life, so far exalted them in the eyes of their associates, that their worthy deeds proved a step stone to office . . . and thus corruption, rebellion, and conspiracy had spread on every side, being fostered and encouraged by a large majority of the state; thus treason and rebellion became general."[59] If anyone doubted the demise of republicanism in Missouri, the state legislature provided the nation with ample evidence by "appropriating $200,000 for the payment of the troops engaged in this unlawful and treasonable enterprise. This last act of unheard outrage," said Pratt, "sealed with eternal infamy, the character of the State of Missouri, and established her downfall, to rise no more. She will be looked upon by her sister States as a star fallen from Heaven, and a ruined and degraded outcast from the federal union."[60]

To ensure this outcome, Sidney Rigdon concocted a plan in the spring of 1839 "to impeach the state of Missouri" for not possessing a republican form of government.[61] Not surprisingly, this plan was short-lived, but Mormon writers continued to characterize Missouri as, in Joseph Smith's words, a "land of tyranny and oppression" and its citizens as "dead to every feeling of virtue which animated the bosom of freemen."[62] While the Saints tried to win support for their cause with sentimental lines about widows and orphans, bleeding humanity, and the love of Jesus, most writers focused their efforts upon turning the Saints into a symbol of Missouri's betrayal of its republican heritage. The old settlers did not kill "Mormons," but rather "murdered many a freeborn son of America."[63] "American citizens," said another writer, "made free by the blood of the Revolution have been driven from their homes—rifled of their property, and made to yield up the ghost, for attempting to worship 'according to the dictates of their own conscience.'"[64]

Mormon appeal writers aimed their salvos not only at American hearts but at their consciences, hoping to shame their countrymen into coming to their aid. In a series of rhetorical questions, they implied that their fellow citizens would engage in a sort of patricidal betrayal of the Founding Fathers if they left Missouri unchastized. "Where is the spirit of our fathers," read one appeal, "who in their patriotism, won the battles of the Revolution, and secured liberty and independence to their offspring?"[65] Another appeal mystically addressed the Revolutionary leaders themselves: "Was it for this you struggled through a covenant made with liberty?"[66] And if appeals to their own heritage did not shame Americans into action, perhaps the fear of European derision would. Jacksonian Americans loved to contrast their republican liberties with the "slavery" endured under the monarchies of Europe. The Mormons cautioned that, if the injustices they suffered in Missouri went uncorrected, all Europe would laugh at America's empty boast of freedom. "O tell it not in Britain," bewailed Parley Pratt, "nor let the sound be heard in Europe, that liberty is fallen: that the free institutions of our once happy country are now destroyed: lest the daughters of Britannia rejoice and laugh as to scorn. Lest the daughters of monarchy triumph, and have us in derision."[67] Noah Packard similarly warned that if Americans turned their backs upon the Saints, "well may the despotic powers of Europe laugh and rejoice in their hearts, in anticipation of beholding the United States of America, fall, and crumble to atoms beneath the ponderous weight . . . [of] her own depravity."[68]

Finally, the Mormons warned their fellow countrymen that the very continuance of American liberty depended upon the restoration of the Mormons' republican rights. Surely tyranny would follow when Americans were either too apathetic or too corrupt to intervene on the behalf of oppressed citizens. "Is there no virtue in the body politic?" asked Joseph Smith. "Will not the people rise up in their majesty . . . and [bring] the offenders to that punishment which they so richly deserve, and save the nation from the disgrace and ultimate ruin, which must inevitably fall upon it?"[69] "If Missouri goes unpunished for crimes," said Parley Pratt, "if myself and friends go unredressed; then farewell to the peace and security of the citizens of this once happy Republic." Employing the ultimate threat, Pratt added that Americans who were too debased to save their fellow citizens from injustice were just as guilty as the Missouri mob, and they would do well to "remember there is a God in Heaven who will avenge the blood of inocence [sic], and especially his own elect, who cry to him day and night."[70]

The Mormon appeals to the nation went unanswered. Many Americans sympathetic to the Saints expressed helplessness before nineteenth-century notions of states' rights. Others simply told the church that the citizens of Missouri could be neither so inhuman or corrupt as to deny them justice, if their case was indeed just. Although deeply aggrieved over their injuries, the Mormons' prognostications of liberty's departure were in good measure rhetorical. Republican virtue was dead in Missouri, and endangered in the rest of the country, but the

Saints' loyalty to American institutions still remained strong. In Illinois the Mormons began yet another church settlement; happy, said Joseph Smith, to once "again take our stand among a people in whose bosoms dwell those feelings of republicanism which gave rise to our nation."[71]

chapter 8

Anti-Mormonism Reappears in Illinois

The Mormon War in Missouri sent thousands of ragged and demoralized Saints streaming into northwestern Illinois during the winter of 1838–39. The citizens in the region received the refugees warmly, providing food and shelter to alleviate their immediate suffering. The cruel treatment of the Saints in Missouri profoundly shocked Illinoisans, who listened with horror to Mormon reports of Governor Boggs's exterminating order, the butchery at Haun's Mills, and the brutality of the militia. Community leaders and local newspapers uncritically accepted the Saints' version of these events as a simple republican morality play in which the forces of mobocracy persecuted an offending people distinguished only for industry and religion. The *Quincy Argus*, for example, on March 16, 1839, denounced Missouri's citizens and public officials as ruthless barbarians who from motives of political ambition, religious bigotry, and greed had "but too well put in execution their threats of extermination and expulsion, and fully wreaked their vengeance on a body of industrious and enterprising men." The Mormons, continued the *Argus*, "had never wronged nor wished to wrong" the citizens of Missouri, but had "ever comported themselves as good and honest citizens," asking only the same "*sacred immunities of life, liberty, and property*" they accorded to their neighbors.[1]

The Saints, for their part, anxiously strove to prove the accuracy of this opinion of their civic virtue. They expressed a heartfelt gratitude to those who took them in and pledged to lift their burden of charity as quickly as possible. On February 27, church leader Elias Higbee suggested at a public meeting in Quincy that those wishing to help the Mormon people regain their self-sufficiency would best do so by renting them farms, hiring their labor, and granting them equal protection under the law. More than anything else, said Higbee, this "would raise us from a state of dependence, liberate us from the iron grasp of poverty, put us in possession of a competency, and deliver us from the ruinous effects of persecution, despotism and tyranny."[2]

Initially, the Saints looked upon Illinois only as a place of refuge, not a new home. Dissent within the church and persecution from without shocked the Mormons into questioning many of their most basic beliefs. The dissenters' fierce resistance to communitarianism, and the general lack of enthusiasm for it by many others, led Joseph Smith, while still imprisoned in Missouri, to forbid all organizations based on common stock principles.[3] More important, although the Saints charged that their enemies were primarily motivated by religious bigotry and economic envy, they well understood that Mormon clannishness in political, social, and economic affairs aroused gentile hatred. This realization caused many within the church, including the prophet, for a while to doubt the wisdom of reinstituting "the gathering."[4] In February 1839, the church leadership turned down a "liberal offer" of Iowa land between the Mississippi and Des Moines rivers for fear of stirring up the same wrath that drove them from Missouri.[5] That the Mormons stayed loosely associated at all during their months of exile was largely due to Brigham Young, who counseled members to settle in small companies throughout the Illinois countryside.[6]

Gradually, however, the Mormons shifted the blame for the Missouri debacle away from fundamental church doctrine and onto the failings or treachery of particular individuals. Finger pointing had, in fact, begun even before the Saints had left Missouri. Sidney Rigdon received the blame for angering the gentiles with his inflammatory Fourth of July address, while Sampson Avard became the scapegoat for Danite excesses. Similarly, the Mormons vilified George Hinkle as a Judas for supposedly having led the prophet into gentile hands and for causing the surrender of Far West, while the dissenters were damned for falsifying charges of Mormon treason at the hearing before Judge King.[7] These accusations were hardly fair, but they allowed the church as a body to regain confidence in its own structure and beliefs. If its troubles stemmed from the actions of a few wicked men, surely such problems could be avoided in the future.

In April, the Saints put to rest their worries about forming another gathering. They accepted the seemingly generous offer of Isaac Galland to sell them the tiny Mississippi riverfront village of Commerce and a part of the adjacent land across the river in Iowa known as the Half Breed Tract. Unfortunately for the Mormons, while Galland had sought them out in the guise of a benevolent sympathizer and prospective convert, his interest in the church extended no further than its coffers. The Saints later discovered that Galland had no clear title to land in the Half Breed Tract. In 1824, the federal government had set aside this land for the racially mixed offspring of whites and Indians. In subsequent years, a series of confused and often fraudulent sales left the tract hopelessly entangled in a web of competing claims of ownership. Galland had merely sold the Mormons his share of the legal quagmire. Partly as a result of this, the church's settlement in Iowa would eventually fade into insignificance. The Illinois town of Commerce posed serious problems for the Saints too, but of quite a different nature. After viewing the town, Joseph Smith rechristened it Nauvoo, a Hebrew word roughly meaning "beautiful plantation." It was indeed beautiful, but also deadly. As the Mormons moved in, they learned to their horror that the whole area was a notorious breeding ground for malaria. The epidemic that soon swept through the church killed far more Saints than the Missourians had.

If the Mormons began their new community under less than ideal circumstances, they nevertheless felt a certain euphoria at making a fresh start away from the clutches of Missouri despotism. Between 1839 and 1841, it was a favorite pastime among the Saints to contrast their past suffering with their blissful existence among the liberty-loving freemen of Illinois.[8] They did not put their Missouri troubles behind them, however. The Saints believed themselves an injured people and expected some sort of restitution for the injustice inflicted upon them. On October 29, 1839, Joseph Smith, Sidney Rigdon, and Elias Higbee left Nauvoo to petition Congress for a redress of their grievances against Missouri. Missouri might have fallen into irredeemable corruption, but Smith believed the rest of the nation had not. Writing eight months earlier from a Missouri jail, the prophet extolled the Constitution as a "glorious standard . . . founded in the wisdom of God."[9] Nor did Smith lack faith that the nation's politicians desired to uphold that standard. Armed with hundreds of Mormon affidavits detailing Missouri's tyranny, the prophet believed he needed only to make the president and Congress fully aware of the violation of the Saints' rights to galvanize the government into action on the church's behalf. Apparently, Smith even went so far as to pledge payment for

Illinois·land based on his expectation that Congress would order Missouri to reimburse the Mormons for their property loss.[10]

Within a few short months, both the president and Congress dashed the Saints' hope for relief. The Mormons had looked for President Van Buren's favor in particular. They had given him their united vote in 1836 and had consistently supported his policies as president. Yet even as Van Buren affirmed the justice of the Saints' grievances, he informed the delegation that he lacked the power to intrude in Missouri's internal affairs. "Gentlemen," he reportedly said, "your cause is just, but I can do nothing for you." According to Smith, the president went on to confess that if he attempted to help the church, he would assuredly lose Missouri's vote in the 1840 election.[11] Whatever Van Buren's true sentiments, the prophet left Washington deeply embittered. Van Buren's words of helplessness soon became infamous among the Mormons and were endlessly and contemptuously repeated as the symbolic expression of all politicians who preferred popularity to justice. Smith had gone to Washington in search of a statesman but found instead a mere "office-seeker" whose "self-aggrandizement was his ruling passion."[12] More prosaically Smith later declared Van Buren, *"not as fit as my dog, for the chair of state."*[13]

Unfortunately for the Saints, Congress proved no more obliging than the president. Once again, the doctrine of states' rights proved the stumbling block to federal action. On March 4, 1840, the Senate Judiciary Committee voted unanimously to table the Mormons' petition, labeling it solely a matter of state concern and, therefore, beyond the jurisdiction of the Senate.[14] At the General Conference of the church a month later, the Saints angrily lashed out at the committee's decision as "unconstitutional, and subversive to the rights of a free People" and called for "all lovers of good government and republican principles" to join them in denouncing it.[15]

From a Mormon perspective, the federal government's failure to punish Missouri implicated the nation in the state's crimes.[16] While the Saints had tirelessly warned Americans of God's impending judgment upon their iniquity, they had previously focused their attack upon the spiritual and moral depravity of their countrymen. These jeremiads had contained political implications that the Mormons occasionally made explicit. Yet with a certain patriotic naiveté, the Saints had retained an almost transcendent faith in the political virtue of the nation's leaders. They had made no systematic attempt to link the country's moral corruption with its national politics. After their rebuff in Washington, they did so.[17] As a republican, Joseph Smith feared that this self-seeking of politicians signaled the beginning of the end of freedom in the United States. As a man of God, he knew that if lawmakers did not return to righteousness, the Lord would destroy His once-favored nation. Upon returning to Nauvoo from Washington, he wrote that he had "witnessed many vexatious movements in government officers, whose sole object would be the peace and prosperity and happiness of the whole people; but instead of this, I discovered that popular clamor and personal aggrandizement were the ruling principles of those in authority; and my heart fails within me when I see, by the visions of the Almighty, the end of this nation, if she continues to disregard the cries and petitions of her virtuous citizens, as she has done, and is now doing."[18] True to his expectation, Smith found evidence of God's chastisement of America five months later in reports of devastating hailstorms, floods, devouring insects, and economic failure. "Since Congress has decided against us," he wrote, "the Lord has begun to vex this nation, and He will continue to do so except they repent."[19] Although the nation stubbornly refused to do so, the Mormons were unwilling to give up hope.

The Saints, however, had no intention of passively waiting for God to make the nation's lawmakers see reason. The Missouri experience took the bloom off early Mormonism. Members of the church became obsessed with the wrongs they had suffered, and in their circumscribed world, their sense of injury remained ever fresh, reverberating from the pulpit to the flock and back again, coloring all of their subsequent thought and action. External events such as the apparent indifference of Washington politicians to the Mormons' plight only rubbed salt into their wounds. Of greater importance, however, was the fact that Missouri seemed bent on persecuting the Saints even in exile. Nettled by the unfavorable publicity generated by the Mormons' expulsion, Governor Boggs sent agents to Illinois in September 1840 to arrest Smith as a fugitive from justice. Although the prophet narrowly escaped capture, this proved only the first of several annual attempts to extradite Smith back to Missouri. In these circumstances, the Saints became afraid as well as bitter. Despite their initial doubts about the gathering, they became more clannish, more hostile to outsiders, and more convinced than ever of their identity as a peculiar people. Ironically, the fear of persecution in Missouri had led the Saints into actions that helped bring persecution upon them. In Illinois, the pattern would be repeated as Mormon defensive efforts provoked fears of tyranny, transforming the once-sympathetic citizens into angry mobs.

It was during this initial period of insecurity and doubt that Dr. John C. Bennett arrived in Nauvoo. The church had always attracted its fair share of opportunists, and Bennett was a prime example. Unlike those who came before him, however, Bennett exuded the air of a man of cultivation and social standing. Most doctors of the day had little or no formal training. Bennett, by contrast, had earned a university degree and had subsequently engaged in a variety of educational projects, including the founding of a medical college in Willoughby, Ohio. After moving to Illinois in 1838, he quickly won appointments, first as brigadier general in the militia and then as the state's quartermaster general. During the Mormon exodus from Missouri, Bennett began to make his way into the inner circle of the church with a series of sympathetic letters to Smith and Rigdon. Upon settling in Nauvoo in the late summer of 1840, he quickly persuaded the prophet he was just the worldly-wise counselor the church needed. Within a few brief months, Bennett superseded Rigdon as Smith's chief lieutenant. When Governor Boggs began his efforts to recapture the prophet, Bennett became the church's chief defender. Writing in the Saints' newspaper, *Times and Seasons*, under the nom de plume "Joab, General in Israel," Bennett flamboyantly excoriated Missouri for its insatiable bloodlust and darkly warned of savage military reprisal should the state continue to hound the Mormons.[20]

While the Saints may have found Bennett's saber rattling emotionally satisfying, they nevertheless realized they needed a more formal means to secure themselves from outside aggression and control. They hoped to fill this need by obtaining a city charter for Nauvoo. Bennett argued that the Mormons should withhold their petition until after they demonstrated their political power at the polls in the 1840 elections. This was hardly necessary. From the moment the Saints arrived in Illinois, both Democratic and Whig politicians had fawned over them. With Bennett acting as lobbyist, the Nauvoo Charter sailed through the state legislature and Council of Revision with bipartisan support in December 1840. Critics would later make much of the fact that the legislature did not even bother to give the act a formal reading.

The Saints considered the charter's passage a great victory for their republican rights. The First Presidency of the church heralded the document as the Mormons' "magna carta," "securing to us, in all time to come, irrevocably, all of those blessings of liberty which of right appertain to all free citizens: it is all we ever claimed."[21] The charter authorized the organization of a city council, a militia (known as the "Nauvoo Legion"), and a university. The city council, composed of the mayor, four aldermen, and nine counselors, was empowered to pass any ordinance not repugnant to the state or federal constitutions. The council also constituted the municipal court over which the mayor presided as chief justice. Among the court's powers was the right to issue writs of habeas corpus for persons arrested under local ordinance. The Nauvoo Legion, on the other hand, was the charter's most unique feature. In addition to militia duties, it also enforced city ordinances at the mayor's discretion. While the Legion received state arms and served at the governor's request in the public defense, it was entirely self-governing. Its self-elected officers formed a court-martial that could pass its own regulations irrespective of those of Illinois, provided these regulations did not conflict with the state or federal constitution.[22]

The legislature's routine passage of the Nauvoo Charter caused little comment from gentiles at the time. Yet before a year had passed, lawmakers would find themselves being castigated as "groveling sycophants" whose "unprincipled pandering" for Mormon favor had given the Saints the means to establish a despotism over northwestern Illinois. While it was true that both Whigs and Democrats had hoped to woo the Mormon vote, this was hardly fair. Even if they had scrutinized the charter, they would have found little that was exceptional. Joseph Smith, in fact, had based it largely upon the Springfield charter approved by the legislature only the year before.

In retrospect, what seemed so insidious to the gentiles about the charter was its easy adaptation to one-man rule. Future governor Thomas Ford, who tried to be fair-minded about the Mormons, called the charter "anti-republican in many particulars," noting that "the great law of separation of powers was wholly disregarded." Although the Saints elected John Bennett as Nauvoo's first mayor, real power lay in the hands of Joseph Smith, who served as an alderman. When Smith succeeded Bennett as mayor in the spring of 1842, that power became all the more apparent. Ford noted that as mayor, Smith "presided in the common council and assisted in making the laws for the city. And as mayor, he was to see these laws put into force. He was ex-officio judge of the mayor's court and chief justice of the municipal court; and in these capacities, he was to interpret the laws, which he assisted to make."[23] Even more frightening in gentile eyes, the Nauvoo Legion elected the prophet its commander. As such, Smith sought and received from Governor Thomas Carlin appointment to the rank of lieutenant general, the first man to hold that rank since George Washington. In addition to these offices, in 1841 Smith established his control over the city's economic affairs as the church's Trustee-in-Trust and, in the following year, took over the editorship of the Saints' newspaper *Times and Seasons*. In another man, this formal concentration of power might have attracted little notice from Illinoisans. But for a leader of a growing and ambitious sect who commanded perfect obedience from his followers as God's spokesman, the charter appeared a blueprint for tyranny.

Equally ominous to outsiders, the prophet sought to enhance the liberal power the legislature bestowed upon Nauvoo. If there existed no force to counter Smith's will within the city, there was within the state. Gradually the prophet moved to limit it. As historian Robert Flanders observed, Joseph Smith interpreted the charter as making Nauvoo a semi-independent city, federated with Illinois much as the state was federated with the national government. While Nauvoo, in the prophet's view, owed certain obligations to the state, it nevertheless reserved to itself certain rights, privileges, and immunities.[24] Smith did not claim this unique relationship at the time of the charter's passage but rather developed it partially in response to what he perceived as growing threats to the Saints' republican liberties. Still, something of this conception was implied from the beginning in the design of the Nauvoo Legion.

The Mormons, of course, hardly saw these things as ominous. They gave great power to Joseph Smith, not because they expected him to become a tyrant, but because they believed he would exercise it wisely. They were engaged in building the kingdom of God and quite naturally looked to God's prophet to rule over it. Similarly, Smith sought to make Nauvoo independent, not to pursue his own lawless will, but to erect a legal barrier against outsiders as the storm clouds of anti-Mormonism gathered over Illinois.

These clouds first appeared in 1841. Settled by a mix of northern and southern migrants, the citizens of Hancock County had earned a statewide reputation for fast dealing and general lawlessness. By the time the Saints arrived, the 5,000 county residents had just passed the first stages of frontier society. The largest town, Warsaw, boasted a mere 300 residents, while Carthage, the county seat, claimed even less. Not only did Nauvoo quickly become the county's leading population center, but within a few years it grew into a small city of at least 11,000, with several thousand more church members living in the countryside. This sudden and unexpected influx of Mormon immigrants startled many old settlers and upset their political and economic aspirations. The citizens of Warsaw in particular keenly felt their town's loss of status and feared Nauvoo's rise would imperil their ambition to become an important Mississippi river port.[25]

The underlying economic tension created by the new Mormon presence in the region was immeasurably exacerbated by the church's involvement in politics. Statewide, Whigs and Democrats struggled on a roughly equal footing for office, although by 1840 the Democratic party showed increasing signs of predominance. In Hancock County, however, the Whigs had successfully resisted this trend. Despite the Mormons' traditional predilection for the Democratic party, they exaggerated the county's political pattern by throwing their unified support to the Whigs in 1840 and again in 1841. When the Saints had first arrived in Illinois, they proclaimed themselves politically neutral. In reality, Missouri governor Lilburn Boggs had seriously weakened the church's allegiance to the Democratic party through his expulsion order. Martin Van Buren sealed this disaffection a year later when he withheld his support during the Mormons' struggle to win a damage settlement from Missouri. Although the Saints' conversion to the Whig party stemmed largely from the antipathy they felt toward certain Democratic politicians, they were drawn to the Whigs for some positive reasons as well. The Illinois Whig congressional delegation had strongly supported the church's petition for redress against Missouri, and a number of prominent Whigs had worked to secure Nauvoo's city charter.[26]

Unfortunately, the Mormons' unified support of the Whig party in 1840 made bitter enemies of the already frustrated Democratic minority in Hancock County, most of whom lived in Warsaw. Nor did it entirely please the Whigs. The Saints had withheld their charter petition until after the 1840 election to impress state politicians with their voting strength. They deeply impressed those in Hancock. Given the rate of Mormon immigration, it became all too clear that those politicians who were not church members or allied with the church would soon have neither office nor influence in the county or congressional district. As a consequence, in the spring of 1841, Democratic politicians in Warsaw began issuing calls for the old citizens to abandon their party labels and unite against political Mormonism. These calls eventually summoned a countywide anti-Mormon convention held the following July.[27]

From the rise of anti-Mormonism in Illinois until the Saints left the state five years later, the most conspicuous leader of those opposed to the church was *Warsaw Signal* editor Thomas Sharp. Young, ambitious, and acid-tongued, Sharp proved a tireless missionary for the anti-Mormon gospel. As fear of Mormon tyranny gradually awakened in the county and spread throughout northwestern Illinois, the *Signal* editor came to speak for the old citizens with almost the same authority as his nemesis, Joseph Smith, had for the Saints.

Sharp began his crusade against the Mormons tamely enough, simply arguing in May 1841 that in its political activity, the church had "stepped beyond the proper sphere of a religious body."[28] Within a month, the attacks became more vociferous. Sharp labeled Smith a jaded despot and his followers fools and fanatics. Unfortunately for the old citizens, he charged, the prophet was not merely content to lord it over his minions, but had larger temporal ambitions. It was precisely Smith's absolute control over the faithful that made him so dangerous to those outside the church. Republican theory demanded that independent citizens obey the prompting of their civic conscience; yet Sharp pointed out that in elections in both Missouri and Illinois, the Mormons had "almost to a man . . . surrendered their own political judgment" to that of their prophet.[29] Given the rapid immigration of church members, he warned, the Saints would soon greatly outnumber the old citizens, and the rights and property of those who first settled in the county would be gone:

> Yes! men who have no minds of their own, but move, act and think at the bidding of one man, are to be our rulers. . . . Are you prepared to see the important offices of Sheriff and County Commissioners selected by an unparalleled knave, and thus place in his hands the power to select jurymen, who are to sit and try your rights to life, liberty, and property? If it comes to this, that Joe Smith is to control the majority of the votes in our county, are we not in effect,

subjects of a despot?—Might we not as well be serfs to the Autocrat of Russia? What need have we of the elective franchise, when a church can rise up in our midst, controlled by the magic of one man, to dispense political favors?[30]

Even more frightening to Thomas Sharp and his neighbors than the Mormons' power at the polls was the church's evident militarism. The long-persecuted Saints looked to the Nauvoo Legion for their safety. As second-in-command, John Bennett served them well, drawing upon his military background to transform the Legion into an impressive military force. Ordinance required that every able-bodied male between the ages of eighteen and forty-five join the militia, and within six months of its formation, 1,500 men were under arms. By 1844, the Legion numbered nearly 4,000 recruits, second in size only to the United States Army. The sheer magnitude of the Mormon militia gave gentiles pause, but they found its machinelike appearance even more intimidating. Typical Illinois militiamen paraded in sloppy dress, lacked discipline, and enjoyed muster day as an occasion for boisterous drinking. The Legionnaires, by contrast, wore snappy uniforms, maintained order, and drilled long and soberly.[31] The men had the look of that peculiarly republican evil, a standing army.

Quite naturally, the old citizens began to wonder why the Mormons needed such a powerful militia. "Ask yourselves," wrote Thomas Sharp, "what means this array of military force which is paraded under the direction of the church. . . . Are they so patriotic as to have no other end than the safety of the state in view?"[32] Spokesmen for the Hancock County anti-Mormon convention suggested that perhaps the Saints maintained such a large armed body "because they well know their principles to be so utterly repugnant to the genius of our republican institutions, that nothing but the point of the bayonet could enable them to live in safety, in any community."[33]

Most old settlers, however, refused to acknowledge any element of self-protection in the Nauvoo Legion's creation, even in defense against the just wrath of an outraged citizenry. In their view, the Mormons meant to use the Legion as an instrument of domination, pure and simple. If the church could not bring Illinoisans into subjugation through conversion or the ballot box, they would use force. One old citizen noted reports spreading through the countryside that Mormons "take the liberty to tell the people they now come with the Bible in their hands but ere long they will come with the sword also by their side."[34] While he found the remark amusing, Sharp thought it telling when Smith warned his critics that if they "did not stop their blab" about his being a military man, he would become President "and then he would show them what a Bonaparte could do."[35] Sharp found even greater significance, however, in the prophet's supposed review of a militia parade of Mormons living around Montrose, Iowa. What military authority, asked the *Signal* editor, did Smith possess outside Nauvoo? "Is this not proof positive that he wishes to organize a military church? Else why should he take so much interest in the military improvement of his followers out of this State? We see in this thing the essential spirit of Mormonism, which is—treason to the Government."[36]

For all their concern, anti-Mormons believed the Nauvoo Legion a potential, not imminent, threat to their freedom. At present, what need did the Saints have of physical force when both Whigs and Democrats kowtowed to the church's interest above those of the public in hopes of winning office? Did not the state legislature's passage of the Nauvoo Charter, granting "powers nearly . . . equal to their own," prove as much?[37] The Mormons' influence seemed even more pernicious in the county, where they held the balance of power between the two parties. The Saints not only could decide elections but dictate the selection of candidates and policies of either party willing to sully its virtue for Mormon favor.[38] Spokesmen for the county anti-Mormon convention accordingly admonished the old citizens to lay aside former party allegiances in the upcoming August elections and "oppose, as independent freemen, political and military Mormonism."[39] If they did not, their liberties would be gone.

Despite the strenuous efforts of Warsaw Democrats and some Whigs, traditional party lines held in the congressional district and much of the county. Outside Warsaw, anti-Mormonism was simply not deep enough to break down customary loyalties. The church's endorsement may have cost the Whigs some votes, but clearly the Saints' support outweighed its disadvantages. Some Democrats, of course, vigorously denounced the Whig-Mormon alliance, but the party leadership generally took a soft line against the church. The Whigs, Democrats, and anti-Mormons all realized the volatile nature of the church vote. Those Democrats not unalterably opposed to the Saints suspected that they might still woo the Mormons back to their party.

Nor were these Democratic hopes unjustified. On December 20,

1841, Joseph Smith publicly declared the church's support for the Democratic nominee for governor, Adam W. Snyder. Smith acknowledged the Saints' support for the Whigs but justified the Mormons' change of heart with an appeal to republican independence. "We care not a fig for Whig or Democrat," he wrote, and added that the Saints would "claim the privilege of freemen" and cast their votes for "the cause of human liberty" irrespective of party.[40] The Saints had voted for William Henry Harrison in admiration of his sterling qualities, said the prophet, but General Harrison was now dead, and his friends were not necessarily the Mormons' friends, or the friends of equal rights.

Adam Snyder won the Saints' favor in good measure because of his highly visible work in shepherding the Nauvoo Charter through the legislature. But as Joseph Smith explicitly stated, it was Stephen Douglas more than any other politician who deserved the credit for leading the Mormons back into the Democratic fold. Douglas had carefully cultivated the church since its arrival in the state. As Illinois secretary of state, he too had played an important role in the charter's passage. After his election to a seat on the state supreme court, he appointed John Bennett as master-in-chancery for Hancock County. Douglas further pleased the Saints by exempting all elders from military duty unless approved by the church, thus underlining the Nauvoo Legion's separation from the regular state militia. Douglas's greatest service for the Mormons by far came in early June 1841 when Missouri agents surprised Joseph Smith near Quincy and arrested him as a fugitive from justice. Immediately following his arrest, Douglas arranged to have Smith appear before him in court on June 10 and promptly set him free on a legal technicality. Whatever the merits of the decision, the jubilant Mormons heralded Douglas as the church's friend and savior. By the time of the 1842 gubernatorial election, Illinoisans associated Douglas with the Saints. The Whig candidate for governor, Joseph Duncan, even went so far as to accuse Douglas of secretly belonging to the church.[41]

When Duncan charged Douglas with being a Mormon, a Whig campaign against the church was already underway. To say that the Whigs did not respond well to the Saints' shift in loyalties would be an understatement. The Whig press swiftly followed Smith's endorsement of Snyder with a barrage of criticism, mostly aimed at the prophet's unrepublican political dictation to his followers. The *Quincy Whig*, for example, declared "that this clannish principle of voting in mass at the dictation of one man, . . . who has acquired an influence over the minds of his people through the peculiar religious creed he promulgates, is so repugnant, to the principles of our Republican form of Government" that it will inevitably engender the bitterest hatred.[42]

The Whigs' criticism of the Mormons, however, reflected more than spite born of Joseph Smith's turncoat politics. Far from lamenting the loss of the Saints' vote, the Whigs saw in the controversy surrounding the church an opportunity to vault themselves back into power. Their party's decline had resulted, in large measure, from a stream of internal improvement and banking schemes they had engineered in the 1830s. Not only had these measures driven the state to the verge of bankruptcy, but Joseph Duncan, the Whig candidate for governor, had presided over their passage during his first term as governor. Duncan and the Whigs now attempted to divert attention from the state's economic woes in a campaign so single-mindedly designed to tie the Mormons around Democratic necks that it was as if, said Thomas Ford, Duncan "expected to be elected governor on this question alone."[43]

Duncan focused his attacks on the supposed antirepublican abuse of the Nauvoo Charter. The Democrats had had control of the legislature at the time of its passage, and Duncan had conveniently been in private life. In a speech delivered in Edwardsville on May 4, Duncan allowed that the Mormons deserved the same privileges enjoyed by other citizens, but demanded the revocation of "*all* extraordinary antirepublican and arbitrary powers which the corruption of a Legislature granted them solely for the purpose of obtaining political support." In proof of the Saints' perfidious use of their charter, Duncan pointed "to one of the ordinances of their city, which provided that if any persons spoke lightly of, or doubted their religion, upon conviction thereof the offender was liable to a fine of five hundred dollars and six months imprisonment."[44] The *Alton Telegraph*, in reporting the candidates' remarks, approvingly noted that Duncan's unveiling of "this disgraceful attempt to form in a republican government, an established religion by legal enactment, created throughout the audience a great sensation, and opened their eyes to the rapid strides that were being made in their very midst towards an arbitrary and monarchical form of government.[45]

The Whig crusade against the Mormons received an unexpected boost from the sensational apostasy of John C. Bennett. Despite his mercurial rise through church ranks, the ambitious Bennett chafed under Smith's leadership. During 1841, relations between the prophet and his first lieutenant gradually became strained. The following year, they deteriorated completely; so much so, in fact, that Smith became convinced that Bennett had contrived to assassinate him during a Nauvoo Legion parade in early May.[46] Bennett's break with the church, however, came over the issue of polygamy. Sometime in early 1841, in imitation of Old Testament practices, Joseph Smith secretly introduced the taking of "plural wives" among his innermost circle.[47] Apparently disregarding the prophet's elaborate justification of the innovation and careful instructions, Bennett practiced the doctrine with amorous abandon. Even worse, Smith discovered that Bennett had deserted a wife and children in Ohio. The prophet initially sought to keep the matter under wraps, fearing that a scandal would further inflame gentile hostility.[48] A series of reconciliations between the two men took place in May, in which Bennett confessed his sins; and under pressure from the church leadership, he made a number of strongly worded statements denying that the prophet had privately justified "illicit intercourse with females" under any circumstances.[49] Given the hard feelings between the two men, however, a permanent split was inevitable. On May 19, the Nauvoo City Council accepted Bennett's resignation as mayor and immediately elected Joseph Smith in his stead. Stripped of his power and glory, Bennett lingered in Nauvoo another month before quietly slipping away in late June.

Bennett made the transformation from Mormon zealot to anti-Mormon zealot the instant he ventured past Nauvoo's city limits. During the summer of 1842, he expended his considerable energy in anti-Mormon lecturing and writing for Whig newspapers. Bennett now professed that he had never believed in Mormonism at all. He had merely feigned conversion out of a patriotic desire to infiltrate the church, the better to expose its nefarious designs.[50] The church, he now disclosed, was a perfect study of tyrannical depravity. Despite Joseph Smith's pious pretensions, the prophet was an infidel motivated by an all-consuming desire for wealth, power, and sexual indulgence. By playing upon the religious superstitions of his fanatical followers, he meant to have all three.

Under Smith's tutelage, Nauvoo had become a cesspool of thievery and sexual debauchery. "The Alpha and Omega of Mormon financiering," wrote John Bennett, was a doctrine known as "milking the gentiles," which in plain English meant swindling nonchurch members. It was through this basic source of revenue that the Saints obtained the necessary funds to "*convert the heathen* of New England," build their temple, and most important, "sustain the Imperial Mormon Pontiff, and his Cabinet, in princely magnificence."[51] If possible, the prophet violated the sanctity of womanhood as freely as he did that of property. Bennett styled Smith as a sensually depraved Mohammed and titillated his readers with tales of the prophet's system of spiritual wifery which, he claimed, even outdistanced "the most luxurious and corrupt empires of pagan antiquity, or . . . those licentious Oriental courts, where debauchery has been, for ages, systematized and sanctioned by law and religion, on the most extensive scale."[52]

Should any person oppose Smith's iniquity, said Bennett, he ran the risk of assassination. Americans denounced the intellectual fetters in which the Pope held Catholics, but his disapproval brought only excommunication, while the prophet's resulted in "cold-blooded Danite murder."[53] The Mormons, he claimed, had quietly resurrected the fanatical brotherhood in Nauvoo and they now numbered two thousand strong, each sworn to obey the prophet as God and ready to execute any "blasphemer" in expectation of a higher heavenly glory.[54] Dramatic evidence for Bennett's charge seemed to have occurred on May 6 when an unknown assailant had repeatedly shot former Missouri governor Lilburn Boggs. Despite two serious head wounds, Boggs survived. Although the motive for the attack at first puzzled authorities, their suspicions fell upon the Mormons when they learned that Joseph Smith's bodyguard, Rockwell Porter, had been in Independence at the time of the shooting. Bennett did his best to make the most of the incident, writing that Smith had prophesied in 1841 that Boggs would die "by violent hands within a year," and had subsequently offered a $500 reward to ensure the prophecy's fulfillment.[55] When Boggs had sufficiently recovered from his wounds, Bennett went to encourage the scarcely reluctant governor to lodge charges against Smith.

Incredible as it seemed, said Bennett, sexual profligacy, stealing, and midnight assassinations were merely incidental to the prophet's greater ambition for political power. Joseph Smith and his henchmen, he warned, darkly conspired to overthrow the governments of the northwestern states and erect in their stead an empire over which the prophet would rule.[56] The gathering at Nauvoo served only as a staging ground, where the Saints would muster their strength until Smith considered it beyond challenge. Once assured of his power, the prophet intended to march upon Independence, where he would build the New Jerusalem he had prophesied. But this was only the first step. Conquest would follow conquest until Missouri, Illinois, and Iowa became "the *nucleus* of the great MORMON EMPIRE."[57] Having established his dominion, the prophet would then stand, sword in hand, above the vanquished citizenry and offer them conversion or death.[58]

In Bennett's view, these tyrannical aspirations were already evident in Illinois. So absolute was the prophet's control over his devotees that in the previous election only six votes in Nauvoo were cast in opposition to the candidates he had anointed.[59] This pernicious political union not only virtually disenfranchised the old citizen minority of Hancock, who had redeemed the county from the wilderness, but spread civic corruption into ever-widening circles by enticing political demagogues to do Smith's bidding in exchange for office. Should this course continue, said Bennett, "the best interest of the country [would] be sacrificed to the ambitious views" of this modern Mohammed.[60] The end result, he predicted, would be the destruction of "our religion and our liberties, [which would] involve us and our country in the most direful and irretrievable calamities." If the American people wished to save the republic, they would have to "quit the forum for the field" and crush the prophet's treasonable designs before it was too late.[61]

The spectacular growth of Nauvoo, the Whig crusade, and Bennett's exposés (published in book form in Boston in the fall of 1842) fanned the flames of anti-Mormon feeling throughout Illinois and gave rise to a germ of national anti-Mormon consciousness. James Gordon Bennett, the editor of the *New York Herald*, took up the Saints as a paper-selling novelty. *Niles' National Register* reported that Joseph Smith had six thousand votes under his command and controlled the balance of power in the state. A United States military officer, after observing a parade of the Nauvoo Legion, wrote a widely reprinted article comparing the Legion favorably with regular troops and asserting that "a western empire is certain."[62]

Despite the Whigs' evident success in defaming the church, their plan to ride anti-Mormonism into power derailed when the Democratic candidate for governor, Adam Snyder, suddenly died in May. The Democrats tried to use this event to undermine the effectiveness of the anti-Mormon issue by replacing Snyder with someone with no known association with the church. Their choice finally fell upon Justice Thomas Ford of the state supreme court. Ford was a man of sterling integrity, likable, but unflamboyant; well-known, but with no popular base within his own party. Although no stern puritan, Ford was in many ways reminiscent of John Quincy Adams. He possessed superior intellectual gifts, had a conservative instinct, and was dispassionate and nonpartisan by nature. Once nominated, Ford undertook a campaign that astonished friend and foe alike. To the amazement of the Democrats, Ford came out strongly for a painful belt-tightening to pay off state debts. The Mormons quickly endorsed him, but rather than quietly accept the Saints' support as the Whigs expected, Ford publicly denounced Joseph Smith and urged the revision of the Nauvoo Charter. If his unorthodox campaigning perplexed and dismayed party professionals, it nonetheless touched a responsive chord among the voters and he won the governorship decisively.[63]

For all the hostility generated toward the church, the Mormons considered the 1842 election a success. The Saints had taken Ford's rebuff of their support lightly and celebrated Joseph Duncan's defeat. Even more gratifying, the elections in the Hancock area proved a clean sweep for the Mormon-approved ticket. William Smith, the prophet's brother, won one of the district's two seats to the legislature, and all the successful candidates for the state legislature, state senate, and county sheriff were all Democrats with close ties to the church. The Saints' electoral victories spread gloom among the old citizens. An exasperated Thomas Sharp bitterly announced that "the recent election clearly demonstrates that the old citizens of Hancock county are the humble subjects of his Royal Highness, Joe Smith."[64] He nevertheless declared that the gentiles would never settle for "political slavery" and defiantly vowed they would do everything in their power short of violence to maintain their rights. Although the Saints, with a good deal of sometimes inadvertent aid from the Democrats, had turned back their enemies in the election, the triumph had come at a fearful price. Anti-Mormonism had taken deep root in the state in 1842 and only awaited sufficient provocation to sprout forth again.

The Saints were keenly aware of this situation. They found satisfaction in their growing city and political power, yet the rebirth of virulent anti-Mormonism in early 1841 had alarmed them. They nevertheless spent little time pondering the root cause of the enmity toward the church; it was the same as it had been in Jackson County, Kirtland, and Far West—and, for that matter, centuries earlier in Rome and Jerusalem. Throughout history, wicked men had always opposed God's work; and, among themselves, the Mormons understood persecution as a sort of perverse affirmation of their true Sainthood.[65] Thomas Sharp was simply another in the long line of evil men ready to do the Devil's work whom the Mormons assigned to the outer circle of hell. The editor of the *Nauvoo Wasp*, William Smith, routinely cursed Sharp as a "monster," a "savage," a "revelator of Ruin," and a "slobberer of slander," who preached that "it is right to disinherit, ravish, and murder on account of religion."[66] To Smith and other Saints, Sharp railed against the church because he was a religious bigot, regardless of what he might claim to the contrary.

Still, the Mormons found it inexpressibly galling that hypocrites like Sharp should accuse them of antirepublicanism. The Saints not only heatedly defended their own republicanism, but attacked that of their enemies. During the 1842 campaign, the *Wasp* charged that the anti-Mormons in Hancock grasped for power solely to deny church members their religious and political rights. The old citizens decried the Saints as antirepublican, but when had the Mormons ever attempted to debar any citizen of his just rights? The Saints had never asked for more than their due as Americans. "We claim no further privileges," said the *Wasp*, "than what the laws and the Constitution of our country grant us; we merely wish to be placed upon a level with other citizens, to enjoy the same privileges and abide the same laws." In their suffrage, the Saints had "merely acted as freemen have an undeniable right to act"—to vote for the man of their own choice. The *Wasp* pointed out that the Mormons had not even attempted to fill the number of political offices to which their proportion of the county's population gave them a legitimate claim. It made no difference to them whether a candidate was a Baptist, Methodist, or Latter-day Saint, so long as he was honest and capable and had the best interest of the community at heart. The old citizens, however, could hardly expect the Mormons to vote for an avowed enemy of the church. "It is not a principle with us, as a community," said the *Wasp*, "to let our religion govern us in matters of politics," but when a faction schemed to deprive them of their rights, the Saints would unite to defend themselves.[67]

The anti-Mormons similarly declared that their religious opinions had no influence on their politics, but that they banded together to protect their rights from church tyranny. Yet the more the old citizens organized their cadres of independent, free-thinking men against the prophet's "enslaved followers," the more they betrayed those characteristics of clannishness and narrow partisanship that they protested. And to complete the irony, as they did so, the Saints denounced them as antirepublican. Thus, in 1842, when anti-Mormon candidates pledged neither to accept support from nor give quarter to any church member, Joseph Smith censured them for manifesting "a spirit of intolerance and exclusion incompatible with the liberal doctrines of true republicanism." The prophet called upon all citizens of Hancock County "to oppose the spirit of dictation which governed the anti-Mormon candidates" and invited them to join with Saints in selecting candidates of integrity, capability, and independence.[68]

The Mormons laid claim to good republican character not only in their politics, but in their daily lives. The *Times and Seasons* noted that from all the "war and rumors of war" ballyhooed by the anti-Mormons, Americans all "across the country are already prepared to hear of the sacking of cities—the march and counter-marching of armies—the burning of towns and villages—the flight of citizens . . . and the monstrous proceedings of Joe Smith and the Mormons." The reality of the situation, said the *Times and Seasons*, could hardly be more different. Through their industry, they had emerged from poverty and sickness to prosperity. In Nauvoo, one found none of the "noise of the Bacchanalian's song, the midnight broils, and the scenes of drunkenness which disgrace so many of our cities and villages." On the outlying farms, "where but a few years ago the red man roamed," one now heard "the cheerful voice of the husbandman while engaged in his laborious but healthy employ—the lowing of herds and the bleating of sheep, give animation to the scene, and give evidence of enterprise and industry."[69] Rather than revoke their charter, the Mormons suggested, the citizens of Illinois should be grateful to the church. At a time when the state suffered under the burden of grievous economic troubles, the Saints had transformed a barren wasteland into a thriving city, contributed thousands of tax dollars to the state, provided a market for farm surpluses, increased property values in the region, raised a crack militia for the public defense, begun manufacturing, and maintained morals as good as any community in the state.[70]

These things should have pleased their fellow citizens, but they did not. Their religion aside, the Mormons believed gentiles most hated them for their republican virtue and Christian morality. Church President William Law had heard the Saints denounced again and again, yet he pronounced himself unable to find any substance in the attacks. Compared with other communities, Nauvoo was nearly faultless. Law defied church critics to find a single instance of a Mormon convicted of a crime, great or small. If the Saints "have broken no law," he reasoned, "they consequently have taken away no man's rights—they infringed on no man's liberties." The real cause of their offense, then, must be "that by industry in both spiritual and temporal things we are becoming a great and numerous people." Every year, the church won tens of thousands "to the glorious liberty of the Gospel of Christ." Thousands of these the church would bring "from foreign lands, from under the yoke of oppression and the iron hand of poverty, and we place them in a situation where they can sustain themselves, which is the highest act of charity toward the poor." In Nauvoo, the Saints dried the widow's tear, fed the orphan, clothed the pauper, and taught all "the principles of morality and righteousness." These acts, said Law, affront the ungodly who find the church's

> moral and religious laws too strict for them . . . cry out, "Delusion,
> false prophets, speculation, oppression, illegal ordinances,
> usurpation of power, treason against the government, &c. You must
> have your charters taken away; you have dared to pass an ordinance
> against fornicators and adulterers; you have forbidden the vending
> of spirituous liquors within your city; you have passed an ordinance
> against vagrants and disorderly persons; with many other high-
> handed acts! You even threaten to vote at the next election, and may
> be . . . you will send a member to the legislature; none of which
> things we, the good mobocrats and anti-Mormon politicians (and
> some priests as well) are willing to bear."[71]

After the 1842 election, it became clear that an attempt would be made in the state legislature to amend or revoke the Nauvoo Charter. Joseph Duncan had gone down to defeat, but all across the state, Whigs had won office calling for the charter's repeal. Nor could the Mormons rely on Governor Ford, who urged the charter's amendment in his inaugural address. In defending the charter, Joseph Smith agreed that if the Saints possessed unusual powers, had robbed others of their rights, or rebelled against the law, they should have their charter modified. But first their critics must prove this to be the case. If they could not, said the prophet, the Mormons would "throw them-selves under the banner of our great republic" and "claim the rights of the free sons of Columbia," trusting to the Constitution to protect them from the assaults of religious intolerance and tyranny.[72]

And to what tyrannical abuse of their charter could faultfinders point? In their effort to enhance their republican image, the Saints took special pains to shun the appearance of having used their chartered privileges to form a powerful combination, poised to sweep away the liberties of their fellow citizens. Under this inspiration, Nauvoo was not touted as a holy city, but a mixed community, much like any other American town or village.[73] The Mormons reminded their detractors that members of all religious persuasions, and even infidels, lived in Nauvoo with their constitutional rights strictly observed. They had even made gentiles officers in the Nauvoo Legion, aldermen on the city council, and regents of the university. For the Legion, they offered no apology. They expressed pride in their citizen-soldiers, heralding them as valiant men who stood ready to defend the republic from tyranny, mob violence, and foreign aggression. If the Legion's discipline, efficiency, and size were crimes, they would gladly plead guilty. Joseph Smith charged that if men from any other community had formed such a militia, they would be lauded as high-minded and self-sacrificing patriots instead of denigrated "as designing persons and traitors to their country."[74] Rather than permit religious prejudice to destroy the state's foremost militia by revoking the charter, the prophet recommended that other Illinois militias imitate the Legion's fine example.

Mormon behavior, unfortunately, belied Mormon arguments. On July 20, 1842, Lilburn Boggs swore out an affidavit accusing Joseph Smith of conspiring to murder him. Three weeks later, Missouri sheriffs arrested the prophet only to see him liberated by the Nauvoo Municipal Court on a writ of habeas corpus. As the indignant sheriffs galloped to Springfield to protest this action, the Nauvoo City Council passed a new habeas corpus ordinance authorizing the municipal court to free any individual arrested "through private pique, malicious intent, or religious persecutions."[75] The Saints, however, avoided a showdown. In Springfield, Governor Carlin assured the Missouri officers of their authority, but they returned to Nauvoo only to discover the prophet had gone into hiding.

The whole affair infuriated everyone involved. Carlin and Missouri governor Thomas Reynolds both offered rewards for Smith's capture. The prophet's wife, Emma, initiated a vigorous correspondence with Governor Carlin, urging him to abandon his aid to those persecuting her husband and staunchly defending the municipal court's interpretation of its habeas corpus power. Carlin, however, was unyielding. The

Nauvoo Charter, he said, gave the city the right to issue writs of habeas corpus in cases arising under local ordinances only. To think that the municipal court had the ability to "release persons held in custody under the authority of writs issued by the courts or the executive of the state, is most absurd and ridiculous: and to attempt to exercise it is a gross usurpation of power that cannot be tolerated."[76]

The attempted arrest of the prophet and the governor's denial of their chartered rights gave sharp rise to a fear among the Saints that their liberties in Illinois might soon be gone. In every direction lay danger. No Mormon believed Smith could receive a fair trial in Missouri; and should a jury, by some miracle, find him innocent, the Saints anticipated his lynching at the hands of a mob. Equally worrisome, many church members feared the old citizens in Illinois would attack Nauvoo under the guise of bringing the prophet to justice. Upon learning of Smith's release by the Nauvoo court, Thomas Sharp fumed that the extradition attempt could not have ended less satisfactorily. If Smith had only resisted arrest outright, Sharp lamented, "we would have had the sport of driving him and his clan out of the state *en masse.*"[77] Sharp's words, predictably, infuriated the Saints. The far-seeing *Wasp* reflected the current anxiety in Mormon thought, viewing them as symptomatic of the decline of republican virtue across the nation. America, said the *Wasp*, was devouring its own offspring. Look at the Dorr War in Rhode Island, the mobs in Philadelphia, the rioting in Cincinnati:

> [While] calamity follows calamity in all the world, Thomas Sharp as an aid to Ex. Governor Boggs, who stands at the *head* of mobocracy and extermination, in these United States, and John C. Bennett, the pimp and file leader of . . . mean harlots . . . flourish with impunity! O virtue! Once the whited robe of millions of freemen! how art thou laid aside to make *sport* for the black coats who drive innocent men women and children from one state to another! O liberty! Once the boasted asylum of the oppressed!—Where are the charms that sages have seen in thy face? Where is the *pledge* for all nations to come and sit under their own vine and fig tree, where there should be none to molest or make afraid?
>
> "Tell it not in Gath, publish it not in the streets of Askelon!" lest the nations of the earth should triumph and say—Take down your Eagle—blot out *E pluribus unum for you drive men, women, and children en masse for Sport!*[78]

Joseph Smith, himself, took no less an extreme view of the situation. In his opinion, the attempt to extradite him to Missouri was an unrepublican attack on the liberties of the Mormons as a whole. Writing to Nauvoo Legion second-in-command, Wilson Law, the prophet charged, "The whole farce has been gotten up unlawfully and unconstitutionally . . . on the part [of] the Governor as others, by a mob spirit, for the purpose of carrying out mob violence, to carry on mob intolerance in a religious persecution." Smith urged Law to reject all other claims and consider the Nauvoo Charter as the supreme authority determining his fate. Should their enemies "carry their pursuits so far as to tread upon our rights as free-born American citizens," the Legion must meet their force "at the point of the sword with firm undaunted valor; and let them know that the spirit of Seventy-Six and of Washington yet lives, and is contained in the bosoms and blood of the children of the fathers."[79]

Despite their apprehension, the Mormons never resorted to the Legion to maintain their republican rights. The prophet remained in hiding for four months. At the end of that time, U.S. attorney Justin Butterfield and Thomas Ford, who had now replaced Carlin as governor, sent the Saints assurances that the charges against Smith would probably not hold up in federal court. This proved to be the case. On January 5, 1843, U.S. Circuit Court Judge Nathaniel Pope dismissed the charges against the prophet. If indeed a conspiracy to murder Boggs took place, Pope ruled, the crime had transpired in Illinois; Smith could not, therefore, be lawfully extradited to Missouri.

During the prophet's stay in Springfield, Governor Ford advised him that it would be better for all concerned if in the future he would "refrain from political engineering." As in the past, Smith retorted that it was persecution, rather than his influence, that drove his people closer together.[80] The prophet nevertheless took Ford's advice. For some time, Mormons and anti-Mormons had discussed dividing Hancock into two separate counties as a means of easing political tension between them. On January 23, Smith used the controversy to announce, "As my feelings revolt at the idea of having anything to do with politics, I have declined, in every instance, in having anything to do on the subject. I think it would be well for politicians to regulate their own affairs. I wish to be left alone, that I may attend to the spiritual welfare of the church."[81]

For nearly six months, the prophet kept his word and avoided political controversy. Smith and his church's retreat from the political scene perhaps helped to save the Nauvoo Charter. Although even in the relative calm of March 1843, the Illinois House did vote to repeal the charter, the movement died in the Senate by a single vote. Smith, in the meantime, turned his attention to building up Nauvoo. If he shunned the outside world, he intended to rule over his own house. "The pagans, Roman Catholics, Methodists and Baptists," he declared, "shall have a place in Nauvoo—only they must be ground in Joe Smith's mill." He bitterly charged that he had been through the "smut machine" in New York, Ohio, Missouri, and finally Illinois, and those who came to Nauvoo must now go through his.[82]

Politics inevitably drew him back in the summer of 1843. When Smith visited his wife's sister near Dixon, Illinois, on June 23, Missouri and Illinois sheriffs arrested him on the old charges of treason. Coincidentally, Cyrus Walker, the Whig candidate for Congress, was campaigning nearby. Walker offered Smith his legal services if, in turn, the prophet would pledge him his vote in the upcoming election. Desperate for help, Smith agreed. Upon learning of the prophet's capture, the citizens of Nauvoo flew into an anxious frenzy and sent posses into the countryside to find him. Ironically, after a series of legal maneuvers and fortuitous circumstances, the Nauvoo Municipal Court proved to have the proper jurisdiction to review the prophet's case. When the rescue party returned with Smith, he was greeted by the Saints, wrote Mormon diarist Joseph Fielding, "as though he had been a mighty Monarch returning from some glorious victory."[83] Walker soon appeared before the Nauvoo court and told its members their habeas corpus power could, indeed, free Smith from arrest; and the prophet was accordingly discharged.

The two frustrated sheriffs left Nauvoo to petition Governor Ford to call out the militia to retake Smith. The sheriffs, however, tarried on their way to Springfield long enough to recount events to sympathetic gentiles, who responded with angry talk of capturing the prophet themselves. Smith himself anticipated an attack on Nauvoo and, once again, warned that it might take an appeal to arms to maintain their constitutional rights. "Some say they will mob us. Let them mob and be damned!" "If the authorities on earth will not sustain us in our rights," he declared, the Saints "will claim them from a higher power . . . for the time has come when forbearance is no longer a virtue; and if you or I are again taken unlawfully, you are at liberty to give loose to blood and thunder."[84]

The Mormons need not have worried. The old citizens never got past talking, and Governor Ford privately decided against ordering out the militia. Cyrus Walker had gone to see the governor to plead the Saints' case, but the mission backfired. Ford viewed Walker's pandering for Mormon favor with ill-concealed disgust and decided to delay announcing his decision to avoid the impression that Walker had influenced him. Unfortunately for the Saints, other Democrats sought to turn the situation to their advantage. Unbeknownst to Ford, a number of Democrats secretly informed the Mormons that the governor's decision would rest upon how church members voted in the congressional election. These rumors were subsequently confirmed to a Mormon agent by a prominent Democrat during Ford's absence from Springfield.[85] In the meantime, the *Illinois State Register* intrigued the Saints by denouncing Smith's arrest as a Whig political trick. Walker's congressional campaign had collapsed, said the *Register*, and the Whigs needed some dramatic act to give it new life. So they manufactured one by sending John C. Bennett to Missouri to revive the treason charges against the prophet. Thus, when the sheriffs came to arrest Smith, Walker just "miraculously *happened* to be within six miles of Dixon," ready, willing, and able to defend the prophet. All of the facts in the case, suggested the *Register*, "produce a strong suspicion, that the whole affair is a Whig conspiracy to compel a Democratic governor to issue a writ against Smith, pending the congressional election, so as to incense the Mormons, create a necessity for Walker's . . . professional services in favor of Smith, to get him delivered out of a net of their own weaving and thereby get the everlasting gratitude of the Mormons and their support of the Whig cause."[86]

Whether or not he was fully aware of the strings being pulled on his behalf, Joseph P. Hoge, the Democratic candidate for Congress, never despaired of winning the Mormon vote. Both Hoge and Walker realized that the election would probably turn on whom the Saints supported. On July 31, a week before the election, both men began four days of campaigning and debate in Nauvoo. Each man reached for new rhetorical heights to outpledge his rival's belief in the Mormons' interpretation of the power of habeas corpus and the sanctity of their chartered rights.

The election caught Joseph Smith in a bind. Walker had blackmailed him into publicly pledging his support, while the Democrats were privately blackmailing him to vote for Hoge. Complicating matters, the church leadership was determined that the Mormons vote en bloc. Several days before the election, the *Nauvoo Neighbor's* editor, John

Taylor, stressed "the necessity of unanimity" among the Saints, warning, "It can answer no good purpose if half the citizens should disenfranchise the other half, thus rendering Nauvoo powerless as far as politics are concerned. In this city we have one interest alone and should not be divided."[87] Just prior to the election, Smith hit upon a scheme that he hoped would permit him to escape his dilemma. On August 6, he appeared before his followers and said he had not come before them to tell them how to vote. "The Lord," he explained, "has not given me a revelation concerning politics. I have not asked him for one." The prophet went on to praise Walker and repledge to him his personal vote. Smith then stunned Walker, the Whigs, and most everyone else by announcing that while he, himself, had not had a political revelation about how the Mormons should vote, his brother Hyrum had. "Brother Hyrum," said the prophet, "tells me this morning that he has had a testimony to the effect that it would be better for the people to vote for Hoge and I never knew Hyrum to say he ever had a revelation and it failed. Let God speak and all men hold their peace."[88]

The Saints could have scarcely concocted a more disastrous strategy had they tried. Out of the more than 15,000 votes cast in the congressional district, Hoge squeaked out a victory of a mere 574 votes.[89] Without the Mormons' unified support, he would have surely lost. The Whig party had dropped its crusade against the Saints during the campaign, but now, beside themselves with rage at Smith's "betrayal," they renewed it with a vengeance. Adding to the uproar, the Mormons neglected to inform their brethren living in and around Quincy of the switch to the Democrats. Stephen Douglas, the Democratic candidate in the congressional district, won the election anyway. Still, the Douglas men angrily suspected that Governor Ford had manipulated the Saints' vote in Quincy, as they believed he had in Nauvoo. Douglas aspired for a seat in the U.S. Senate, and his followers surmised that Ford had attempted to throw the election to the Whigs to discredit Douglas and clear a path for his own senatorial ambitions. The subsequent rancor in the Democratic party later hindered Ford's effectiveness in dealing with the coming Mormon crisis and turned a good many Democrats against the Saints.[90] In the end, the 1843 election proved decisive in mobilizing public opinion against the Saints. "From this time forth," wrote Ford, "the whigs generally and a part of the democrats, determined upon driving the Mormons out of the State."[91] The substantial body of previously moderate citizens who had stood between the church and its critics now rallied to the anti-Mormon standard.

Anti-Mormonism had many facets; by and large, it grew out of a fear of tyranny produced by the Saints' clannishness at the polls. Yet, in Illinois at least, Mormon clannishness alone was not enough to build a general consensus against the church. Other despised groups, such as the Irish, tended to vote in blocs as well. But these groups found a measure of protection by firmly wedding themselves to one of the two great political parties. The Saints, by contrast, held themselves aloof from both the Whigs and Democrats, changing their political loyalties from one election to the next. Their erratic behavior left potential allies perpetually insecure, created resentment, and made the prophet seem the unprincipled opportunist his enemies claimed.[92] The obsequious behavior of Hoge and Walker, furthermore, struck gentiles generally as a disgusting confirmation that the church was drawing the body politic into its own corruption. "Junius Secondus" spoke for many of his fellow citizens when he observed, "It is truly humiliating to see talented and able men go and act the spanial to a set of base miserable rascals who are abusing the great privileges that was bought with the noblest blood that ever flowed. It is a low pitiable, contemptible kind of electioneering that old Tom Jefferson would have been ashamed of—when a body of men acting under the garb of religion . . . shall decide our elections and act together as a body politically, we may as well bid a farewell to our liberties and the common rights of man."[93]

If by the late summer of 1843 many Illinois citizens wished the Saints gone, Hancock's old settlers became increasingly ready to engineer the desired result. Frustrated Democrats in Warsaw had issued the first appeals for a bipartisan anti-Mormonism in 1841. After the 1843 election, Whig politicians in Carthage took the lead, sponsoring mass rallies on August 9 and again on September 6 and 7. In a "he has caused" style echoing the Declaration of Independence's charges against George III, spokesmen for the old citizens accused Joseph Smith of a variety of despotic acts, ranging from authoring Nauvoo city ordinances subversive to the rights of free citizens, to shielding Mormon thieves and harassing their gentile accusers, to abusing the power of habeas corpus to escape justice. Still, however tyrannical the gentiles judged these deeds, they meant little compared with the prophet's rapidly growing power to impose his will outside of Nauvoo:

We have had men of the most vicious and abominable habits, im-
posed upon us, to fill our most important county offices, by his dic-
tum, in order, as we verily believe, that he may the more certainly
control our destinies, and under himself, through the instruments of
these base creatures of his ill-directed power as absolute a despot
over the citizens of this county, as he is, over the serfs of his own
servile clan. And to crown all, he claims to merge all religion, all law,
and both moral and political justice, in the knavish pretension that
he receives fresh from heaven, divine instructions, in all matters per-
taining to these things; thereby making his depraved will, the rule
by which he would have all men governed.[94]

In the present emergency, continued the old citizens' spokesmen, it
was imperative that all men set aside their private affairs and party
distinctions and rise to the common interest. While the spokesmen
deprecated lawless violence, they noted that the Mormons had proved
"unwilling to submit to the ordinary restraints of the law." It thus
became clear that "the time is not too far distant, when the citizens of
this county will be compelled to assert th[eir] rights in some way . . .
peaceable if we can, but forcibly if we must." In the meantime, the
old citizens forswore support for any politician who elicited Mormon votes; offered Missouri officials their services as a posse to arrest Joseph Smith; and called for the creation of county and inter-
county corresponding committees to coordinate their efforts against
the church.[95]

During the fall of 1843, the crisis gathered. All sense of restraint
among the old citizens began to deteriorate. While "respectable people" anxiously awaited fresh Mormon provocation, toughs from Missouri as well as Illinois beat, stabbed, kidnapped, and shot at Mormons
caught out alone. Groups of gentiles took to night riding and plun-
dered and burned isolated Mormon farms. Fear verging on panic
seized the church. Rumors spread that Missouri would make another
attempt to arrest the prophet, and many anticipated that the new
legislature would try to revoke the Nauvoo Charter.

The Saints matched the new militancy of the old settlers with a
different sort of militancy of their own. On December 8, the Nauvoo
City Council passed an ordinance mandating life imprisonment for
any person attempting to arrest Joseph Smith on the Missouri treason
charges, and forbade the governor's pardoning of anyone so convicted, unless the governor had first obtained the consent of Nauvoo's
mayor—who was, of course, Joseph Smith.[96] Four days later the coun-

cil empowered the mayor to create a police force of forty men.[97] On December 21, the city council passed yet another ordinance imprisoning and/or fining any legal officer attempting to arrest a Nauvoo resident without first having his writ countersigned by the mayor.[98] Thomas Ford later commented that "when these ordinances were published they created general astonishment. Many people began to believe in good earnest that the Mormons were about to set up a separate government for themselves in defiance of the laws of the state."[99] If any gentile entertained lingering doubts, these dissolved on December 21 when the Saints announced their intention to seek protection from their enemies by petitioning the United States government to make Nauvoo a federal territory.[100]

Nor were Illinoisans far from the mark. Kingdom building was much on the minds of the Mormons, and only feebly symbolized by their desire to transform Nauvoo into a federal territory. Four years before, they had fled mobocratic rule in Missouri for freedom in Illinois, merely to find that freedom illusory. Paradoxically, both the Mormons and their enemies viewed themselves as oppressed republicans, struggling to retain their liberties. As 1843 drew to a close, the old citizens spoke of invoking the right of revolution against tyranny, while the Saints stood ready to proclaim their political independence as the only means left of saving their freedom.

chapter 9

To Redeem the Nation

In the 1840s, fearful gentiles accused the Mormons of conspiring to establish a theocratic empire. The Saints retorted that their political activity was guided by a single aim, to uphold their republican rights in the face of mobocratic oppression. With considerably more dispassionate rhetoric, more sophistication, and certainly more charity, recent historians have split along the same partisan lines.[1] But the truth is that both sides were right—at least partially so. Mormon behavior reflected the deep ambiguities in Mormon thought. By late 1843, the Saints began to echo classical republican theorists who had gloomily predicted the inevitable decline of all republics. While the Mormons never ceased to think of themselves as republicans, they sometimes proposed authoritarian solutions to the problem of republican degeneracy. During this trying period, church members were chronically uncertain of their direction and behaved inconsistently. At one moment, they strutted like arrogant empire builders, dreaming of theocratic rule over a vice-ridden world. At the next, they proposed to join other well-meaning citizens in reforming the Republic. At still another time, they humbly asked only for their liberties and the opportunity to lead quiet, industrious lives. By ignoring or downplaying these contradictions, both the church and its enemies, and later historians, were able to build the case they desired.

Whether as an island of safety amid a disordered America, or as an impregnable empire, the Mormon church from its creation was an expression of a longing for security. In the early 1830s, the Saints had found psychic refuge primarily in fantasies of Christ's imminent return and in church fellowship. Their apocalyptic visions were essentially apolitical. True, they expected to rule as Christ's regents during the millennium, and as they waited, they fully intended to exercise their civic rights. In the process, many Mormons, not least of all Joseph Smith, found temporal power to be to their liking. The essential politicization of the church, nevertheless, had its genesis in persecution. The long years of hostility eventually drove the Saints to the conclusion that only in a separate political state or in national political ascendancy could they grasp the security they wanted. Even more startling, by the 1840s, the intensity of their opposition encouraged compensatory dreams of earthly glory.

Throughout their lengthy troubles, the Mormons continued to point to persecution as proof of their sainthood. The godly had always suffered and always would. Paul said, "They that will live godly in Christ Jesus, must suffer persecution," and the Mormons nodded knowingly.[2] On December 27, 1843, Martha Haven, a recent convert, wrote home to her parents that she liked Nauvoo and preferred it to "the East even if we are driven. . . . We know that if we suffer affliction with the people of God, we shall also reign with them. We know the Saints in all ages have suffered, the Bible says we shall suffer persecution. It is true that this is the place to try people."[3] The Saints facilely laid these trials at the feet of the Evil One. If God was planning for the last days, Satan was no less busy. With a sense of awe, Joseph Fielding noted in his journal, "There seems to be a Power or Influence exerted against every thing the Saints take in hand to do."[4]

This "Influence" found its concrete manifestation in anti-Mormons and Missouri sheriffs. In Fielding's view, the prophet's 1843 release from arrest was nothing less than an "Escape from the Hands of the Wicked."[5] Two years earlier, the *Times and Seasons* had pursued a similar, if more elaborate, line of thought, rhetorically asking if men really persecuted the Mormons because they "violated the laws, trampled upon the constitution, wrested the rights of individuals or communities, and pursued a lawless demoralizing course." The answer was no. Rather, hatred for the church sprang from rebellion against the Lord: "Whenever God has made known his will to the world, by far the greatest part of mankind has discarded it, and acted on entirely different principles than those revealed, consequently hatred and animosity have sprung up in the bosoms of those who love darkness rather than light, towards those who professed to adhere to the principles of truth." The Saints recognized that some of their tormentors appeared to be honest in spite of their wicked acts. The *Times and Seasons* explained this away, observing that through the Devil's wiles the ungodly "could feel themselves perfectly justified in persecuting the saints, trampling all law and order under their feet, and could without blushing, say their prayers both morning and evening, and appear as pious as angels."[6]

Satan's legions had punished God's chosen people and spread chaos, misery, and pain throughout the world since his fall from heaven. But the Mormons were the Saints of the *latter* days. Lucifer's fury would increase as his time grew short. The distress of past ages would be tame compared to the days at hand. The Mormons blended this belief in the millennium's advent with their fears of the Republic's ruin. On October 15, 1842, the *Times and Seasons* editorialized:

> If this, to the Saints of God, may indeed be called a day of adversity, we shall do well to take the admonition of Solomon, and "consider"; if we see mobocracy and lawlessness prevailing; if we see our laws and constitutions trampled under foot; if we see our once happy country bleeding at every pore, and her own sons pushing the dagger to her vitals; if we see these glorious principles of liberty, for which our fathers fought, and bled, and died, trampled under foot by a set of lawless miscreants—and mobocracy, anarchy and confusion taking their place, let us consider that in "*the last days* PERILOUS TIMES SHOULD COME."[7]

Every mob, riot, and national division echoed the hoofbeats of the four horsemen.

Paradoxically, the Saints had gathered in the happy expectation of their Savior's coming; yet as republicans, they mourned the signs of their nation's end. In one frame of mind, all of the "wars and rumors of wars" lightened their hearts; in another, it burdened their souls. No doubt, a good part of their gloom stemmed from their participation in those "wars." It is certainly easier to view discord serenely from a distance. The Mormons, nonetheless, loved their country, and the nation seemed intent upon cannibalizing itself. Faction was pitted against faction, politicians intrigued for their own advantage, bigots and murderers roamed the streets in search of victims. Anti-Mormonism, in their view, was only one, if the most important, piece in this pattern of national decay. In an editorial entitled "The Present Age," the *Wasp* ably captured the Saints' all-consuming fears of national anarchy:

> O, vile and degenerate age!—how art thou fallen from the night galaxy of years wherein the cry of the oppressed was never made in

vain! The whole world seems tottering on the verge of some mighty revolution. . . . High and dignified places in the departments of Government are being filled with demagogues and fawning aspirants, promising all things and performing nothing beneficial to the public commonwealth. Men disregarding the prosperity of organized Governments, are bolstered up by party clamor and entrusted with the general weal, doing nothing for the interest of their Constituents; but constantly glutting themselves upon the "loaves and fishes" of office, bloating their private purses out of the revenue of the people and squandering the public domain. Our penitentiaries are crowding with convicts; plunder, burglary and highway robbery, seem to be the order of the day, and business for this hangman is daily increasing. In our beloved America, State is arrayed against State in some petty contest for pecuniary advantage; districts are involved in difficulties with districts; communities disturbed by the clamor of strife and party litigation; and, in fine, the whole country is overwhelmed in the turbulent whirlpool of vice and sordid avarice. The seeds of discord and disunion are sown among us, secretly threatening the dismemberment of the Union . . . the spirit of strife and envy is spreading with lightning rapidity, and the American enchantresses—Freedom, Liberty, and the Rights of Man— we fear will prove incompetent long to support the equilibrium of the nation.[8]

The Mormons understood their adversarial relationship with gentile foes as a struggle between the Children of Light and the Children of Darkness. They also regarded it as a struggle for the soul of the Republic. The Saints believed themselves the direct political descendants of the Founding Fathers. On June 1, 1841, the *Times and Seasons* noted that amidst oppression, corruption, and self-seeking politicians, the American revolutionaries had won liberty and had successfully bequeathed it to a grateful posterity. Now, in similarly trying circumstances, the Mormons, with "a love of liberty as strong, a courage as great, a spirit as indomitable, as the fathers of the revolution," labored to complete their ancestors' work by winning true religious liberty for the people.[9]

In 1841, the Saints had optimistically expected to emerge triumphant over the dark forces opposed to the church. It would be a tough fight, but one they would eventually win. By late 1843, they were no longer sure. All of Illinois, and perhaps the whole nation, seemed bent on destroying the church. With few friends, and many enemies, the Mormons increasingly doubted that the Constitution could save them from a mobocratic majority. In a sermon delivered to the church on October 15, 1843, Joseph Smith said:

> I am the greatest advocate of the Constitution of the United States there is on earth. In my feelings I am always ready to die for the protection of the weak and oppressed in their just rights. The only fault I find with the Constitution is, it is not broad enough to cover the whole ground.

> Although it provides that all men shall enjoy religious freedom, yet it does not provide the manner by which that freedom can be preserved, nor for the punishment of Government officers who refuse to protect the people in their religious rights, or punish those mobs, states, or communities who interfere with the rights of the people on account of their religion. Its sentiments are good, but it provides no means of enforcing them. It has but this one fault. Under its provision, a man or a people who are able to protect themselves can get along well enough; but those who have the misfortune to be weak or unpopular are left to the merciless rage of popular fury.[10]

The fact that even this most perfect of documents contained this "one fault" reinforced the prophet's strong millenarian views. No human form of government, even a republic, could save man from his own folly. In reviewing the whole sweep of history for his followers, Smith found only an endless cycle of anarchy and tyranny in the rise and fall of nations. "Monarchical, aristocratical, and republican governments of their various kinds and grades," he stated, "have, in their turn, been raised to dignity, and prostrated in the dust." In the present age, America enjoyed the premiere place in the world, but even she had fallen into the slough of political chaos and economic hardship. The universal "perplexity" of nations, he argued, "speak[s] with a voice of thunder, that man is not able to govern himself, to promote his own good, nor the good of the world." The Saints, however, should not despair. Within the pervasive anarchy and despotism of history had appeared glimmering rays of goodness, peace, and justice through the Lord's intervention. Fortunately, the time was near when they would take an active and continuing part in governing the earth. "The world," Smith said, "has had a fair trial for six thousand years; the Lord will try the seventh thousand Himself." In the meantime, he enjoined the church to cling to the Lord's guidance through revelation for their salvation.[11]

In the waning months of 1843, the tension between the Mormons' self-conception as ardent nationalists and as millenarians reached a breaking point. During 1844, they would make one last dramatic attempt to save the Republic, but, half-hidden from public view, the Saints gave a decisive new political emphasis to their millenarian beliefs. The church considered the attacks upon it as a symptom of the internal corruption that would soon bring about the country's collapse. While the Mormons lauded themselves as the last true republicans and loyal defenders of the Constitution, they judged the nation's government too weak to fulfill their vision of a just and humane society. American republicanism had been mankind's last best hope for secular salvation. Now that it had proved inadequate to the task, God alone could restore righteousness to the earth.

In a utopian fantasy entitled *The Angel of the Prairies*, Parley Pratt brilliantly summarized this strain of Mormon thought. Completed in January 1844, Pratt said he had written it "as a reproof of the corruptions and degeneracy of our Government, in suffering mobs to murder, plunder, rob and drive their fellow citizens with impunity." "It also," he modestly noted, "suggested some reforms."[12]

The Angel of the Prairies is the first person account of a restless young New Englander who sets out to explore the West. The farther he travels, the more he is enchanted with the scenery—Niagara Falls, the Great Lakes, and delightful fields and forests. But it is only when he reaches the prairies that he dissolves into complete rapture. There he encounters a yeoman's idea of paradise. "The landscape was sufficiently diversified in hills and valleys and other gentle elevations, neither presenting the dull monotony of a level plain, nor the rough and abrupt appearance of hills too steep for easy cultivation." The possibilities of the region stuns the narrator. The land, he speculates, would support "an empire more extensive, numerous and wealthy, than some of the most renowned kingdoms of the old world." Why then, he wonders, have no people stepped forward to claim the region as their own? It would seem that mankind "would rather seek a precarious subsistence in the streets of some overgrown and populous town, or kill and conquer the inhabitants of some miserable country already overpeopled." Yet in mulling over these ideas, the young man concludes that "such vast riches would not always be overlooked by the enterprising and the industrious."[13]

With these thoughts still in mind, the New Englander comes upon a remote cottage and is given shelter for the evening. During the course of the night, a being that calls itself the "Angel of the Prairies" appears to him. The angel knows of the young man's reflections and offers to show him the future of the prairies through the power of a "curious glass." The land in question extends from Lake Michigan and the Wabash River in the east to the Great American Desert in the west, from Iowa and Wisconsin in the north to Central America in the south. The angel informs him that they now stand in the "central position" of the American continent. "Here is the spot which is destined for the seat of empire, and here shall ambassadors of all nations resort with a tribute of homage to a greater than Cyrus."[14]

Pratt thus sets the stage for the fictional birth of a Mormon empire. Notice that he retains, as he does until near the end, a fidelity to republican values. He leads his traveler away from the overcivilized eastern part of the United States, which seems to suffer from the same decay Americans ascribed to Europe. In the West, this evil might be shunned by an industrious people ready to exploit the land's bounty. Americans interpreted world history as the steady westward migration of imperial power. In earliest times, Iran, Egypt, and Greece held imperial sway over the world, only to lose it, in turn, to Rome, Western Europe, and finally the United States. The Angel of the Prairies affirms this theory in principle, but rebukes the belief of "some narrow minded mortals" who suppose that the seat of empire, after progressing for thousands of years, had now found a resting place where it would tarry forever. The permanent seat of empire would not be the first settlements along the Atlantic coast, but the center of the North American continent.[15]

In a second vision, the angel reveals to the New Englander the region's coming glory. Now, instead of a flower-filled prairie, he "beheld an immense city . . . thronged with myriads of people, apparently of all nations. In the midst of this city stood a magnificent temple, which, in magnitude and splendor, exceeded everything of the kind before known upon the earth."[16] The angel leads the traveler into the temple and to the great hall within. There, it is implied, sits Joseph Smith upon a throne. Now venerable with age, the crowned prophet is clothed in dazzling white robes, and a shaft of light plays about his head. The New Englander is struck by "something in his countenance which seemed to indicate that he had passed long years of struggle and exertion in the achievement of some mighty revolutions, and had been a man of sorrows and acquainted with grief. But like the evening sun after a day of clouds and tempest, he seemed to smile with a dignity of repose."[17] Seated immediately below the prophet, similarly dressed and looking only slightly less venerable, are the other two members of the First Presidency. On a third level sit twelve personages, obviously the Twelve Apostles, and upon the floor are some thousands of white-robed Saints lauded as "kings and priests presiding among the sons of God." This, says the angel, is "the Grand Presiding Council organized in wisdom, and holding the keys to power to bear rule all over the earth in righteousness. And to the increase and glory of their kingdoms there shall be no end."[18]

From the great hall, the angel guides the young man back to the prairies to show him the great changes these men have wrought. The transformation proves even greater than he had envisioned: "Cities, towns, palaces, gardens, farms, fields, orchards, and vineyards extended in an endless variety where once I beheld little else but loneliness and desolation."[19] As he turns west and gazes at the land lying between the Mississippi River and the Rocky Mountains, he numbers among the happy people 35 million Indians. Once savage and degraded, "the light of Truth" had redeemed them, and they now enjoyed "all the blessings of peace, plenty, civilization, cleanliness, and beauty."[20] Turning in the opposite direction, the New Englander is startled to discover the old republic gone. The region "seemed no longer identified as States, with their former geographic boundaries and political forms of government." He nevertheless concedes that the amalgamation of the states into the "great central and universal government" had made the inhabitants more numerous and wealthy and given them institutions "far superior in excellence, glory and perfection to the former."[21]

By this point in Pratt's narrative, it is obvious that the Mormon millennium has arrived. Joseph Smith and the Saints have set up a world government over which they rule in Christ's stead. In the land of peace and plenty he has envisioned, Pratt imaginarily fulfills the Book of Mormon prophecy that the Indians would reclaim the spirituality of their Nephite ancestors. Furthermore, it is noteworthy that the Saints' New Jerusalem divides the country allegorically, as well as literally, at the very point that separated the previously uncivilized Indians in the West from the overcivilized people in the East, neatly adjusting both to a republican mean. In this regard, it should be emphasized that republican values color Pratt's kingdom of God in yet another way. The citizens of his paradisaical empire are wealthy and happy, but their millennial glory apparently precludes luxury and sensual delights in favor of devotion to farms, orchards, towns, and even cleanliness. Finally, one observes that Pratt has abolished states in his millennial kingdom, thus eliminating the doctrine of states' rights that mobo-cratic governments like Missouri's hid behind.

The young traveler acknowledges to the Angel of the Prairies that the new empire is in every aspect an improvement upon the American republic, but until that moment, he had always believed in "the future greatness and primacy of our national institutions." How was it possi-ble that they should fall? The angel's response perfectly summarizes the Mormons' dark republican analysis of the country's imminent col-lapse from its internal corruptions and their wishful scenario for the future:

> The American system was indeed glorious in its beginning, and was founded by wise and good men, in opposition to long established abuses and oppressive systems of the Old World. But it had its weaknesses and imperfections. These were taken advantage of by wicked and conspiring men, who were unwisely placed at the head of government, and who, by a loose and corrupt administration, gradually undermined that beautiful structure. In their polluted hands justice faltered, truth fell to the ground, equity could not en-ter, and virtue fled into the wilderness. A blind, sectarianized and corrupt populace formed themselves into numerous mobs, over-turned the laws, and put at defiance the administration thereof. These were either joined by the officers of Government or secretly winked at and encouraged by them, until the injured and persecuted friends of law and order, finding no protection or redress, were forced to abandon their country and its institutions, now no longer in force, and to retreat into the wilderness, with the loss of a vast amount of property and many valuable lives. These carried with them the spirit of liberty which seemed as a cement to form them into union, and thus was formed a nucleus around which rallied by degrees all the virtue and patriotism of the nation. Thus rallied and reorganized, the bold and daring sons of liberty were able to stand in their own defense, and to hurl defiance upon their former ene-mies. Thus the spirit of freedom had withdrawn from the mass and they were abandoned, like King Saul of old, to destruction. Divi-sions and contentions arose, and multiplied to that degree that they soon destroyed each other, deluged the country in blood, and thus ended the confederation under the title of *E Pluribus Unum*.[22]

The Mormons, in Pratt's fantasy, did not have to win their "mighty empire of liberty" by the sword. They needed only to ready themselves to pick up the pieces after America's villains did themselves in. (Pratt's story might be offered as indirect evidence that the Saints intended to use the Nauvoo Legion strictly for their self-protection in the coming civil wars.) Once in power, they combined the "wisdom of former experience with the light of truth which shone into their hearts from above" to lay "the foundation of the perfect form of government."[23]

Pratt's fictional triumph of the Mormons in America marked only the halfway point in the march to his religious utopia. The church's victory over the forces of darkness on the planet came about roughly as it had in the United States. The establishment of a wise and righteous government in America, says the angel, attracted all "the good, the great, the noble, the generous and patriotic lovers of truth" to the New World's shores. The departure of this virtuous remnant from the Old World (clearly Europe) immeasurably increased the decadence of those countries. Jealous of America's prosperity and success, the "corrupt powers" leagued together and sent a powerful "Armada" to crush the new government and plunder her people. The "sons of liberty," however, were more than equal to the challenge. After fierce fighting, the wicked belligerents offered their unconditional surrender. Generous in victory, the conquering Saints gave the citizens of the Old World "new liberal laws and institutions, broke off the fetters of their old masters, and utterly forbade the use of arms or the art of war." The more distant nations of the earth watched these events with growing excitement until they, too, "saw the beauties of liberty, and felt the force of truth, till finally, with one consent, they joined the same standard. Thus, after one short century, the angel concludes, "The world is revolutionized; tyranny is dethroned; war has ceased forever; peace is triumphant, and truth and knowledge cover the earth."[24]

Welcoming the destruction of the United States, even on paper, troubled Pratt and his brethren. Once again the question arose, how could the Saints be good Americans and work for a new millennial order? Pratt solved this problem by connecting the aspirations of the Founding Fathers with the Mormons' millennial achievements. In his narrative, the young New Englander is saddened by the angel's story. It seems tragic that the once beautiful republic, built upon the blood and sweat of his ancestors, should have withered under "the corruption of its own degenerate sons." On further reflection, however, his sadness passes into joy. True, the republic had fallen, but even as it fell some of the Founders' children had kept alive the dream of liberty.

These true sons eventually vindicated their fathers by establishing "a government more permanent, strong and lasting, and vastly more extensive and glorious, combining strength and solidity, with the most perfect liberty and freedom."[25] Nor had they simply brought new freedom to the United States. Their heroic efforts "had burst the chains of tyranny and broken the bondage of the growing millions of all nations and colors." Why, then, the young man asks himself, should he mourn? "The labors of our fathers were not in vain. On the contrary, the results have been a thousand times more glorious than their most sanguine expectations. The spirit of their institutions has been enlarged and perfected; while the dross had been separated and destroyed, and the chaff blown to the four winds."[26]

Clearly, Pratt's millennial utopia rests upon republican aspirations; yet he and his brethren have lost their faith in republican means to accomplish republican ends. He makes this plain at the end of his narrative. His Saints succeed gloriously in erecting the perfect world order. Pratt's young man, however, remains mystified as to how they succeed in bringing universal peace and happiness when all mankind before them had failed. The angel solves the mystery by taking the New Englander into a sacred library within the "Temple of Freedom" and giving him a volume entitled, "A true and perfect system of Civil and Religious Government, revealed from on High." Reading the preface, the young man learns that, as the earth's Creator, the Lord alone possesses the rightful authority and power to rule over it. Governments not based upon revelation vary only in their imperfection, ultimately rendering them "liable to corruption and abuse."[27] Only God's government begins and ends in perfection. As the New Englander comes to the end of the preface, the angel reclaims the volume, telling him he has learned enough for the present:

> Son of mortal, you now understand the nature of the government you have beheld. You see it is not a human monarchy, for man-made kings are tyrant. It is not an aristocracy, for in that case the few trample upon the rights of the many. It is not a democracy, for mobs composed of the mass, with no stronger power to check them, are the greatest tyrants and oppressors in the world. But it is a theocracy, where the great Elohim, Jehovah, holds the superior honor. He selects the officers. He reveals and appoints the laws, and He counsels, reproves, directs, guides and holds the reins of government. The venerable Council which you beheld enthroned in majesty and clad in robes of white, with crowns upon their heads, is the order of

the Ancient of Days, before whose august presence thrones have
been cast down, and tyrants ceased to rule. You have understood the
secret purposes of Providence in relation to the prairies and the
West, and of the earth and its destiny. Go forth on your journey, and
wander no more; but tell the world of things to come.[28]

With these words, the visitation ends. In the classic device of utopian
fiction, Pratt's narrator suddenly awakes at his landlord's call and real-
izes he has been only dreaming.

Parley Pratt's theocratic dreams, however, were hardly idle. The
Mormons emerged from the pessimism of 1843 militant and ambitious.
The mood reached a rhetorical peak at the General Conference of the
church in April 1844. At the Conference, the Saints spoke highly of the
revolutionary generation's heroism, but like Pratt, they now openly
dismissed their accomplishments as ephemeral. Apostle John Taylor
informed his brethren that their achievements would, in fact, super-
sede those of their ancestors. The Founding Fathers had "stood in
defense of their rights, liberty and freedom. But where are now those
principles of freedom?" The Mormons, he said, were "exiles in a land
of liberty." The glory of the nation had departed, the tree of liberty had
been blasted. "We, as Republicans," he continued,

> look back to the time this nation was under the iron rule of Great
> Britain, and groaned under the power, tyranny and oppression of
> that powerful nation. We trace with delight, the name of a Washing-
> ton, a Jefferson, a LaFayette, and an Adams, in whose bosoms
> burned the spark of liberty. These themes are dwelt upon with de-
> light by our legislators, our governors and presidents; they are the
> subjects which fire our souls with patriotic ardor.
>
> But if these things animate them so much, how much more great,
> noble and exalted are the things laid before us! . . .
>
> [The revolutionaries] were engaged in founding empires and estab-
> lishing kingdoms and powers that had in themselves the seeds of de-
> struction, and were destined to decay. We are laying the foundation
> of a kingdom that shall last forever—that shall bloom in time and
> blossom in eternity. We are engaged in a greater work than ever oc-
> cupied the attention of mortals. We live in a day prophets and kings
> desired to see, but died without the sight.[29]

The rapidly expanding scope of Mormon ambition was even more
apparent when Joseph Smith addressed the Conference on April 7 and
8. On the eighth, the prophet announced that God had revealed to

him that "*the whole of America is Zion itself from north to south*," that is to say, the entire Western Hemisphere, not simply Independence, or Nauvoo, or even the western empire feared by gentiles and touted by the "Angel of the Prairies." Smith suggested that as soon as the Saints had completed the Nauvoo Temple and received their endowments, they should begin building stakes in New York, Boston, and across the land. Yet if the Mormons would soon hold temporal power over the continents, how much greater would be their spiritual power? John Taylor had merely told the Saints that their attainments would exceed those of the Founders, indeed of all men before them. On April 7, Smith promised them that through their own efforts, by moving "from grace to grace, from exaltation to exaltation," they could become gods.[30] The quest for temporal and spiritual power was no less on the prophet's mind a month later, when he boldly declared: "I calculate to be one of the instruments of setting up the kingdom of Daniel by the word of the Lord, and I intend to lay a foundation that will revolutionize the world." Smith assured his listeners that the Saints' triumph would not come from the marching of Mormon armies. "It will not be by the sword or gun that this kingdom will roll on: the power of the truth is such that all nations will be under the necessity of obeying the Gospel."[31]

Unbeknownst to all but a few Saints, the prophet had already begun laying the foundation for a "political kingdom." On April 2, 1842, Smith had received a revelation commanding him to do so, although almost two years passed before he took any action. One scholar has explained the delay as a necessary waiting period during which the Saints received special religious endowments conferring upon them the proper authority to build the kingdom.[32] This may be true in part, but the driving force behind what may be viewed as their incipient nationalism derived from their concern over deteriorating Mormon-gentile relations and their despair of obtaining protection from either the state or federal government.

The actual organization of a separate temporal government inadvertently grew out of a search for a Mormon homeland. For years, both friends and enemies of the church had suggested the Saints emigrate to the Far West where they might live in peace under a government of their own choosing.[33] By the fall of 1843, many Mormons had accepted the possibility of abandoning Nauvoo and grown more amenable to the idea. On October 1, 1843, the church leadership sent George J.

Adams to Russia, probably with instructions to solicit Russian opinion on the feasibility of founding an independent Mormon state within their borders.[34] Other missions, closer to home, followed. On February 20, 1844, Smith ordered that scouting parties be sent to California and Oregon to "hunt out a good location; where we can remove after the temple is completed, and where we can build a city in a day, and have a government of our own, get up into the mountains, where the devil cannot dig us out, and live in a healthful climate, where we can live as old as we have a mind to."[35]

By far the most important of these early exploratory missions originated with Lyman Wight. For some time, Wight had headed a church lumber camp at Beaver Falls, Wisconsin. Frustrated with operations, Wight and others wrote the prophet on February 15 requesting permission to disband the camp. Instead of returning to Nauvoo, Wight proposed that he and his brethren emigrate to Texas and begin a southern gathering.[36] The Mormon leadership, in turn, proved so struck with Wight's suggestion that they began toying with the idea of moving the entire church to Texas. Since winning its independence from Mexico in 1836, Texas had claimed the Rio Grande River as its southern border. The Mexicans hotly disputed this claim, insisting upon their rightful ownership of all land south of the Neuces River. The church leadership hoped to turn this situation to their advantage. On March 14, they sent Lucian Woodworth to convey to Texas officials their offer to settle in the disputed area and act as a buffer between the two antagonists. In exchange, they asked that the Texas government recognize their settlement as an independent nation. Curiously, the initial meeting between Woodworth and Texas officials went well. Bishop George Miller called Woodworth's report "altogether as we could wish it."[37]

A dramatic turn in church affairs eventually ended the Saints' interest in Texas. The consideration of Wight's proposal, however, occasioned the creation of the political kingdom of God. On March 14, Joseph Smith secretly organized a "special council" to review Wight's suggestion and, more generally, to determine, in his words, "the best policy for this people to adopt to obtain their rights from the nation and insure protection for themselves and children; and to secure a resting place in the mountains, or some other uninhabited region, where we can enjoy the liberty of conscience guaranteed to us by the Constitution of our country, rendered doubly sacred to us by the precious blood of our fathers, and denied to us by the present authorities, who have smuggled themselves into power in the States and Nation."[38] While true enough, the prophet's words do not begin to tell the story. This council was no mere planning group, but the nucleus of a world government, born of revelation two years before. At that time, the Lord had rather perversely saddled the council with the long and cumbersome title, "The Kingdom of God and His Laws, with the Keys and power thereof in the hands of his servants, Ahman Christ."[39] The Saints soon exchanged this mouthful for the appellation, "Council of Fifty," designated as such from its approximate membership.

The prophet headed the Council of Fifty, but the Mormons did not regard it as a religious organization per se. They intended it rather as a political body, separate and distinct from the priesthood. As we have seen, the Saints believed even the best earthly governments fell into irremediable error. God alone could provide the perfect government, and any other usurped His rightful authority. The Council of Fifty was specifically designed to restore the Lord's government to the earth. Council members believed that Christ would return at the advent of the millennium, but that his stay would be brief. Earthly rule, then, would fall upon their shoulders. In symbolic anticipation of their rule, the prophet had himself crowned king and installed council members as princes of God's government. John D. Lee's diary description, written several years after the Council's creation, provides one of the earliest accounts of its self-conceived mission: "This Concil aluded to is the Municipal department of the Kingdom of God set up on the Earth, from which all law emanates, for the rule, government & controle of all Nations Kingdoms & Toungs and People under the whole Heavens but not to controle the Priesthood but to council, deliberate & plan for the general good & upbuilding of the Kingdom of God on earth."[40]

Although the prophet's regal pretensions offended some Council members, the Saints had no intention of erecting a monarchy.[41] In typical American fashion, Joseph Smith charged the Council with writing a constitution as its first order of business. They took the Constitution of the United States as their guide. The Saints had long cherished the American Constitution as a gift from God, but their experience had shown it deficient in some respects that they now labored to rectify. To aid their efforts, the prophet gave the Council long lectures on political theory, yet they quickly abandoned their effort as hopeless.[42] Smith expressed little surprise at their failure. According to Lee, the prophet "said that no legislature could enact laws that would meet every case, or attain the ends of justice in all respects."[43] Only men inspired by God could do that. The Lord, said Smith, had foreseen their difficulties and did not wish a written constitution: "Ye are my Constitution and I am your God and ye are my spokesmen."[44] The Council thus became known as the "Living Constitution."

The Council failed to write a constitution, but it did produce some working rules. The Saints never liked the cacophony of American society, and the Council sought to promote perfect harmony within its own ranks. Their rules required that each man considered for membership receive the unanimous approval of all sitting members before he could join. Similarly, all measures brought before the Council needed a unanimous vote for passage. Members freely and openly discussed all proposals, but once the group's general will became known, dissenters either suppressed doubts or resigned from the Council. Whatever a member's personal feelings, he was expected to give enthusiastic support to all Council decisions. Finally, should a deadlock occur over an important issue, the prophet resolved the impasse by means of revelation.[45]

The Council of Fifty did make one important bow to political pluralism. The Saints did not intend the Council to be an exclusively Mormon organization. When America and the world plummeted into the chaos preceding the millennium, the Saints expected many people who did not share their religious views to flock to their standard of virtuous and orderly government. Only gradually would the countries of the world be absorbed into the kingdom of God. In the meantime, all honest nonbelievers deserved a voice in the government. The Mormons therefore decided they would invite the most important representatives of other nations and peoples to sit on their Council. Consequently, shortly after the Council of Fifty's organization, the Saints solicited three non-Mormons to join their ranks. The three men selected were obscure individuals, but the Saints meant it as a gesture of things to come.[46]

Smith viewed the Council of Fifty as a nascent world government. In the short run, however, he assigned it a number of practical tasks. The Council, for example, organized Mormon efforts to find a new homeland (it would later direct the Saints' exodus from Nauvoo); it coordinated efforts to obtain redress for their grievances against Missouri; and it directed missionary efforts to the Lamanites. The Council undertook yet another task, far more important than the rest. It managed Joseph Smith's campaign for president of the United States.

Actually, the prophet's decision to run for president predated the organization of the Council of Fifty. On October 1, 1843, Smith published an editorial in the *Times and Seasons* entitled, "Who Shall Be Our Next President?" In the article, Smith rehearsed the Mormons' familiar grievances against Missouri and their outrage at the seeming indifference of the nation's politicians. The prophet accordingly pledged to investigate each of the likely candidates for president and declare the Saints' support for the one who backed their demand for justice. "If the voice of suffering innocence will not sufficiently arouse the rulers of our nation to investigate our cause," he coolly suggested, "perhaps a vote of from fifty to one hundred thousand may rouse them from their lethargy."[47]

On November 4, Smith wrote the five probable candidates for president. Noting the Mormon's suffering at the hands of Missouri, the prophet asked each candidate for "an immediate, specific, and candid reply to *What will be your rule of action relative to us as a people*, should fortune favor your ascension to the chief magistry?"[48] After the candidates responded, Smith deemed their answers entirely unsatisfactory, and he wrote back angry letters denouncing corrupt and vacillating politicians and bewailing America's ruination. He even ventured to lecture John C. Calhoun on the Constitution, which he encouraged the South Carolinian to read.[49]

With all other choices ruled out, Joseph Smith and the Twelve Apostles decided on January 29 that the prophet would run for president. There were actually a number of realistic reasons for Smith's candidacy. For one, the Mormons had nothing to lose. The success of either of the leading presidential contenders, Henry Clay or the hated Martin Van Buren, offered the Saints no real hope of assistance in their claims against Missouri, or protection from their enemies in Illinois. As *Nauvoo Neighbor* editor John Taylor put it, "Under existing circumstances we have no other alternative [than to run our own candidate;] if we throw away our votes, we had better do so upon a worthy, rather than unworthy individual, who might make use of the weapon we put in his hand to destroy us with."[50] But it was more than a matter of going down to honorable defeat. Smith's candidacy offered potential benefits as well. Fawn Brodie rightly observed that by entering the presidential race, Smith hoped "not only to win publicity for himself and his church," but "to shock the other candidates into some measure of respect."[51] Furthermore, as Klaus Hansen has suggested, by 1844 the Mormons' practice of selling their vote to the highest bidder had sorely offended both Whigs and Democrats. By giving their votes to the prophet, they could escape the dangers of a cross fire between the parties.[52] The Saints, said John Taylor, were tired of being "made a political target for . . . filthy demagogues," and "we refuse any longer to be thus bedaubed for either party."[53]

This line of discussion seems to suggest that the Mormons did not take Smith's candidacy completely seriously. At times the prophet did treat it lightly. When he and the Apostles decided he should run, Smith joked, "There is enough oratory in the church to carry me into the presidential chair on the first slide."[54] Later, he laughingly told his followers, "When I get hold of the Eastern papers, and see how popular I am, I am afraid I shall be elected."[55]

These statements, however, belie the life-and-death earnestness with which the Saints regarded the prophet's campaign. The Mormons threw their entire energies into the election because they believed that only by electing Joseph Smith president could they save the Republic. Willard Richards made this clear in a letter to James Arlington Bennett: "Your views about the nomination of General Smith for the Presidency are correct. We will gain popularity and external influence. But this is not all: we mean to elect him, and nothing shall be wanting on our part to accomplish it; and why? Because we are satisfied, that this is the best or only method of saving our free institutions."[56] During every presidential election since the nation's founding, partisans claimed that the Republic hung upon the victory of their candidate. After losing the contest, members of the defeated party begin preparing for the apocalyptic showdown at the next election. The difference between the Mormons and conventional gentile politicians lay in the Saints' already well-developed millenarian views. If the Council of Fifty was the Mormon signal of despair over American government, Joseph Smith's presidential run was the nation's last best hope to save its republican virtue.

The Mormons came to their millenarianism, in large part, through their bleak republican assessment of the state of the nation. In an explosion of campaign speeches and articles, the Saints argued that anarchy pervaded every corner of American society. To illustrate their position, they pointed to the widespread violence directed against Catholics, blacks, abolitionists, and, of course, themselves. In a typical statement of Mormon views, Parley Pratt angrily observed,

> In the face of our glorious Constitution, and under the shade of the "Stars and Stripes" of our free republic, American citizens are exiled from their native states, dispossessed of their property, and men, women, butchered in cold blood, solely on account of their religious sentiments (as was the case with the Latter Day Saints), and abolitionists are mobbed and shot, and their Halls burned: or Catholic churches convents and libraries, are burned and destroyed—black men burned at the stake or tree, and white men hung—all, without the shadow of law; and when the authorities are applied to for redress of wrongs and justice in the premises; they are met with the *very* consoling and democratic response, *"Your cause is just, but we can do nothing for you,"* (as was the case with the Saints), or *you commenced the disturbances, so help yourselves, there is no Government for you* (as was the case with the Catholics and abolitionists).[57]

Mob violence hardly exhausted the Mormon list of signs of America's internal corruption. They frequently cited, in addition, the mistreatment of the Indians, the cruelty of slavery, the suppression of the Dorrites in Rhode Island, Southern disunionism, economic woes, false imprisonment, an inflammatory press, and even steamboat explosions as testimony to America's decay.[58]

Such a staggering myriad of social ills led the Mormons to doubt that the Republic could save itself from its own iniquity. In his campaign pamphlet *Views of the Powers and Policy of the Government of the United States*, Joseph Smith declared, "No honest man can doubt for a moment, but the glory of American liberty is on the wane; and, that calamity and confusion will sooner or later, destroy the peace of the people."[59] Orson Spencer observed that the country's recent history had "been replete with evils that ordinarily precede the extinction of a nation or a revolution through the shedding of blood." Americans, he suggested, should take warning from ancient Rome's self-destruction from corruption and effeminate luxury: "Ancient Rome was never more inflated with pride and boasting—never more imperious towards her enemies and scornful to her own subjects than just before she was overrun and trodden down by the savage hordes of Northern Europe. A highly civilized people enervated by luxury and corruption like the people of the United States might become an easy prey to the savage hordes West of the Mississippi." Should the Indians fail to tidy up his historical parallel with Rome, Spencer speculated that the Republic's fall might as easily come from a slave uprising, invasion by a foreign power, or a civil war among factions.[60]

The history of the nation's declension since the heroic days of the Founding Fathers had always been a favorite theme of Mormon critics of American politics. During the presidential election campaign, they used it with unhappy abandon. The United States had entered nationhood in the full bloom of republican virtue. The guiding motives of revolutionary statesmen and citizens alike was their overriding concern for the good of the entire community. Unfortunately, said Mormon campaigners, as time passed the vigilance of the citizenry waned, and scheming and ambitious men introduced innovations that threatened to deflower the nation's virtue. "Such was the transcendent power of the primitive virtues of the American people" following the revolution, said Orson Spencer, that "they obtained a glorious succession of wise and beneficent rulers. And the nation grew in wisdom and stature beyond a parallel. The sterling virtues of the people for a long time overawed base tyrants. But at length the volcanic fires of misrule broke out in aristocratic and licentious minds."[61] Joseph Smith in his *Views of the Powers* celebrated the history of the nation from Benjamin Franklin through the first seven presidents as the triumphal progression of republican government.[62] The prophet spoke for all Mormon commentators in denominating Andrew Jackson's administration "the *acme* of American glory, liberty, and prosperity."[63] Yet in the decade that followed the Old Hero's retirement from office, the degeneration of America's political leadership was rapid and complete. William Smith observed that where the Founding Fathers had pledged their lives, fortunes, and sacred honor for their principles, present-day demagogues pledged the same for private gain and party advantage.[64] The Saints placed the blame for America's political debasement squarely upon the shoulders of Martin Van Buren, whose presidency, they believed, had opened the door to these evils. After "sixty years," wrote Joseph Smith, "our blooming republic began to decline under the withering touch of Martin Van Buren. Disappointed ambition; thirst for power, pride, corruption, party spirit, faction, patronage; perquisites, fame, tangling-alliances; priestcraft and spiritual wickedness in *high places*, struck hands, and reveled in midnight splendor."[65]

The Mormons warned that the unrestrained ambition of politicians held dire consequences for the citizenry as a whole. Aspirants for office thought nothing of corrupting the virtue of the people. Party leaders, Joseph Smith said, were ever ready "to foment discord in order to ride into power on the current of popular excitement."[66] While most citizens remained good at heart, Orson Spencer fumed, "Men in high places have raised the wind and dust that have vexed the eyes of the nation. They have sought to obtain and keep an unholy elevation above the people at the expense of virtues and rights that should forever hand their names down to insignificance and contempt."[67]

In their censure, the Saints played no favorites. Democracy and Whiggery, Parley Pratt said, "are only other names for mobocracy."[68] The corruption of America's politicians led Pratt to declare that "Washington is a stink . . . in the nostrils of God and all good men, and except this nation speedily reform and hurl down such men," it would be hurled down itself.[69]

Like other republicans, the Mormons believed that once civic corruption set in, it claimed the liberties of the people at an ever increasing rate. Good republicans, consequently, stood ready to counter corruption at its first appearance, in fear that if it went unchallenged, it would set a precedent for further expansion. Thus, Parley Pratt scorned the controversies of conventional politicians over the tariff and the national bank as unimportant. "It is the security of person, liberty and property that is of the first importance; until this is provided for no person is safe. The Catholics may be the sufferers today, the Mormons tomorrow, the Abolitionists next day, and next the Methodists or Presbyterians."[70] Similarly, Orson Spencer wrote, "Something must be done to check the growing turbulence and riotous disposition that pervades our land. If not, the evil which now, by efficient measures might be subdued, will grow into a monster to undermine the fair fabric of liberty and consummate the ultimate overthrow of our national happiness."[71] In the current crisis, the Mormons believed their duty lay in calling upon their fellow citizens to set aside partisan feeling and rise to defend the public interest. Now was the time for all good men to come to the aid of their country. The Saints never wearied of exhorting Americans to begin the work of reformation: "Oh! Freemen why will you sleep? awake from your lethargy, the spirit of Washington calls upon you—let it not be said that we are slaves—that we are machines for the exaltation of ambitious tyrants, who have no other claim upon you than of having tarnished the honor and glory of our once happy country and sold their country for office."[72] When the American revolutionaries spoke of revolution, they did not mean the overturning of the government, but a return to first principles, a restoration of civic virtue. In that same spirit, Parley Pratt told delegates to Smith's presidential convention in New York, "We can bear it no longer. We must—we will revolutionize this corrupt and degraded country, so as to restore the laws and rights of the citizens, or we must perish in the attempt."[73]

The Mormons, however, doubted that simply tossing the rascals out would save the country. Desperate times called for a hero whose indomitable will could turn back the tide of corruption and restore liberty to the people; a man, in other words, possessing the qualities of "*virtù*," rather than the simpler "virtue." The Mormons, of course, saw those very qualities in Joseph Smith. One writer said Smith combined "the courage of a Napoleon" with "the wisdom of a Solomon."[74] Others compared him to Andrew Jackson or George Washington. If Americans would elect Smith president, said one writer, "our once blooming republic will again thrive and flourish as in the days of primeval glory, when a Washington broke the chains of slavery from her neck and raised her to a full-fruition of national immunity."[75] A. Young agreed, calling Smith "the man who will carry out the principles to the letter. He it is that God of Heaven designs to save this nation from destruction and preserve the Constitution."[76]

The Saints expected that if Joseph Smith were elected president, he would do for the nation much the same as he had done for the church. Most Saints had been confused and embittered by the religious, social, and economic anarchy in American life. They came to the church, in part, for the order it provided. Smith as president would extend this order to an unruly nation. Above all, the prophet would transcend faction and party interests. In advocating Smith's election, "Libertas" wrote, "We have, long enough, had a president over a party; we have, long enough, had a president over office holders and Aristocrats. Let us now have a President over the whole *people*."[77] Playing upon the slogans of other campaigns in which the candidate from one region identified with the views of another, the Mormons recommended their prophet as "not a Southern man with Northern principles, or a Northern man with Southern principles; but an independent man with American principles."[78] The Mormons thought Smith so ably exemplified republican disinterestedness, of course, because they identified his perspective with God's. Smith, himself, pledged to bring "theodemocracy" to the nation. In a widely reprinted letter to Francis Blair's *Globe*, Smith wrote:

> As the "*world is governed too much*" and as there is not a nation or dy-
> nasty, now occupying the earth, which acknowledges Almighty God
> as their lawgiver. And as "crowns won by blood, by blood must be
> maintained," I go emphatically, virtuously, and humanely, for a
> THEODEMOCRACY, where God and the people hold the power to
> conduct the affairs of men, in righteousness. And where liberty, free
> trade, and sailor's rights, and the protection of life and property
> shall be maintained inviolate for the benefit of ALL. To exalt man-
> kind is nobly acting the part of a God; to degrade them is meanly
> doing the drudgery of the devil.[79]

Naturally the beauty of Smith's theodemocracy was lost upon non-Mormons who viewed it simply as an unholy desire to join church and state in religious tyranny. This the Mormons hotly denied. John Taylor wrote that the Saints "shrink from the idea of introducing any thing that would in the least deprive us of our freedom or reduce us to a state of religious vassalage." Yet in their zeal to prevent a religious despotism, said Taylor, politicians had taken the division of church and state too far and "thrust God from all our political movements." It did not make sense to the Mormons that God should be compartmental-ized as if He had no interest in the secular affairs of men. Such a sentiment was indisputably unscriptural. If the advocates of the separa-tion of church and state had ever bothered to read their Bibles, said Taylor, they would "find that God in ancient days had as much to do with governments, kings, and kingdoms, as he ever had to do with religion."[80] Both Taylor and "Libertas" argued that to keep a godly man from office was to reserve politics for the wicked. "All the great Reformers and learned Doctors," wrote Libertas, "have told us that ecclesiastical and civil government must never be united; and warned us to be careful how we mingle religion with politics. Therefore we must have a Deist and Infidel, or an Atheist, at the head of the govern-ment: lest forsooth, if we have a Christian, Church and State will be United." Americans, he continued, had taken their advice and tried to make do with ungodly men "until we are now on the very verge of anarchy and ruin; and the people smarting under their wrongs and oppression, are sounding throughout the length and breadth of the land, the trumpet of Reform."[81] In reality, this clash between the reli-gious political consciousness of the Saints and their more secular countrymen was less than it seems. Though serious, it was mostly a matter of emphasis. Most Americans made God, in effect, a servant of the Republic. The Mormons, by contrast, made the Republic a servant of God. The Mormons cherished republicanism, but thought only religion could make it work the way it was supposed to.

Despite some novel suggestions, the prophet's program for implementing theodemocracy hardly portended a religious dictatorship. Some of his proposals he merely pinched from other parties. For example, he followed the Whigs in arguing for the reestablishment of a national bank and the creation of bank branches in every state. To end the decadent luxury enjoyed by an army of parasitic officeholders, the prophet urged that the size of Congress be cut in half and its pay reduced to two dollars a day plus board: "That is more than a farmer gets, and he lives honestly." If he seemed ungenerous toward congressmen, he showed greater charity toward criminals, asking that all convicts be freed with the injunction to "go thy way and sin no more." Smith hoped to cut through the knotty slavery issue by freeing the slaves and reimbursing their masters through revenue from the sale of public land. If he had his way, there would be much land to sell. An ardent expansionist, the prophet opposed British claims to Oregon and advocated the annexation of Texas and, if it could be managed peacefully, both Canada and Mexico. Finally, in a proposal most dear to Mormon hearts, Smith suggested that the president be given the authority to suppress mobs and protect the constitutional rights of all citizens irrespective of the wishes of a state governor, who, Smith noted, might be a mobber himself.[82]

Most recent historians have argued that, while not certain of the prophet's victory, the Mormons judged it by no means unlikely.[83] On April 24, the *Nauvoo Neighbor* boasted that the Saints could put, "independent of any other party, from two, to five hundred thousand voters, into the field."[84] The church leadership sent every available elder out on the campaign trail, preaching Mormonism and Joseph Smith's election. Bishop George Miller argued, "If we succeeded in making a majority of the voters converts to our faith and elected Joseph President, . . . the dominion of the kingdom would be forever established in the United States."[85]

A more practical, but certainly still visionary, measure was the Mormons' hope to build a coalition of the oppressed. The land teemed with those who had had their rights taken away from them—Catholics, abolitionists, the Dorrites of Rhode Island, and many others. By joining hands with those suffering under similar circumstances, the Saints believed they might create an electoral majority. To that end, the prophet's election committee wrote a letter to Hugh Clark, a Catholic alderman in riot-torn Philadelphia, soliciting Catholic support for Smith's candidacy. "The Mormons and Catholics," observed the committee, "are the most obnoxious to the sectarian world of any people and . . . have suffered from the cruel hand of mobocracy for their religion under the name of foreigners." With their aid, Joseph Smith would "stay this growing evil," and return to Catholics the freedom that was theirs by right.[86]

The Saints took an even brighter view of their electoral prospects when they reflected that most Americans were probably not really wicked at heart, but rather duped and misled by evil leaders. If the Mormons could only lift the veil and show them the truth, virtue would be restored. "There are now thousands of persons," wrote A. Young, "opposing the very spirit and letter of . . . [the] Constitution ignorantly and are serving party with more than triple the zeal, that they ever manifested towards their divine master. Those persons are many of the honest, truly so, and need only to be convinced of their error, and will immediately embrace the truth. . . . There is yet sufficient virtue and discernment in the nation," Young decided, "to save it."[87]

In spite of their various secular strategies, most Mormons expected God to provide the winning margin. Apostle Willard Richards said, "Our Elders will go forth by hundreds or thousands and search the land, preaching religion and politics; and if God goes with them, who can withstand their influence?"[88] Brigham Young was already certain the Lord was with them; He had been with them all along. God had broken John Bennett's power. He had caused Joseph Duncan to lose the election for governor. He had just recently made Missouri governor Thomas Reynolds commit suicide to deliver the Saints from his persecutions. God would stay by their side in this election.[89] When asked how he could possibly win it, Joseph Smith himself replied, "The Lord will turn the hearts of the people."[90]

To the extent that newspapers and politicians around the country noticed Smith's candidacy, they did so lightly. In Illinois most gentiles simply regarded it as further proof of Smith's megalomania. (It was bad enough, they said, that he thought he was God, but now he

wanted to be president too.) Moreover, contrary to Mormon expectations, it simply worsened the political situation in Illinois by loosening
restrictions on those still hoping to exploit the Mormon vote. Thomas
Ford viewed Smith's presidential candidacy as the Saints' crowning
folly and probably best summarized gentile opinion when he wrote,
"This folly at once covered the Mormons with ridicule in the minds of
sensible men, and brought them into conflict with the zealots and
bigots of all political parties."[91] One of the latter, revivalist Peter
Cartwright, shared the Saints' sanguine expectation that citizens across
the land would flock to the prophet's standard. "When Joe Smith was
announced a candidate for the President of these United States," wrote
Cartwright, "almost every infidel association in the Union declared in
his favor."[92]

Whether or not every infidel association, or God's influence on the
hearts of the people, would have given Smith the presidency became
irrelevant with the prophet's assassination in June. The Mormons were
confident enough in Smith's victory to suspect "that a strong political
party numbering in its ranks many of the prominent men in the nation
. . . had conspired to murder the prophet to prevent his election."[93]
The Mormons had supported Smith's candidacy as a last chance to
redeem the nation from its corruption. When he died, the Saints'
dilemmas of balancing their duties to the Republic and their devotion
to the kingdom of God came to an end.

chapter 10

America the Corrupt

By the winter of 1843–44, the vast majority of gentiles in northwestern Illinois believed that war with the Saints was inevitable. The old citizens now lamented their earlier denunciation of violence against the church in Missouri. One old settler called Governor Boggs's extermination order "one of the brightest pages in the history of Missouri" and regretted only that it had driven the Saints to Illinois.[1] Violence now appeared the only recourse left to preserve the old settlers' rights from Mormon tyranny—as it had been in Missouri. Church members had made their franchise meaningless, while Joseph Smith's despotic manipulation of the Nauvoo Charter, in particular the writ of habeas corpus, placed both the prophet and his followers beyond the reach of the law. If the old citizens' liberties could be maintained only by extralegal means, so be it. They felt themselves fully justified both by their republican heritage of rebellion against oppression and by natural rights doctrines.

The gentiles were unified in their anti-Mormonism, but divided in their tactics. The more hot-blooded among them insisted upon an immediate commencement of hostilities; the more conservative wanted to wait for new provocation from the Saints. While no man's anti-Mormonism ran deeper than *Warsaw Signal* editor Thomas Sharp's, he counseled patience to his ardent friends. Sharp understood that any overt action against the Saints was premature and would split the anti-Mormon consensus. Waiting did not trouble him; he had faith events would sooner or later play into the anti-Mormons' hands and provide a basis for action. He was right.[2]

On December 29, 1843, Joseph Smith told Nauvoo's new forty-man police force, "All the enemies upon the face of the earth may roar and exert all their power to bring about my death, but they can accomplish nothing unless some who are among us . . . join with our enemies, turn our virtues into faults, and, by falsehood and deceit, stir up wrath and indignation against us, and bring their united vengeance upon our heads." The prophet was not speaking hypothetically. "We have," he declared, "a Judas in our midst."[3] When Smith withheld the name of the "Judas," all Nauvoo became abuzz with speculation as to who the traitor might be. The suspicion of most Saints fell upon President William Law, the prophet's second counselor.

Law's disaffection with Smith's leadership was deep and comprehensive, but it had its origins in Nauvoo's economic life. In 1841, the prophet had become Trustee-in-Trust for the church, and as such exercised an autocratic control over Nauvoo's development, even threatening to excommunicate anyone who purchased land without his prior consent. By and large, Smith's motives were praiseworthy. Church projects, such as the temple and the Nauvoo House (a hotel), were meant for the good of the whole community; and much of the money he made from his real estate speculations enabled him to give land to the poor. The prophet, however, tarnished his good intention by inextricably merging his personal economic affairs with those of the church and mismanaging both badly.[4]

The prophet's economic strong-arm tactics and his confused finances angered William Law and led him to suspect that Smith himself had pocketed donations collected to build the temple. A Canadian convert of substantial wealth, Law had ambitions of his own. He owned a steam mill and a hemp farm, and, more important, he had heavily invested in real estate with his business partner, Dr. Robert Foster. Law and Foster's housing interests soon incited the prophet's wrath by competing with church operations for materials and labor. Not only did they purchase lumber originally cut for the temple and the Nauvoo House, but they paid workers real wages, while church laborers received only city scrip. When Nauvoo House workers deserted church work for Law and Foster's private projects, Smith fell into a rage. In an angry address to temple workers on February 21, 1843, the prophet denounced rival developers and singled out Foster's promotions, in particular, as "all for personal interest and aggrandizement." Smith reminded the laborers that God had commanded the construction of the Nauvoo House, and he declared that the Saints' salvation depended upon its completion. If any man lacked enough to eat, the prophet said, he would split with him his last morsel of food, and he added, "If the man is not satisfied, I will kick his backside."[5]

Law and Foster's discontent with Smith soon expanded into other areas. Law, for instance, sharply disapproved of the prophet's meddling in political affairs. Yet Law and Foster's final break with Smith came over neither politics nor economics, but polygamy. The prophet had secretly encouraged plural marriage among his closest associates since 1841. Most initiates had responded to what they considered an onerous duty with reluctant acquiescence. Smith's marital unorthodoxy, however, became even more extreme when he asked that certain of his followers offer him their wives for marriage.[6] On occasion, he went so far as to approach the desired woman without her husband's knowledge. Not surprisingly, this practice caused considerable anxiety even among the prophet's staunchest friends. Both Law and Foster already regarded polygamy with open disgust; and when they discovered that Smith had made illicit proposals to their wives, they finally went into active opposition against him.

William Law was only the most important of a significant minority of church leaders who became disaffected with the prophet's leadership and ready to challenge his rule. With Law at their head, a group that included Robert and Charles Foster, Bishop William Marks, Nauvoo High Council members Austin Cowles and Leonard Sobey, Nauvoo Legion major general Wilson Law, and Francis and Chauncey Higbee, quietly began organizing opposition to the prophet in March 1844. Despite their secrecy, news of the meetings leaked out; and Smith made their quarrel public. Character assassination, charges and countercharges, and ugly threats ensued from both camps.[7] On April 15, Robert Foster learned that his church membership was to go on trial on the twentieth. Deciding to turn it into a show trial on polygamy, Foster mustered forty-one witnesses on his behalf. To circumvent this effort, the High Council secretly met on April 18 and excommunicated Foster, Law, and Law's wife and brother for unchristianlike conduct.[8]

Law, Foster, and their friends repudiated Joseph Smith, not Mormonism. Like David Whitmer and many Kirtland dissenters, and Cowdery and Corrill in Missouri, they viewed Smith as a fallen, not false prophet, who apostatized from Mormonism's true teachings. On April 28, the Nauvoo dissenters appointed William Law their president and formed their own church, organizationally identical to the one from which they had been excommunicated. As the true guardians of the faith, they called "upon the honest in heart" to join them in vindicating "the pure doctrines of Jesus Christ, whether set forth in the Bible, Book of Mormon, or Book of Covenants," and withdrew the hand of fellowship from those who taught doctrines to the contrary.[9]

The dissenters lured only about three hundred of the approximately fifteen thousand Mormons in the Nauvoo area into their schismatic church. They were, nevertheless, confident that once they had made the prophet's iniquity generally known, the loyalty of many more would follow. In late May, William Law, Joseph Jackson, and Robert Foster appeared before a grand jury in Carthage and obtained an indictment against Joseph Smith for adultery, polygamy, and false swearing. The leading dissenters also pooled their resources to purchase a printing press and secured the services of Sylvester Emmons, a non-Mormon city council member, to edit a newspaper they intended to call the *Nauvoo Expositor*.

As it turned out, the *Expositor* published only one issue, on June 7, 1844. That issue, however, offered a comprehensive explication of the dissenters' views. These views struck at the root of the society the prophet was attempting to create. In essence, Joseph Smith's vision of Nauvoo was that of an organic godly commonwealth, republican, yet socially hierarchical, in which the lower ranks deferred to their chosen church and city leaders as the Lord's representatives. The leadership, in turn, sought to promote a moral community and a rough equality of condition. Like the dissenters in Ohio and Missouri, the prophet's new opponents held a more libertarian view of society. Most of the leading dissenters were economically and socially secure and did not need the emotional props Smith offered. Consequently, they judged the prophet's plural marriage doctrines and his involvement in economics and politics as an unwelcome intrusion into the private sphere of the individual. If Smith's beliefs built on those of his New England ancestors, the dissenters more closely reflected contemporary America's concern for personal liberty at the expense of communal duty and the growing restrictions it placed upon religion in politics. "We do not believe," they said, "God ever raised up a Prophet to Christianize a world by political schemes and intrigue." Smith's political activities thus seemed wrong, whatever his goals, and his methods, darkly symbolized by his political revelations, struck dissenters as positively villainous. When Law, Foster, and others began to question Smith's involvement outside the sphere of religion as defined by society, it appeared to the prophet that they were striking at the very foundation of the community. His opposition, in turn, gave rise to a new charge that he impinged on the rights of free speech and conscience—all personal liberties the age held dear. Viewing the situation as a whole, the *Expositor* thus declared that through "paradoxical dogmas, new systems of government, new codes of morals [and] a new administration of the laws by unlettered and corrupt men," Smith and his lieutenants were "pursuing a course subversive to the best interests of the country and dangerous to the well-being of the social compact." Patriotism demanded that they rise against these tyrannical innovations. In the manner that Smith and his gentile enemies used to justify their actions, Francis Higbee added that to do anything less would be to betray the memory of the Republic's founders.[10]

The appearance of the *Nauvoo Expositor* posed a formidable challenge to the Mormon hierarchy. John Bennett's apostasy two years before had damaged the church's reputation and demoralized the Saints. Bennett, however, was clearly unscrupulous, and his opportunistic conversion to anti-Mormonism discredited him in the eyes of most church members. When Bennett, for example, revealed that top church leaders had been practicing polygamy, the prophet denied it, and the Saints believed him, dismissing the apostate's charge as another of his vile lies. Although spite and frustrated ambition played a role in Law and his circle's opposition to Smith, the dissenters were generally men of integrity who were ready to fight for their beliefs on more principled grounds. They could not be as easily dismissed as Bennett had been. Moreover, as former church officials themselves, they knew much about the secret doctrines and inner workings of the hierarchy. The first issue of the *Nauvoo Expositor* had blasted plural marriage and had hinted at Smith's coronation as king of the Council of Fifty, announcing that the dissenters would "*not* acknowledge any man as king or law-giver to the church; for Christ is our only king and lawgiver."[11]

If Joseph Smith had publicly acknowledged polygamy and some of the other charges leveled against him, he could have easily retained the loyalty of most church members. He feared, however, that many might find polygamy, as well as some other recent doctrinal innovations, "too strong a meat" for their taste and that schism and apostasy would result. This proved to be the case when perhaps thousands left the church or followed schismatic leaders who repudiated these doctrines after Smith's death. Even more worrisome, the church leadership dreaded the effect the *Expositor*'s disclosures might have on gentile opinion. The Mormons had endowed the Nauvoo Charter with al-most mystical properties as the bulwark against their enemies. The year before a bill for its repeal had failed in the legislature by a single vote. The controversy generated by the dissenters' crusade against the charter seemed to ensure that the next attempt at repeal would be successful. Of far more pressing concern, however, was the church leadership's fear that the dissenters would use the *Expositor* to incite anti-Mormons to open violence.

On June 8 and 10, the Nauvoo City Council met to discuss the situation. To keep the church intact, Mormon leaders had to avoid debate on the actual merits of the *Expositor*'s charges. As they had done with earlier dissenters, church leaders expended great energy crudely defaming their opponents as criminals and degenerates. While virtu-ally all agreed that the *Expositor* should be silenced, council members grasped for a defense against the charge that they were infringing upon the freedom of the press. They answered this issue in the first instance by denying that the *Expositor* had any legitimate claim to constitutional protection. Mormon leaders affirmed their willingness to let the truth be published, however unpleasant, yet as Joseph Smith declared, "the Constitution did not authorize the press to publish libels."[12] The "Ordinance Concerning Libels" passed by the city coun-cil at the time of crisis denounced the "wicked and corrupt men" who were "degrading and converting the blessings and utility of the press to the sin-smoking and bloodstained ruin of innocent communities."[13]

The church leadership, in the second instance, attempted to justify action against the *Expositor* by arguing that the community's right to peace and safety transcended the newspaper's right to continued op-eration. Behind the whole proceeding lay the specter of the Missouri expulsion. "What the opposition party want[s]," the prophet told the city council, "is to raise a mob on us and take the spoil from us as they did in Missouri." Smith declared that he "would rather die tomorrow and have the thing smashed, than live and have it go on, for it was exciting the spirit of mobocracy among the people, and bringing death and destruction upon us."[14] By the end of the city council's debate, however, it looked upon demolition of the *Expositor* as a patriotic act rather than a violation of the First Amendment. Councilor William Phelps went so far as to compare wrecking the press to the Boston Tea Party. With shouts of approval greeting his words, Phelps asserted that no one had had his rights violated then, and no one was having his rights violated now.[15] Mustering a quote from Blackstone, the city council resolved to abate the press as a civic nuisance. The resolution was followed by swift action. Under the direction of City Marshal John P. Greene, members of the Nauvoo Legion broke into the *Expositor*'s office, smashed the press, and pied the type.

There was no painless way for the Mormon leadership to defuse the problems posed by the *Nauvoo Expositor*. Still, one could hardly imagine a course better designed to play into the hands of their enemies. Thomas Sharp and the anti-Mormons had closely monitored the developing rift in Nauvoo and had maneuvered the full weight of gentile support behind the dissenters.[16] Writing on May 29, Sharp charged that Smith was conspiring to murder his church opponents and gravely warned that if "any of his enemies be assailed, or the blood of one of them assailed, it will be a signal for general hostilities. The feeling in this county," he continued, "is now lashed to its utmost pitch, and it will break forth in fury upon the slightest provocation."[17]

As soon as the press was destroyed, the dissenters sped to both Carthage and Warsaw carrying the news. In Carthage, William Law and Robert Foster secured warrants against Joseph Smith and others for inciting a riot. When a Carthage constable arrested the prophet and attempted to take him back to the county seat, a Nauvoo court interceded on Smith's behalf and released him on a writ of habeas corpus. The *Expositor*'s demolition and Smith's subsequent release from arrest whipped gentiles into a frenzy of outrage. Time and again the old citizens had stood by while the prophet escaped "justice" through the fraudulent manipulation of Nauvoo's habeas corpus ordinance, various legal technicalities, and flight. This time Smith had gone too far. The prophet's refusal to submit to "proper" arrest, observed John Taylor, led the old citizens "to believe we were in open rebellion against the laws and the authorities of the state."[18]

In Warsaw, the news of the *Expositor*'s destruction gave Thomas Sharp all the provocation he had longed for. For anti-Mormon moderates, the situation seemed at last to have lost that last hint of moral ambiguity that had heretofore restrained them from violence against the church. Now certain of unified public support, Sharp let all his sanguinary desires burst forth in a call to arms: "We have only to state, that this is sufficient! War and extermination is inevitable! CITIZENS ARISE, ONE AND ALL!!! — Can you *stand* by, and suffer such INFERNAL DEVILS! to rob men of their property and rights, without avenging them. We have no time for comment, every man will make his own. LET IT BE MADE WITH POWDER AND BALL!!!"[19]

To chart a course of action, the old citizens held mass rallies in Carthage on June 13 and in Warsaw on the following day. Anti-Mormons had called Joseph Smith a tyrant for years; but in their eyes, the moment to choose between freedom and despotism had now arrived. A consensus to use violent force against the Saints was apparent. In Carthage, the old citizens resolved to hold themselves "in readiness to co-operate with our fellow citizens to exterminate, utterly exterminate, the wicked Mormon leaders, the authors of our troubles." Yet for all their willingness to adopt radical measures, the old citizens professed conservative ends. No one, they insisted, had greater respect for the law than they did, it was simply that "the Law had ceased to be a protection to our lives and property . . . to seek redress in the ordinary mode would be utterly ineffectual."[20] At the Warsaw meeting, Thomas Sharp endeavored to give this practical argument for violence greater intellectual foundation by invoking higher law. "When our Political rights are gone," he told his listeners, "and legal remedies fail what shall we do? What can we do, but throw ourselves for protection on that arm which God and Nature intended every man should use as a last resort." Overthrowing Smith's tyranny would be difficult, he warned, but failure meant political slavery. If the old settlers wanted victory, they must call forth their best feelings of republican citizenship and set "aside sect, prejudices, and all former grudges, and unite . . . in the cause of Virtue and Liberty!"[21]

In declaring war on the Saints, anti-Mormons assured themselves that they were not acting as a mob. Rather, this was a legitimate uprising of civic-minded patriots defending their community from Mormon despotism. In Nauvoo, preparations for battle went on under the same republican rhetoric. While the old settlers asserted their fear of despotism, the Saints asserted their fear of lawless mobocracy. On June 18, Joseph Smith called out the Nauvoo Legion and placed the city under martial law. In what proved to be the last public address of his life, the prophet insisted that the Saints had never broken any of the country's laws. The Mormons, he said, were a moral and industrious people who had transformed a bleak prairie into beautiful cities and farms. Now bigoted men, masking their lust for plunder with wicked lies, threatened to rob them of the fruits of their labor and the rights belonging to all Americans. While the outcome of the struggle might be in doubt, Smith declared the Legion would never disgrace the Founding Fathers' bloodshed by tamely submitting to "lawless marauders." The prophet went on to call upon all men "whose hearts thrill with horror to behold the rights of freemen trampled under foot, to come to the deliverance of this people from the hand of oppression, cruelty, anarchy and misrule to which they have long been made subject."[22]

While Smith might call on the nation's freemen to "loose the iron grasp of mobocracy" on Nauvoo, the actual source of such deliverance was another matter. The Saints had already written Governor Ford and President Tyler when Apostle Willard Richards desperately resorted to beseeching James Bennett to raise volunteers in New York and hasten to Nauvoo. Richards told Bennett that he believed there were still "virtuous men and patriots" in the nation to sustain the Saints in their rights. Surely it was in the self-interest of Bennett and other good men to help the Saints, for in the not too distant future, they, too, would face mobocracy if its progress were not now checked. Richards nevertheless made it clear that even if their fellow citizens turned their back on the church, the Saints were prepared to go it alone, even to the point of republican revolution: "And if the mob cannot be dispersed, and the Government will not espouse our righteous cause, you may soon, very soon, behold the second birth of our nation's freedom; for live without the free exercise of thought, and the privileges of worshipping God according to the dictates of our conscience, we will not!"[23]

Between these two sets of committed republicans came Governor Thomas Ford. Unready to shoulder full responsibility for their interpretation of events, the anti-Mormons at Carthage had cautiously sent two men to Springfield to seek Ford's approval. They need not have bothered. Ford had left Springfield for Carthage immediately upon hearing of the *Expositor*'s destruction. No less than the old settlers, Ford was outraged by the press's demolition and had decided to call out the militia, if necessary, to apprehend those responsible. This intention notwithstanding, Ford was appalled upon his arrival to find the militia mustered and actively planning to attack Nauvoo. Roving bands had already driven Mormon farmers in outlying areas into the city, and only fear of the formidable Nauvoo Legion had kept further violence in check. If some old citizens sought the governor's approval, virtually none sought his presence. Anti-Mormons suspected Ford's aims in light of the Saints' past political support for him, and he thus found his authority in Hancock County scarcely respected. The old citizens looked upon the governor as an impediment, rather than a help, in bringing Smith to justice and driving the Saints from the state.[24]

The Mormons were more pleased with Ford's arrival. They, too, hoped for a peaceful settlement of the crisis. The governor, however, soon dashed their hopes by insisting that Smith submit to a new trial in Carthage. While Ford believed that tension would diminish once the old citizens regained their faith in the normal operation of the law, the Saints feared for their prophet's life should he venture from Nauvoo. Under these circumstances, Smith agreed to comply with the governor's demand only if Ford would allow the Nauvoo Legion to accompany him as a bodyguard. The governor flatly refused this condition, fearing the onset of civil war should Mormon and gentile militiamen meet. Rather than face a lynch mob, the prophet, his brother Hyrum, and a few loyalists fled Nauvoo for the Iowa side of the Mississippi River.

Smith's flight from the city caused great consternation among some church leaders, who compared the prophet to a shepherd who deserted his flock to the wolf's fury. At their urging, Emma Smith wrote her husband, pleading for his immediate return. Bowing to this pressure, the prophet recrossed the river. Upon his arrival in Nauvoo, Smith was greeted with fresh assurances from the governor that he would have the state's protection should he give himself up voluntarily. At last the prophet agreed; and, on June 24, he set off for Carthage in the company of a small group of friends. Smith's appearance in Carthage electrified the old settlers, and it was only with great difficulty that order was maintained among the massed militias. The hearing on the charges of riot went quickly, and the Saints raised the necessary bail to secure the prophet's release. Before Smith could leave town, however, his enemies had him rearrested, claiming he had committed treason against the state by placing Nauvoo under martial law in order to fend off capture. By delaying the hearing on this new charge, anti-Mormons succeeded in forcing the prophet to remain in Carthage.

Up to this point, probably only the presence of Governor Ford had kept Smith from being mobbed. Yet on June 27, the governor decided to address the citizens of Nauvoo. Ford was not unmindful of the old citizens' hatred of the prophet, but he seriously underestimated the danger. Smith's safety seemed secure. Ford had placed the prophet in protective custody in the local jail and had assigned the local militia, the Carthage Greys, to guard him. The governor took the further precaution of disbanding the almost mutinous Warsaw militia and ordering it home. Members of the militia, however, did not return home, but reassembled just outside of Carthage. Exhorted to action by Thomas Sharp and others, the militiamen determined to return to the jail. By a prearranged conspiracy, they fought a mock battle with the Greys, stormed the jail, seriously wounded Apostle John Taylor, and shot to death the prophet and his brother Hyrum.

The murder of Joseph Smith temporarily abated active hostility between the old citizens and the Mormons. Immediately upon the prophet's death, gentiles in Hancock County braced themselves for the Nauvoo Legion's swift and fierce retaliation. It never came. The shock of their loss sent the Saints into quiet mourning for the passing of the greatest man to have ever walked the earth save Christ alone.[25]

If most Americans bothered to think about Joseph Smith in 1844, they regarded him as a grasping megalomaniac who either dreamed of building an empire in the West or madly aspired to rule the nation by becoming president. With the growth of Nauvoo, the foundation for a national anti-Mormonism had come into being. Yet "respectable opinion" still failed to take him or his followers seriously. As it had mocked him in life, it now mocked him in death. The *Niles' National Register* announced his murder, sighing, "Alas, for human greatness! One of the nominated candidates for the next presidency is already a lifeless corpse." The *Register* put down the prophet's pretensions to power as a symptom of the oddity of the times and argued that his only real miracle had consisted of "deluding thousands to his mystical faith." However, despite its flippant assessment of Smith's talents and ambition, the *Register* sharply condemned his murder as "shocking," "cowardly," and "disgraceful."[26] Editors across the land agreed. They, too, had little use for the prophet, but bewailed his death as part of a rising tide of violence engulfing American society.[27]

The old settlers retreated from violence after Smith's death, but not because they had second thoughts about what had been done. By and large, the non-Mormon citizenry of Hancock felt well pleased by the prophet's murder and seemed more than willing to kill him again should he rise from the grave. They were infuriated by the attack on them by newspapers and politicians outside of Illinois. Those who criticized them simply did not understand the situation. In the months that followed they accordingly set out to demonstrate three things: first, that the killing of Smith and their opposition to the church did not spring from religious bigotry; second, that they had acted in a manner becoming to republican citizens; and third, that Mormon tyranny had been a real, not imaginary, menace.

As usual, the indefatigable Thomas Sharp took the lead in defending the old citizens. Sharp argued that he had never heard of a single instance in which the old settlers had molested Mormon worship or interfered with their preaching when and where they chose. The old citizens, he suggested, felt a complete indifference to the Saints' religious creed in the abstract and opposed it "only so far as it inculcates the principles of rascality and treason to the Government, as we aver it does."[28] As proof of his fellow citizens' indifference to the particulars of Mormon theology, he pointed to the tolerance shown William Law and other dissenters. Their beliefs, he observed, were "perfectly rediculous and absurd," but as long as "they conduct themselves as good citizen[s]" and "avoid . . . anti-republican clannishness . . . we believe they should be treated with the same respect and consideration that other citizens are."[29] The cry of religious persecution, said Sharp, is one that evokes great sympathy. Just as many Americans believed the Mormons had been religiously persecuted in Illinois, in 1839 the citizens of that state accepted at face value Mormon claims that they had been persecuted by Missourians and sympathetically gave them refuge. Sharp continued, "Five years have passed, and the helpless band of exiles that sought our hospitality in the inclement season of winter, have become the most powerful people that ever organized a distinct community under our republican institutions."[30]

Far from persecuting a religious minority, the old citizens had heroically resisted Mormon despotism. "When in the name of the Lord they oppressed us," wrote Sharp, "it was the oppressor, and not the *priest* we resisted."[31] One old citizen styling himself "Hancock" claimed for anti-Mormons the right of rebellion against tyranny and invoked "the noble spirit which led to the American Revolution of '76" in support of their cause.[32] A committee representing the citizens of Warsaw went even further. On July 25, Governor Ford warned Warsaw residents that if they did not end their lawlessness he would use force to restore order. The committee, in turn, replied with a heated defense of their actions and defiantly vowed they would continue to fight for their rights. "The object of law," they told the Governor, "is to secure justice, but it sometimes so happens that it fails of that end. We have taught that submission to tyrants, is treason against Heaven. The patriots of the revolution never suffered half the wrongs from George the third, that the citizens of Hancock, have from Joe Smith."[33]

The prophet had to die at the hands of the community, argued Thomas Sharp, because his crimes could be punished in no other way. Smith's killing was an execution, not a murder. Arguments from critics that the prophet was already in jail and the law was operating properly offered no satisfaction. It was an indisputable fact that Smith had had complete control over Nauvoo and, within its city limits, had dispensed justice or injustice as suited him. After the upcoming August election, moreover, he would have obtained complete control over the county as well. As it stood, the Saints and their sympathizers held nearly all county offices already. The sole exceptions were two of the three county commissioner posts; after the elections they would have held these as well. These commissioners impaneled both petit and grand juries. When the prophet finally came up for trial after the election, Mormon commissioners could have simply packed the jury with their brethren. Thus, Sharp asked, what satisfaction could it have afforded the old citizens of Hancock, "to know that Joe was in jail?"[34] It would have been impossible to convict him of any crime. This was simply a case that legislators, no matter how wise, could neither foresee nor provide for. The old settlers, therefore, had to fall back upon their natural rights. Men might piously prattle about the law, said Sharp, but "they never can, and they never will prevent freemen from taking the law into their own hands when they feel they are aggrieved and that they have no legal remedy. . . . If the law had provided a remedy for the evils under which the people of Hancock were laboring, we should have been the last to justify a resort to illegal violence. But we had no law to read our case—the alternative was to wear the yoke of a tyrant, or dethrone him."[35]

Arguing on much the same line as Sharp was *Alton Telegraph* coeditor George T. M. Davis whose *Authentic Account of the Massacre of*

Joseph Smith, the Mormon Prophet offered the most systematic account of the old settlers' views. Although he spiced his work with hitherto little known facts about Smith's coronation as king by the Council of Fifty and other Mormon secrets, Davis essentially drew together the conventional anti-Mormon interpretations of the Saints' residence in Illinois. In an age, he wrote, where men thirst after the marvelous, the prophet and his depraved confederates succeeded in assembling a good portion of the fools, fanatics, and criminals from America and Europe in Nauvoo. Within a mere four years, the city boasted fifteen thousand people all ready to give unquestioning obedience to Smith's claim of absolute religious authority. This total sway over his minions soon gave the prophet the power to corrupt the virtue of ambitious politicians who, placing preferment over principle, showered him with favors and even greater power. With these powers, Smith sought to create the nucleus of a movement that would one day overturn the Republic, and in the meantime oppressed the citizens of Hancock County until they could bear it no longer. Thus, if the heated feelings of injustice expressed by "the vox populi was any criterion to judge by, an attack upon the Smiths" at the Carthage jail "was an inevitable consequence."[36] Davis wished to make plain that this was not the work of lawless rabble, but involved "some of the most estimable, wealthy, and intelligent citizens of Hancock county."[37] Why should these long-suffering citizens be held at fault when the Mormons had shown themselves unable to live in peace with the citizens of New York, Ohio, and Missouri, as well as Illinois?[38] In the end, said Davis, one must judge the deaths of Joseph and Hyrum Smith as "the unlawful killing of two as wickedly depraved men, as ever disgraced the human family."[39]

The *St. Louis New Era* also offered its services in tutoring eastern newspapers in the facts of Mormon iniquity. The root cause of the anti-Mormonism that had led to Smith's death, said the *New Era*, was the Saints' clannishness. In first moving to Illinois the Mormons, "instead of trying to form a component part of the community, . . . set themselves up as a separate people, peculiar for holiness and the favor of heaven, and . . . branded all others as Gentiles. This array and separation on their part, soon caused a counter array on the part of all other citizens." Mormon separatism, however, was only the initial cause of offense. The prophet's fanatical horde of worshippers finally made their presence intolerable because in their zealotry they became an extension of Smith's political will and pliant tools in the commission of any crime. With this unchecked power behind him, the prophet transformed Nauvoo into a perfect despotism. "Such a despotism," declared the *New Era*, "whether it be civil or religious, cannot exist in the midst of a free Republic, but will inevitably arouse the indignation of the surrounding country, and no laws, no parchment constitutions, no forms of legal proceedings,—can protect it from hostility and violence of the citizens who come in contact with them. Whether this is right or wrong it is so." Smith's murder, therefore, was a natural manifestation of the community's outrage. The *New Era* now warned that should the Mormons attempt to "maintain and exercise the same despotism that Joseph Smith did in his life time, it will most inevitably lead to fatal collisions with the citizens of the surrounding country, and their expulsion or extermination will be unavoidable." Yet the *New Era* ended on a hopeful note. Now that their prophet was gone, the Mormons had an opportunity to rectify the situation. If the Saints would relinquish their tyrannical city charter, disband their Legion, and submit to the nation's laws, they might yet live in harmony with their fellow citizens.[40]

Indeed, many old settlers believed that Smith's death would spell the demise of Mormonism. They had long viewed the prophet's pretensions to divine authority as the key to Mormondom. The act of tyrannicide, then, would effectively destroy the church at a single stroke. A writer in the *Morgan Journal* typically expressed these feelings when he wrote, "We had hoped, that with the death of the Prophet the troubled waters would be stilled, and that the Mormons would gradually desert Nauvoo, and diffuse more generally throughout the country."[41] According to George T. M. Davis, the Carthage conspirators similarly thought that if the Smith brothers "were out of the way, no other man or set of men, could spring up in the community at Nauvoo, who would have control sufficiently over the will of the populace, as to direct them in the perpetration of outrages against others, as Joe and Hyrum Smith had done."[42] With the greater advantage of hindsight, Thomas Ford later wrote that some people believed Mormonism "would perish and die away with its founder. But upon the principle that 'the blood of the martyrs is the seed of the church,' there was now really more cause than ever to predict its success. The murder of the Smiths, instead of putting an end to the delusion of the Mormons and dispersing them, as many believed it would, only bound them closer than ever, gave them new confidence and an increased fanaticism."[43]

According to republican theory, the despot who corrupted the will of the Saints was gone. Unfortunately, Mormon slaves insistently remained slaves even without their prophet. For years, moderate gentiles like Ford had pointed out that illegal violence created martyrs and strengthened the church, but this notion of martyrdom never set easily with most anti-Mormons. Perhaps they simply wanted to attack the Saints too much. There were, however, theoretical considerations as well. Acknowledgment of the power of martyrdom granted too much credence to Mormon sincerity. Like many Americans today who argue that the Russian masses yearn to be free, but have had their spirit crushed by their Communist masters, anti-Mormons argued that once they released the Saints from Smith's grasp, the church members would again become like other citizens. The assumption that most Mormons did not "really" believe in the humbuggery and wicked doctrines practiced in Nauvoo rested, in good measure, upon the currency given to charges that church leaders employed deceptive means in winning converts. Gentiles noted that outside Nauvoo the Mormons taught only the "first principles" of the church, which in actuality amounted to no more than popular doctrines espoused by Campbellites and conventional denominations. Only when safely lured to Nauvoo did converts learn the true "fullness of the gospel"—polygamy, blind obedience, and world domination. Once proselytes were removed from general society, Mormon leaders used social pressure, brainwashing, and, if necessary, the iron rod to keep them faithful.[44]

Even after Smith's death, then, anti-Mormons instinctively clung to the old categories of knaves and dupes to describe the church rank and file. The subsequent Mormon succession crisis became for them merely "a contest for the dictatorship" of the church.[45] When the Apostles finally obtained the support of the majority of the Saints, the old citizens put them down as the same old villains that had always surrounded the prophet. Still, one senses that the rise of a collective leadership cost the anti-Mormon critique some of its edge. The old citizens needed a tyrant to keep their theory at least roughly reflective of reality. When it gradually became clear that Brigham Young, acting as the senior Apostle, had taken full command of the church, things appeared to be back on track. Anti-Mormons soon verbally horsewhipped Young with the same fervor they had once reserved for his predecessor. If dates and names were removed, one could not tell the difference between the attacks on Young and those on Smith. Thus, "Juvenal" wrote that the Mormons "are a unit in opinion and action, deaf to the voice of reason, acknowledging no law save Brigham's will, slaves of the most servile casts."[46] Thomas Sharp, too, painted yet again the picture of broken-spirited Saints who groaned under the oppressor's yoke, writing that he would

> venture the prediction that if the spell, which blinds the deluded fanatics at Nauvoo should ever be broken—if the wand, by which the villainous leaders of the Mormon rule the great masses of their follower[s] should lose its magic—if the inhabitants of Nauvoo should scatter and no longer live in dread of the power of those who now rule them with a rod of iron, that there will be told by the released slaves of Mormonism, tales of oppression, of seduction, depravity and crime which will astound the world. As things now stand every seceder from the Mormon church seems to have a seal upon his lips—he is afraid to speak; but this fact alone fully establishes the dread character of the despotism that rules at Nauvoo.[47]

It is curious that Mormon followers were simultaneously portrayed as aggressive zealots and passive victims. Moreover, the seceders' silence, which Sharp found so telling, might have equally proved that there was no despotism in the city. But Sharp apparently was not listening. Many of those who left the church in the wake of Young's rise to power lambasted the Apostle with words as scurrilous as Sharp ever uttered.

Brigham Young and the Apostles may have kept despotism intact among the Saints, but many old settlers held others responsible for keeping Mormon despotism in the state. Anti-Mormons had hoped Smith's death would lead to the dissolution of the church, but regardless of whether the church continued to exist, they wanted the Saints out of Nauvoo. Much to their annoyance, they found their efforts to drive the church from the state undercut by a number of non-Mormons who, for reasons of pacifism, neutral-mindedness, or ambition, refused to countenance their actions. Enemies of the church branded these men "Jack-Mormons," sometimes accusing them of being church members at heart, but lacking the courage of their convictions. Many old citizens came to hate them more than the Saints. Before long, rabid antichurchmen expressed their determination to expel or exterminate Jack-Mormons along with the Saints.[48]

Jack-Mormon sins were manifold. Most obviously, many anti-Mormons feared that the existence of a bloc of friendly, or at least not overtly hostile, citizens would encourage the Saints to stay in Illinois. Jack-Mormons made church opponents look bad in the large community as well. Their willingness to work with the church undercut propaganda efforts to portray the Mormons as irrational fanatics with whom no compromise was possible. Furthermore, by refusing to sanction anti-Mormon violence, Jack-Mormons undermined church opponents' claims to embody the will of the community.

Whatever really motivated the Jack-Mormons, church enemies ascribed their motives to lust for political office. If anti-Mormons held them in contempt for soiling their own civic virtue for advancement, they loathed them for selling the liberty of their neighbors in the process. Sharp charged that Jack-Mormons would "do any manner of dirty work for a dirty gang, for the sake of a few political crumbs. They are men who would disgrace any party; and who could never succeed in their ambitious views, if it were not, that unscrupulousness gains them the favor of the Mormons. Poor, loathsome despised wretches, scorned and insulted—the condition of Mormons is *tolerable* to theirs."[49] Although church opponents first adopted the term "Jack-Mormon" only in the summer of 1844, they applied it retroactively to any politician who had ever sought Mormon favor. Some even went so far as to lay the entire blame for the troubles between themselves and the Saints entirely at their feet. "An Old Citizen of Hancock," for example, claimed that Jack-Mormons had caused Smith's death by years of flattering and fawning over him until he became drunk with his own sense of power and had rashly brought about the events that led to his killing.[50]

Church opponents began their crusade against Jack-Mormons with the upcoming August elections specifically in mind.[51] Anti-Mormons expected that the Saints or those favorable to them would succeed in winning those last few offices not already under church control. In fact, some of the old citizens standing for office did have close ties to the Mormons. Daniel Wells, for instance, ran for county coroner. When his status as a gentile no longer proved of use, he followed the church to Utah, where he formally became a member. Similarly, Jacob Backenstos, a personal friend of Joseph Smith, became the church-approved candidate for the state legislature. Still, Minor Deming's candidacy for county sheriff was equally objectionable to anti-Mormons; Deming was truly neutral in the contest between antagonists and hoped to bring peace through an impartial administration of the law.

An impartial administration of the law, of course, was the last thing anti-Mormons wanted. Not only did they intend eventually to drive the Saints from the state, but many feared that a new sheriff and new county commissioners would demonstrate a fresh vigor in bringing those responsible for the murders of Joseph and Hyrum Smith to trial. Railing against Jack-Mormons was, in part, an attempt to intimidate these candidates into refraining from fully exercising their powers of office. When this effort failed, church opponents turned to more forceful measures.

On September 7, a circular appeared in Carthage and Warsaw calling for a "Great Military Encampment." Those promoting the encampment announced that participants would engage in a "wolf hunt" designed to keep up "a proper military spirit" among the citizens. In the past, "wolf hunting" had served as a euphemism for raids against isolated Mormon farm communities. On this occasion, however, those calling for the encampment had scheduled it to coincide with the upcoming impanelment of grand jurors. Sheriff Deming, the county commissioners, and potential jurors were left to draw the implication.[52] Yet the wolf hunt never came off. Fearing new violence, Governor Ford issued a call for troops to help keep peace in the troubled county. In an effort to fend off any imputation of partisanship, Ford asked John J. Hardin, a prominent Whig politician, to direct the operation. It took Hardin and his men until October 25 to reach Hancock County, but the news of their coming successfully derailed anti-Mormon plans. Although Hardin remained the entire winter, he soon felt free to send the majority of his troops home.

Securing the peace, however, had been Ford's initial object only. He meant to use the militia, if necessary, to back up Deming's efforts to bring Smith's murderers to trial.[53] Indeed, only three days after Hardin's arrival, nine men were indicted for the prophet's murder, four of whom had been active in organizing the wolf hunt. Of the original nine, four fled and successfully escaped arrest. The remaining five were men of substantial property and community influence: Thomas Sharp, editor of the *Warsaw Signal*; Jacob C. Davis, an Illinois state senator; Mark Aldrich, a land speculator and former state representative; Levi Williams, a prosperous farmer; and William Grover, a rising young attorney. With the exception of Sharp, all of the defendants were officers in the Warsaw militia.[54]

When the alleged conspirators finally went on trial in Carthage on May 19, 1845, the Mormons looked on with comparative indifference. They expected little from "gentile justice," and for safety's sake, church leaders dissuaded their followers from offering testimony. Perhaps it was just as well. Writing five months before the trial, Sharp noted that the Smith brothers' murder had sprung from patriotic motives, and he fully believed that they would be formally accepted as such by the community.[55] He was right. Things augured well for the defense right from the start. The purportedly pro-Mormon jury impaneled by the county commissioners was dismissed by the trial judge, and men widely believed to be sympathetic to the defendants took its place. Although an able man, the prosecutor presented a spiritless case, and his one star witness proved to be an inept self-promoter. Finally, while details of the conspiracy were widely known in the gentile community, no one cared or dared to step forward. The verdict, thus, was never really in doubt. After three hours of deliberation, the jury found the defendants not guilty. John Hay, who grew up in Hancock County, later observed, "There was not a man on the jury, in the court, [or] in the county, that did not know the defendants had done the murder. But it was not proven, and the Verdict NOT GUILTY was right in law. And you cannot find in this generation an original inhabitant of Hancock county who will not stoutly maintain that verdict."[56] Among the old citizens, at least, a sense of justice prevailed.

Preoccupation with the conspiracy trial and the presence of Hardin and his men helped keep relations between the Saints and the old citizens relatively peaceful through the end of 1844 and into the summer of 1845. While Thomas Sharp and a host of others continued to blast away at the church in the pages of the *Warsaw Signal*, the Mormons betrayed no sign that they might soon leave Illinois, and their enemies made no overt effort to force them. There was, however, no reason to believe that this period represented anything but a lull in the conflict. The root causes of anti-Mormonism remained as strong as ever; and, in September 1845, a new and final wave of violence swept through western Illinois.

The trouble began on September 9 when citizens representing the villages of Lima and Green Plains met in a schoolhouse to talk over ways to rid their neighborhood of a small Mormon community called the Morley settlement. During the course of the meeting, shots were fired through the schoolroom window. Both Mormons and non-Mormons alike believed the incident staged, but it nevertheless provided a sufficient, if transparent, cover for those anxious to attack church members. Soon 150 Mormon homes and farms in the area lay in ashes. After futilely attempting to raise a posse of old citizens to put down the mob, the new county sheriff, Jacob Backenstos, turned to the Saints. Shortly thereafter, during an ambush on Backenstos by gentile extremists, a Mormon shot and killed Frank Worrell, the man once in charge of guarding Joseph Smith in the Carthage jail. Full-scale civil war was at last at hand. Backenstos and the Mormons soon overran Carthage and the Saints began sacking the countryside. Nine counties in western Illinois responded with a call to arms to drive the church from the state. Once again, Governor Ford hurriedly intervened with a state militia to reestablish the supremacy of the law. At the same time, Ford sent Congressman Stephen Douglas and newly elected Congressman John Hardin and two others as commissioners to manage the conflict. In rather blunt terms, the commissioners informed the Mormons that nothing short of their departure would ever bring peace to Illinois and strongly urged them to leave. With almost surprising swiftness, the Saints, in turn, agreed to go. In reality, Mormon leaders had quietly, but actively, been planning to abandon Nauvoo for over a year and a half. Making public their intent was merely acknowledging a fait accompli. On September 24, the church formally announced its decision to leave the state the following spring. While anti-Mormon firebrands still cried for action, this was enough to quell further violence.

That even an uneasy peace had stretched from July 1844 to September 1845 proved invaluable for the Saints. Anti-Mormons hoped that Joseph Smith's death would destroy the church. But before 1844, Mormonism had grown into a self-perpetuating movement that would survive whether Smith became a fallen prophet, as the dissenters maintained, or a dead one. Still, Smith's murder did sow considerable confusion among the Saints. The most immediately troublesome question was who would now lead them. The events in Carthage had caught the church leadership off guard. Most of them were in the East campaigning for the prophet's presidential candidacy and learned of his assassination only weeks after the fact. In July, the church fell into chaos, and the situation hardly improved when the elders returned around the beginning of August. A paucity of leaders was replaced by an embarrassing abundance, each seemingly ready to assume the solemn duty of guiding the church. Joseph Smith, himself, had planted the seeds of this disorder. By word or deed, the prophet had established eight possible ways others might succeed him. Thus, with no clear line of succession, a multitude of rival claimants touted themselves as Smith's legitimate heir.[57]

Initially, the two most important factions were the one led by Sidney Rigdon, the sole remaining member of the First Presidency, and the Twelve Apostles, led by Brigham Young. After a brief period of Machiavellian intrigue, the contest for supremacy came to a dramatic head at a special conference of the entire church on August 8. In a sense, the struggle between Rigdon and the Twelve was decided on a supernatural basis. While Young spoke, many Mormons believed they saw "the mantle of Joseph" fall upon the senior Apostle, and Smith's very voice seemed to emanate from Young's mouth. By the conference's end, the majority of the Saints readily gave their allegiance to the Twelve.

Yet there were more than supernatural forces at work in the ultimate division of the church. A substantial Mormon minority never became reconciled to the new order, and they chose to follow Rigdon or some other would-be leader out of Nauvoo. In reality, this split occurred along the same lines as every major schism in the past. Most of the Saints who rejected Brigham Young and the Twelve Apostles also disapproved of those idiosyncratic features of the church that most sharply divided it from traditional American religious life—the maintenance of a separate theocratic community, political revelations, special temple ordinances, plurality of gods, and polygamy. These seceders disliked the church's authoritarian intrusion into what they considered their personal affairs and expressed a desire for greater individualism among the Mormons. In good measure, they reflected this in their strong commitment to the Christian primitivism of the early church. By contrast, the Twelve promised to uphold faithfully Smith's doctrinal innovations. The Saints who followed Young had always welcomed the comprehensive scope of church direction for the security it gave them. Equally important, by 1844 Mormonism had effectively socialized its adherents into new traditions, so that they became increasingly impervious to the growing latitudinarian thrust of antebellum America.[58]

Those who followed the Twelve Apostles soon found greater reason for their alienation from gentile society. The ascendancy of the Twelve coincided with the end of Mormon power within Illinois. The Saints had become political poison, and the legislature made debate of an act to repeal Nauvoo's city charter the top priority of its new session in December. The Senate bill went so far as to characterize the Mormons as religious revolutionaries, practicing "the Mohometan faith under a name little varied from the original, the tendency [of which] strikes at the very foundation of our society." The bill charged that through such charter abuses as the unlawful use of habeas corpus to shield Joseph Smith from justice, the improperly authorized destruction of the *Nauvoo Expositor*, and the defiance of legitimate authority, the Saints had brought the state to the brink of civil war.[59] Despite Governor Ford's plea to the legislature to amend the charter's excesses rather than repeal it outright, the tide of anti-Mormonism sweeping across the state made moderation toward the Saints impossible. In January 1846, by wide bipartisan margins, both the Senate and House passed legislation disincorporating Nauvoo.

The charter's revocation did not surprise the church, but it exacerbated its sense of vulnerability. The Mormons had revered the charter as their primary defense against their enemies, and they hotly denounced its abrogation as "not only cruel and tyrannical but unprecedented in all civilized nations."[60] With Nauvoo legally deprived of its militia, courts, police, and city council, Brigham Young turned a blind eye to the letter of the law and devised a new city government out of the church's ecclesiastical machinery. For the most part, these new measures were taken circumspectly. The Legion, however, was another matter. The Saints openly refused to disband their militia; their safety depended on it too much.[61]

In the months following Smith's death, it became clear that church members had come to loathe their country. The loss of their sacred city charter and the continued threat of renewed violence only strengthened this feeling. In the opinion of Thomas Ford, Mormon sermons had degenerated into mere fanatical ravings against American society, dishing out a venomous spite toward everything and everyone outside the church's fold: "Curses upon their enemies, upon the country, upon the government, upon all public officials were the lessons taught by the elders to inflame their people with the highest degree of spite and malice against all who were not of the Mormon church or its obsequious tools."[62] Ford was not far from the mark in his description of Mormon feeling, but the Saints were not aimless in their denunciations. They were consistently guided in their views by their understanding of republican ideology and millenarian prophecy.

The Mormons had denounced the wickedness of contemporary America from the founding of the church, but for all of their bewailing of the nation's sins, they had been reluctant to declare the irrevocable end to its republican virtue. Their rejection of American society came only step by step during the course of their arduous and, too often, deadly struggle with their neighbors, and it became complete only with their departure from Nauvoo. In New York and Ohio, the Saints had supposed themselves attacked by a number of ungodly men, not all Americans. When the citizens of Jackson County forcibly ejected them from their new Zion, they directed their anger only at those who had taken an active part in the expulsion. After Governor Boggs offered them the choice of extermination or exile five years later, they broadened their indictment to the whole state of Missouri. To be sure, on each of these occasions, the Mormons issued dire prognostications about the fate of the Republic should its citizens persist in their indifference to the rights of the weak. But behind their jeremiads lay, however faint at times, the hope for repentance and reform.

After the summer of 1844, the Mormons still occasionally showed signs that they did not view Americans as irredeemably corrupt, and they called upon them to put down the spirit of degeneracy engulfing the nation. Just two months before the church agreed to leave Illinois, for instance, the *Nauvoo Neighbor* declared, "Many people know the Mormons are exiles in their own realm—the boasted 'asylum of the oppressed'—and if there remains one particle of the 'spirit of '76': any essence of the 'sons of liberty,' and only fire enough or patriotism to find old paths, the voice of the people will cure the country of *national suicide*."[63] These half-hearted appeals, however, generally lacked the fervor of earlier efforts. In a sense, the Saints had to call for a restoration of virtue; as long as they remained within the United States, what else could they do?

Yet with the rise of violent anti-Mormonism in Illinois, culminating in the prophet's lynching, it became impossible for the Saints to pretend that their troubles were merely local. Liberty in America had begun its death rattle. Thomas Sharp, George Davis, and others justified Joseph Smith's murder by pointing out that violence had followed the church wherever it went. The Mormons, they said, were too odious to make up a legitimate part of the republican community. The Saints reversed this logic and used it to document the nation's fall from republican glory. The Mormons refused to celebrate the Fourth of July in 1845, much to the church's censure by its critics. As the *Nauvoo Neighbor* explained, "So many accidents have been perpetrated upon the Latter-day Saints, for the past fifteen years, that 'Independence' or, as it is commonly called, *the Fourth of July*, had a very few charms as a nation's birthday, or as a patriotic holiday. The 'extermination from Missouri'; the ASSASSINATION, at Carthage, of JOSEPH AND HYRUM SMITH, *with impunity*; and the repeal of our city charters, by might to rob us of right," made the nation's celebration of freedom only an empty echo.[64]

The Mormons had always been almost wilfully blind to how reasonable men could view them as antirepublican. They extolled the Constitution as divinely inspired and endlessly praised the Founding Fathers, whose virtuous character they claimed they shared. So certain were they of their own civic virtue that their moments of introspection were few and far between. Still, however much it was tainted with hypocrisy and self-deception, the Saints' republicanism, mingled with millenarianism, provided them with the means to understand their plight. In the Saints' view, the United States was no longer menaced by anarchy, it had succumbed. The vox populi had turned into the "vox turbae— the voice of the rabble."[65] History taught republican theorists that once corruption had become well advanced, it was self-perpetuating, and patriots could no longer turn it back. The *Nauvoo Neighbor* now gloomily pronounced the nation's fate: "All republics have found an incurable malady in party factions; ambition and revenge, will triumph over patriotism and generosity; and then anarchy and confusion, generally sweep the country of liberty and right, and barbarity, degradation, ruin, and wretchedness ensues. From all appearance, the United States has seen its best days."[66] A month later, the *Times and Seasons* was even more emphatic: "The glory of America has departed;—the virtue of freemen has been corrupted; and the good name of liberty has been filched from 'the asylum of the oppressed' by wicked men in high places."[67]

The Saints carefully avoided basing their republican critique of the country solely on their own experience. In a strategy they had perfected in years past, they argued that their suffering was only one symptom of the mobocracy sweeping the nation. This gave them the advantage of deemphasizing the specialness of their own situation, while magnifying the degradation of freedom. The Mormons, for example, frequently pointed to the recent nativist riots in Philadelphia as another instance of the nation's plunge into anarchy. "The freemen of the United States, in the assassination at Carthage jail, and native American slaughter, and burning churches in Philadelphia, degraded themselves below the wild Indian of the forest!" America's liberty had become death, said the *Nauvoo Neighbor*, and villains would soon force others exercising their rights of conscience to drink from the same cup of oppression the Saints had been the first to taste: "The blow aimed at Mormonism, does not satisfy its votaries with the blood of its victims: no, the Catholics are threatened next; foreigners next; and so on; for revolutions never go backward. The Presbyterians, Methodists, Baptists, Quakers and all other denominations, when they come in the way of self made power, must succumb or die; the government unless in its agony, it cuts the canker out by the roots must crumble to pieces."[68]

Although Americans continued to sing the praises of their rights and liberties, the *Nauvoo Neighbor* said, these blessings had become empty forms.[69] Real republicanism had ended when the blackleg replaced the patriot in the places of national honor, and the mobocrat on the street replaced the citizen at the ballot box. The old citizens liked to claim that they had suffered much more under Mormon tyranny than their forefathers had under the British. In a curious parallel, Parley Pratt described the Saints' suffering in similar terms. In his view, the Constitution and the nation's laws were "a dead letter." The wicked men entrusted with upholding them either refused to do so, or only enforced them selectively against the church. "Under these circumstances," Pratt said, "it must be obvious to all men of common intelligence that we as a people are in the midst of revolution of far more importance than were our fathers the founders of this nation." While their ancestors had to fight foreign oppressors, the Mormons had "to struggle with our own rulers and country to keep them from committing suicide, or in other words to preserve our country and rights from destruction by the hands of our own citizens."[70]

The time had come for the Saints to lead a peaceful counterrevolution to restore the nation to its "first principles." The Constitution might be dead, but the Mormons believed that its resurrection was possible. By rising to do "our first work again," they declared, Americans might yet have "some hope of regaining that fame we once enjoyed as republicans."[71] How the Saints might accomplish that revolution was, of course, problematic. One way was through political manipulation. Pratt urged the church to maintain its political union, suggesting it could meet the crisis by holding the balance of power between the two parties. The Mormons could then regain their right by forcing one or the other of the parties back into civic virtue. Yet even if this strategy failed, and Pratt thought it might, it did not really matter what the Democrats or Whigs did. The rapid decay of both corrupt parties, combined with the geometric growth of the church, made the question ultimately irrelevant. If they "neglect their duty as they have done," Pratt said, "we will let them, and their adherents go to ruin together, while we hold on to the spirit and union of '76 till we are sufficiently powerful to restore the supremacy of the Constitution and laws."[72] The *Nauvoo Neighbor* spoke with even less qualification than Pratt when it declared that nothing except the religious triumph of the Saints could halt the nation's degeneracy: "There is nothing but Mormonism that will save this generation from wretchedness and ruin. Now mark it; if fifty years find this nation prosperous without Mormonism, Joseph Smith was a false prophet, and there is no God!"[73]

The Mormons knew that such bold words would never be brought to the test. For Joseph Smith was a true prophet, God did exist, and the Saints could put their trust in Him to see that they triumphed over their adversaries. In this vein, talk of growing church membership and the balance of power became irrelevant. The end of American republicanism had a millenarian meaning for the Mormons. The fall of the United States heralded the fall of the world.[74] More than anything else, it was this reflection that gave balm to the church's wounded spirit. For fifteen years, they had labored mightily under the heavy burden of slander, betrayal, and violent persecution to spread the gospel and warn of coming tribulation. Now as the last days finally approached, they could find bliss amidst the turmoil, as God began to fulfill the words of His servants.[75]

Such anticipations of the apocalypse abounded in Mormon newspapers and sermons, but perhaps the most interesting never appeared before the public. In late April 1845, the Saints wrote a series of hat-in-hand letters to President Polk and the nation's governors, asking for relief on the grounds of humanitarianism and shared republican sentiment.[76] This was actually their second communication directed to political leaders. The first, written only three weeks earlier, was prudently never sent, but it clearly reveals the Mormon state of mind at its extremity. Boldly entitled, a "Proclamation of the Twelve Apostles to all the Kings of the World, To the President of the United States of America, To the Governors of Several States, And to the Rulers and Peoples of all Nations," it announced that the kingdom of God had arrived on earth. The appearance of the kingdom, which the Apostles identified with the Mormon church, had set the world into commotion, and in the gathering struggle, there would be no neutrals. The Twelve thus warned the world's rulers,

> You cannot, therefore, stand as idle and disinterested spectators of the scenes and events which are calculated, in their very nature, to reduce all nations and creeds to *one* political and religious standard, and thus put an end to Babel forms and names and to strife and war. You will therefore either be led by the good Spirit to cast in your lot, and to take a lively interest with the Saints of the Most High, and the covenant people of the Lord; or, on the other hand, you will become the inveterate enemy and oppose them by every means in your power.[77]

Not surprisingly, gentiles interpreted the somewhat milder published expressions of this belief as treasonous. Unquestionably, such a fierce millenarianism led the Saints into some decidedly antirepublican opinions. Church members, however, refused to debate their eschatological hopes within a republican/antirepublican context. If at times the Mormons seemed to preach holy war against their enemies, it was a war in which, they said, they wished to take no part. More typically, the Saints suggested that the wicked would either destroy themselves or fall victim to God's wrath. On the other hand, if belief in the overthrow of carnal governments was treasonous, then the Bible taught treason, and they were willing to be thought traitors.[78]

Perhaps because of their well-developed millenarianism, the church took the fresh outbreak of anti-Mormon violence in September 1845 with surprising calm. The *Nauvoo Neighbor*, of course, strongly denounced gentile mobbing, but nevertheless took it simply as another "sign of the times."[79] A sense of resignation had gripped the Saints. When in late September Congressmen John Hardin and Stephen Douglas pressed the church to leave Illinois, the Mormons were ready. Brigham ruled out any further appeal to higher authorities: "We have told such tales to our father the president and to all the high-minded governors until we are weary of it."[80] One could not appeal to a politician's sense of republican virtue if he had none. In his journal, Erastus Snow wrote, "Regarding this as a door [from] which we could make a peaceful exit from this corrupt nation and establish ourselves independent of them, it was unanimously resolved in the councils of the church to adopt the alternative insisted upon by our enemies."[81]

The Mormons had had enough of the United States and determined to seek a new homeland somewhere well outside the nation's western borders. Their impending physical break with the country finally permitted a psychological break as well. Fleeting prayers for the resurrection of civic virtue in America died on Mormon lips. In their place came direct avowals of contempt for the land of their birth. In a farewell to his brethren in the East, Apostle Orson Pratt wrote,

> Being included with my family, among the tens of thousands of American citizens who have the choice of death or banishment beyond the Rocky Mountains[,] I have preferred the latter. It is with the greatest joy that I forsake this republic; and all of the saints have abundant reasons to rejoice that they are counted worthy to be cast out as exiles from this wicked nation; for we have received nothing but one continual scene of the most horrid and unrelenting persecution at their hands for the last sixteen years. If our heavenly father will deliver us out of the hands of the bloodthirsty Christians of these United States and not suffer any more of us to be martyred to gratify their holy piety, I for one shall be very thankful. Perhaps we may have to suffer much in the land of exile, but our suffering will be from another cause—there will be no Christian bandit to afflict us all day long—no holy priest to murder us by scores—no editors to urge on house-burning, devastation and death. If we die in dens and caves of the Rocky Mountains, we shall die where freedom reigns triumphantly. Liberty in a solitary place, and in a desert, is far more preferable than martyrdom in these pious states.[82]

Characteristically, Brigham Young was even more blunt. On September 26, two days after the church agreed to leave Illinois, he declared, "I never intend to winter in the United States [again] . . . we do not owe this country a single Sermon." This nation is "as corrupt as Hell from the president down clean through the priests and the people."[83]

The Mormons had done their duty to the nation, but its degeneracy could not be checked. The Saints' garments were now clean, and they could depart without guilt.[84] It was as "the nation of Israel" that Brigham Young and the Twelve would lead their "captive people" out of bondage. This was more than simply a metaphor. Not only did they identify themselves with the ancient Israelites, but their alienation from the United States had brought them to the brink of nationhood.[85] Their struggle and suffering had made more than a "peculiar people"; it made them a separate one, possessing a unique identity and sacred history.

Even before the first wagon left Nauvoo, the Mormons' new home in the West became a land of milk and honey. Mormon poets and hymnists of variable talent turned out inspirational pieces contrasting mobocratic America with the liberty, equality, and freedom to worship God they would soon enjoy.[86] While Orson Pratt wrote grimly of the Saints' regaining their rights in Rocky Mountain caves, his brother, Parley, heralded the church's future home as a place of equal rights amidst earthly abundance:

> The Lord designs to lead us to a wider field of action, where there will be more room for the saints to grow and increase, and where there will be no one to say we crowd them, and where we can enjoy the pure principles of liberty and equal rights.

> When we settle a country where the air, the water, soil and timber is equally free to every settler without money or price, the climate is healthy, and the people free from unjust and vexatious lawsuits, mobocracy, and oppression of every kind, we can become vastly more wealthy, have better possessions and improvements, and build a larger and better Temple in five years from this time than we now possess.[87]

Immediately following the General Conference of the Church in October 1845, the Mormons began working diligently to make their escape. The problems involved in the undertaking were immense. Farms, homes, and shops went at rock bottom prices—when the Saints were lucky enough to find purchasers. The Church found even more troubling the herculean task of finishing their temple. God had warned Joseph Smith that the Mormons would be "cut off with their dead," if they failed to receive their "endowments" in the completed temple. A climate of fear added to these problems. Throughout the fall of 1845, Brigham Young and other church leaders periodically went into hiding to avoid arrest on counterfeiting charges. Rumors also spread that the United States government would bar their emigration to the Far West in fear that the church would aid England in its claim to Oregon Territory. The Saints had hoped to wait until the spring thaw to begin their departure. In the face of rumors and legal harassment, they scuttled these plans. On February 5, 1846, the Mormon exodus began when the first emigrants crossed the frozen Mississippi River.[88]

Brigham Young, himself, left Nauvoo on February 12. After sixteen years, Americans had pronounced the Saints unfit to live among them. Young knew better. The very people who charged the Mormons with antirepublicanism were casting out the nation's only true republicans.

It was Americans who were unfit to live with the Saints. In Iowa, Young told his brethren that Nauvoo would stand as an enduring symbol of the Saints' civic virtue and the corruption of those who hated them: "Our homes, gardens, orchards, farms, streets, bridges, mills, public halls, magnificent temple, and other public improvements we leave as a monument of our patriotism, industry, economy, uprightness of purpose and integrity of heart; and as a living testimony of the falsehood and wickedness of those who charge us with disloyalty to the Constitution of our country, idleness, and dishonesty."[89] Across the Great Plains, America's last republicans would venture west, where freedom would be reborn, and where they would no longer suffer as exiles in a land of liberty.

Notes

Introduction

1. Joseph Smith, The Book of Mormon, p. 84.
2. For one of many such examples, see *Evening and Morning Star*, July 1834.
3. Stout, *On the Frontier*, 1:73–74.
4. My treatment of republican ideology represents a distillation of a wide variety of works on the subject. For the historiographical development of the concept of republicanism, see Robert Shalhope's discussion in "Toward a Republican Synthesis," pp. 49–80, and in his article, "Republicanism and Early American Historiography," pp. 334–56. I have included citations to more recent studies relevant to the use of classical republicanism in my bibliography, including those hostile to the concept.
5. The phrase is Shalhope's, "Toward a Republican Synthesis," p. 63.
6. Morgan, "The Puritan Ethic and the American Revolution," in his book *The Challenge of the American Revolution*, pp. 88–138; the persistence of the jeremiad tradition in American history is the theme of Bercovitch, *The American Jeremiad*.
7. Berthoff, "Independence and Attachment, Virtue and Interest," pp. 97–124.
8. See, for example, Bushman, *Joseph Smith and the Beginnings of Mormonism*; Shipps, *Mormonism*; Flanders, "To Transform History"; and Hansen, *Mormonism and the American Experience*. For a recent exception to this general view, see Moore, *Religious Outsiders and the Making of Americans*.

Chapter 1

1. Although it emphasizes the Mack line, the most indispensable source on Joseph Smith's ancestors is Lucy Mack Smith, *Biographical Sketches*, pp. 15–44; the best secondary account is found in Bushman, *Joseph Smith and the Beginnings of Mormonism*, pp. 9–29.
2. Lucy Mack Smith, *Biographical Sketches*, pp. 45–73.
3. Berthoff, *An Unsettled People*, Chap. 10 passim; Hansen, *Mormonism and the American Experience*, pp. 1–3; Donna Hill, *Joseph Smith*, p. 45.
4. Joseph Smith, "Joseph Smith's 1832 Account of His Life," p. 3.
5. Howe, *Mormonism Unvailed*, p. 257.
6. Ibid., p. 260. The use of these affidavits to assess the Smiths' New York reputation has come under sharp attack from Mormon church historians, most notably Richard Anderson. These historians argue that the anti-Mormon investigator who solicited these testimonies, Philastus Hurlburt, sought only information damaging to the Smiths and made no attempt to obtain an accurate portrait. Furthermore, the repetition of a number of key phrases betrays Hurlburt's hand in preparing the statements, ensuring a negative slant. Jan Shipps, on the other hand, has defended the accuracy of the attitudes contained in the documents, pointing out the appearance of similar information in newspaper articles by other writers three years prior to the publication of *Mormonism Unvailed* (1834). Anderson, "Joseph Smith's New York Reputation Reap-

praised," pp. 283–314; Shipps, "The Prophet Puzzle," p. 13; see also Marvin S. Hill, "Secular or Sectarian History?," pp. 87–89.

7. Joseph Smith, *History of the Church*, 1:9.

8. Arrington and Bitton, *The Mormon Experience*, p. 18.

9. Donna Hill, *Joseph Smith*, pp. 21–31.

10. Marvin S. Hill, "The Shaping of the Mormon Mind in New England and New York," pp. 353–56; Hatch, "The Christian Movement," pp. 545–67.

11. Donna Hill, *Joseph Smith*, p. 44.

12. Lucy Mack Smith, *Biographical Sketches*, p. 57.

13. Ibid., p. 59.

14. Joseph Smith, The Book of Mormon, pp. 19–20.

15. William Smith, *William Smith on Mormonism*, pp. 6–7.

16. Paul E. Johnson, *A Shopkeeper's Millennium*, p. 108.

17. Marvin S. Hill, "Joseph Smith's First Vision," pp. 92–93; Joseph Smith, *History of the Church*, 1:2–3.

18. Marvin S. Hill, "Joseph Smith's First Vision," p. 93.

19. Joseph Smith, *History of the Church*, 1:4.

20. Ibid., p. 6. What actually occurred during Joseph's "first vision," or even if it occurred at all, is the subject of an intense debate. The account I have given is in accordance with the official version of the church, first recorded in 1838. In the 1960s, earlier accounts of the first vision surfaced in the Mormon Church Archives. The most important of these accounts was written by Joseph in the winter of 1831–32. In this, the earliest version known to exist, Joseph gave his age at the time of the vision as sixteen, not fourteen, and recorded only one personage, "the Lord," as present. Although the element of sectarian strife is apparent, Joseph's emphasis is more personal, dwelling on the forgiveness of his sins. In another account written on November 9, 1835, the details of the vision are sharper and not too dissimilar to the official 1838 version. Undoubtedly, Joseph tailored his story as time went on, accenting the points he found more useful rather than what actually occurred. Yet one wonders why, if God had visited him, he was not even impressed enough to remember his own age clearly at the time it occurred. Indeed, Fawn Brodie believed the inconsistencies in his various accounts smacked of fraud. Still, in all the accounts, the central thrust remains the same. Joseph disliked sectarian confusion, feared for his soul, and, one way or another, threw off his burden of doubt as a result of this experience. The various accounts of Joseph's first vision may be found in Jesse, "Early Accounts," pp. 275–94; for contrasting opinions on the first vision, see Brodie, *No Man Knows My History*, pp. 405–12.

21. Marvin S. Hill, "Joseph Smith and the 1826 Trial," pp. 223–44.

22. Mulder and Mortensen, *Among the Mormons*, p. 37.

23. Marvin S. Hill, "Secular or Sectarian History," pp. 85–86; see also Alan Taylor's excellent article, "Joseph Smith's Treasure Seeking."

24. Marvin S. Hill, "The 'Prophet Puzzle' Assembled," pp. 101–5.

25. Joseph Smith, *History of the Church*, 1:11.

26. Ibid.

27. Ibid., p. 12.

28. Ibid., p. 14.

29. Joseph Smith, *Joseph Smith's 1832 Account of His Life*, p. 11.

30. Lucy Mack Smith, *Biographical Sketches*, p. 85.

31. Ibid., p. 99. See also Marvin S. Hill, "The Role of Christian Primitivism," p. 47.

32. Joseph Smith, *Joseph Smith's Diary, 1832–34*, p. 26.

33. Lucy Mack Smith, *Biographical Sketches*, pp. 160–61.

34. Hansen, *Mormonism and the American Experience*, p. 16.

Chapter 2

1. Campbell, *Delusions*, p. 13.

2. Finding republicanism in the Book of Mormon is not new, as Campbell's state-ment, written in 1831, indicates. Indeed, a quarter of a century ago Thomas O'Dea, in one of the best interpretations of the Book of Mormon ever written, claimed, "Ameri-can sentiments permeate the work. In it are found the democratic, the republican, the anti-monarchical, and egalitarian doctrines that pervaded the climate of opinion in which it was conceived and that enter into the expressions and concerns of its Nephite kings, prophets, and priests as naturally as they later come from the mouths of Mor-mon leaders preaching to the people of Utah" (O'Dea, *The Mormons*, p. 32). In support of this contention, O'Dea listed the republican and egalitarian principles he found in a variety of passages, including expressions of antimonarchicalism, election of prophet-judges by the voice of the people, hatred of oppressive taxation and lawyers, a crude respect for human rights, and separation of church and state (pp. 32–35).

Recently, O'Dea's position has come under sharp attack from Richard Bushman. Bushman charges that the supposedly republican and antimonarchical sentiments that O'Dea discerned in the Book of Mormon are spurious, bearing only a superficial resemblance to the attitudes held by Americans in the 1820s. He first identifies what he considers the three most prominent beliefs held by Joseph Smith's contemporaries concerning the American Revolution: first, that the Revolution represented heroic resistance to tyranny; second, that revolutionary antimonarchicalism sprang from en-lightened ideas of human rights; and third, that the control of power necessitates special constitutional arrangements (Bushman, "The Book of Mormon," p. 6). Bush-man then compares these attitudes with those ascribed to the Nephites in the Book of Mormon under roughly similar circumstances. The result is a perfect picture of incon-gruity. "Instead of heroically resisting despots, the people of God fled their oppressors and credited God alone with deliverance. Instead of enlightened people overthrowing their kings in defense of their natural rights, the common people repeatedly raised up their kings, and the prophets and the kings themselves had to persuade the people of the inexpediency of monarchy. Despite [King] Mosiah's reforms, Nephite government persisted in monarchical practices, with life tenure for the chief judges, hereditary succession, and the combination of all functions in one official" (p. 18). Bushman consequently concludes that "the innermost structure of Book of Mormon politics and history are biblical, while American forms are conspicuously absent" (p. 20).

Professor Bushman has done a fine job of refuting the traditional view of non-Mormon critics like Campbell who had so casually detected "republican government and the rights of man" in the Book of Mormon. Still, the earlier critics were right. The innermost structure of the Book of Mormon is not biblical, at least in Bushman's sense, but republican; far more deeply republican, however, than earlier scholars had imag-ined. When Joseph Smith wrote the Book of Mormon, he consciously modeled it on the Bible. He would indeed have set down a crude religious history of pre-Columbian America if the book's essense had been merely a thinly disguised version of American political thought. One would expect the republican or American elements to creep in and appear more subtly. Often the various Americanisms in the Book of Mormon come out distorted because Smith merged them with biblical, theocratic values. By concen-trating on only one aspect of these values, Bushman is able to rule out any connection between Smith's political environment and that of the "ancient" Nephites. Moreover, while Bushman tests the Book of Mormon for republican values that Americans held toward the Revolution, a broader republicanism permeates the work. Joseph Smith, like most Americans, unself-consciously carried with him the cultural baggage of re-publican ideology. The republicanism of the Book of Mormon lies not so much in notions such as the "separation of powers," but in the republican social and moral code.

3. Joseph Smith, The Book of Mormon, p. 72.
4. Ibid., p. 560.
5. Ibid., p. 403.
6. Ibid., p. 203.
7. Ibid., p. 403.
8. Ibid., p. 405.
9. Ibid., p. 307.
10. Ibid., pp. 156–57.
11. Ibid., p. 168.
12. Ibid., p. 193.
13. Ibid.
14. Ibid., pp. 164–65.
15. As quoted in Lee, *Mormonism Unveiled*, p. 163.
16. Joseph Smith, The Book of Mormon, pp. 164–65.
17. Ibid., p. 219.
18. Ibid., p. 203.
19. Ibid.
20. Ibid., p. 218.
21. Ibid., pp. 218–19.
22. Ibid., p. 218.
23. Ibid., p. 219.
24. Ibid.
25. Ibid., p. 225.
26. Ibid., p. 407.
27. Ibid.
28. Ibid., p. 408.
29. Richard Bushman brushes away the more concrete evidence of popular elections in the Book of Mormon as not necessarily republican. There were times, he argues, when the acclamation of the king in European history was not merely ritualistic either. He cites as his examples the approval of William III by the English House of Commons in 1688; Marc Bloch's view that feudal kings were sometimes named from the predestinate family by leading personages and natural representatives of the realm; and a reference to the selection of Omri "by common consent" as the commander of the army of Israel (1 Kings 16:16 NEB). Yet the "elective" element, such as it was, in the examples of William III and Omri is notable because it is unique. By contrast, the Nephites show a fidelity to the elective process in their selection of chief judges and generals and in their judgments on political measures. Second, both the selection of the king in feudal society and Parliament's acceptance of William III lack the specific popular element explicitly present in the Nephite elections by the "voice of the people." Finally, examples from medieval and early modern Europe seem slender reeds to cite as analogies for a truly biblical people. See Bushman, "The Book of Mormon," p. 15.
30. Joseph Smith, The Book of Mormon, p. 367.
31. Ibid., p. 344.
32. Ibid., p. 358.
33. Ibid., p. 351.
34. While Bushman has conceded that this episode might appear to the "casual reader" to possess a "republican flavor," he insists that "the details of the story, beginning with the peculiar designation, 'the title of liberty,' are strangely archaic." Yet terms such as "liberty," "freedom," and "rights" are pervasive in the Book of Mormon and employed in a manner that would have puzzled a premodern people. A comparative examination of the Bible for similar usages, for instance, yields no politically meaningful result. See Bushman, "The Book of Mormon," p. 15.

35. Joseph Smith, The Book of Mormon, p. 397.

36. Ibid., pp. 399–401.

37. Morgan, *The Challenge of the American Revolution*, p. 92.

38. Joseph Smith, The Book of Mormon, p. 230.

39. Ibid., p. 321.

40. Ibid., p. 466.

41. Ibid., p. 251.

42. Ibid., p. 222.

43. Ibid., pp. 221–22.

44. Ibid., pp. 222–23.

45. Ibid., pp. 178–79.

46. Ibid., p. 424.

47. Ibid., p. 425.

48. Ibid., p. 423.

49. Ibid., p. 237.

50. Ibid., p. 180.

51. Ibid., p. 439.

52. Ibid., p. 73.

53. Ibid., p. 270.

54. Ibid., p. 175.

55. Ibid., p. 357.

56. Ibid., pp. 28–29.

57. Ibid., p. 29.

58. Ibid., p. 60.

59. Ibid., p. 29.

60. Ibid., p. 60.

61. Ibid., p. 81.

62. Ibid., pp. 84, 541, and passim.

63. Ibid., p. 554.

64. Ibid., p. 109.

65. Ibid., pp. 58–59, 108, 109, 113.

66. Ibid., p. 33.

67. Ibid., p. 497.

68. Ibid., p. 66.

69. Ibid., p. 67.

70. Ibid., p. 534.

71. Ibid., p. 501.

Chapter 3

1. Berthoff and Murrin, "Feudalism, Communalism, and the Yeoman Freeholder," pp. 256–88; Gross, *The Minutemen and Their World*; Berthoff, *An Unsettled People*, pp. 83–124.

2. The best general discussion of these economic changes and their social consequences is found in Berthoff, *An Unsettled People*, pp. 126–232.

3. Berthoff, "Independence and Attachment, Virtue and Interest," pp. 97–124.

4. Wood, "Evangelical America and Early Mormonism," pp. 367–75.

5. Berthoff, *An Unsettled People*, pp. 177–203.

6. The Mormon church changed its name from the Church of Christ to the Church of Latter-day Saints on May 4, 1834, and changed that name to the Church of Jesus Christ of Latter-day Saints on April 6, 1838.

7. Yorgason, "Social and Geographical Origins of Early Mormon Converts," p. 282.

8. Douglas, *The Feminization of American Culture*, pp. 25–26, 33.

9. My following treatment of the break between masters and their laborers is indebted to Paul E. Johnson, *A Shopkeeper's Millennium*.

10. Marvin S. Hill, "The Rise of Mormonism," pp. 426–27.

11. Pollack, "In Search of Security," p. 62; Yorgason, "Social and Geographical Origins of Early Mormon Converts," p. 282.

12. Marvin S. Hill, "The Rise of Mormonism," pp. 421–28.

13. Hatch, "The Christian Movement," pp. 545–67.

14. John Whitmer, *John Whitmer's History*, pp. 1–2.

15. Parley Parker Pratt, *A Voice of Warning*, p. 94.

16. A Book of Commandments, 1:3.

17. *Evening and Morning Star*, March 1833.

18. A Book of Commandments, 48:57.

19. Ibid., 4:5.

20. Orson Pratt, *The Prophetic Almanac*, p. 1.

21. Parley Parker Pratt, *A Voice of Warning*, p. 9.

22. Marvin S. Hill, "The Role of Christian Primitivism," pp. 8–12; Hatch, "The Christian Movement," pp. 545–67; Wood, "Evangelical America and Early Mormonism," pp. 378–81.

23. Marvin S. Hill, "Mormon Religion in Nauvoo," pp. 177–78.

24. As quoted in David Whitmer, *An Address to All Believers*, p. 31.

25. Joseph Smith, *History of the Church*, 1:312–16.

26. Kelley, "Ideology and Political Culture," pp. 536–37.

27. Arrington and Bitton, *The Mormon Experience*, pp. 41–43.

28. A Book of Commandments, 40:22.

29. Arrington and Bitton, *The Mormon Experience*, pp. 42–43.

30. Pollack, "In Search of Security," p. 276.

31. Fielding, "The Growth of the Mormon Church," pp. 153–56.

32. *Evening and Morning Star*, February 1833.

33. For an excellent discussion of the development of Mormon church organization, see Fielding, "The Growth of the Mormon Church," pp. 109–29.

34. "Lectures on Faith," in Doctrine and Covenants, Sec. 3:23.

35. Hansen, *Mormonism and the American Experience*, pp. 34–35.

36. Brodie, *No Man Knows My History*, p. 100.

37. Pollack, "In Search of Security," pp. 274–77.

38. O'Dea, *The Mormons*, p. 165.

39. Hansen, *Mormonism and the American Experience*, pp. 121–22.

40. Hunter, "Autobiography," p. 322.

41. Arrington, *Great Basin Kingdom*, p. 6.

42. Acts 2:44–45.

43. Marvin S. Hill, "The Shaping of the Mormon Mind," pp. 366–68.

44. Joseph Smith, The Book of Mormon, p. 574.

45. The crucial section of the revelation on the law of consecration and stewardship is found in the Book of Commandments, 44:26–29; for a discussion of the law and its subsequent modifications, see Arrington, "Early Mormon Communitarianism," pp. 341–69, and Cook, *Law of Consecration*.

46. Doctrine and Covenants, Sec. 75:1.

47. Joseph Smith, *History of the Church*, 1:364.

48. A Book of Commandments, 50:19–20.

49. Ibid., 48:2.

50. Doctrine and Covenants, Sec. 87:5.

51. Ibid., Sec. 6:37–38.

52. Arrington, *Great Basin Kingdom*, p. 5.

53. *Gospel Reflector*, January 1841.

54. Parley Parker Pratt, *A Voice of Warning*, p. 3.

55. Klaus Hansen, who usually writes perceptively about early Mormon history, views the Saints' attitude toward nature as an illustration of the "profound cultural differences between Mormons and Gentiles." To his mind, Jacksonians held a romantic view of nature, glorying in rough-hewn mountains and untamed wildernesses. (See Hansen, *Mormonism and the American Experience*, pp. 68–70.) This romanticism found its best expression in the celebrations of unspoiled nature by intellectuals and artists like Henry David Thoreau and Thomas Cole. Hansen argues that Mormonism, in striking contrast, was a quest for order and could not abide this untidiness of nature beloved by other Americans. But romantic intellectuals, like Thoreau, do not represent orthodoxy by which to measure dissent from the mainstream of society. They themselves were dissenters. The great body of Americans still retained their allegiance to the older republican values. (See Berthoff, "Peasants and Artisans, Puritans and Republicans," pp. 587–88.) These values balanced the dangers of raw nature against those of over-refined society. Just as they scorned the savagery of the Indians, Jacksonians rejected the overcivilization of Europe. Thomas Cole, in fact, is typical of this. As Hansen himself points out, Cole lauds in his great painting *The Course of Empire* neither the unimproved wilderness nor luxurious urban society, but the yeoman pastoralism suspended between the two extremes. (See Hansen, *Mormonism and the American Experience*, p. 69. Strangely, Hansen perceives Mormon fears of overcivilization as common to larger society, yet he fails to understand that their attitudes toward nature were equally common.) Romanticism may have better explained the dramatic changes of the Jacksonian era, but Americans embraced no more than its bastard cousin, sentimentality. (See Ann Douglas's discussion in *The Feminization of American Culture*.)

56. Parley Parker Pratt, *A Voice of Warning*, p. 40.

57. Isa. 40:4.

58. *Nauvoo Neighbor*, September 10, 1845.

59. Mulder, "Mormonism's Gathering," p. 253.

Chapter 4

1. This charge is ubiquitous in early Mormon writings. For an example of attacks on the anti-Mormon clergy in New York, see Joseph Smith, *History of the Church*, 1:86.

2. Ibid., p. 87.

3. "A. W. B." letter to the editors, *Evangelical Magazine and Gospel Advocate*, April 9, 1831, as quoted in Donna Hill, *Joseph Smith*, p. 113.

4. Spirited animosity between the Mormons and the Campbellites continued until the time of the Saints' departure from Ohio; see, for example, Sidney Rigdon's vitriolic attack on alleged Campbellite slanders in *Messenger and Advocate*, January 1837.

5. *Painesville Telegraph*, December 7, 1830.

6. On gentile reaction to Mormon self-righteousness, see Marvin S. Hill, "The Shaping of the Mormon Mind," p. 358, and Marvin S. Hill, "The Role of Christian Primitivism," pp. 117–20; see also Underwood, "'Saved or Damned.'"

7. In developing this version of anti-Mormonism, I have sometimes used evidence from those who did not live near Mormon settlements in New York or Ohio between 1830 and 1837, but who I feel closely fit the pattern of the anti-Mormonism of those who did live near the settlements. Nationwide political anti-Mormonism was insignificant until the Saints assembled in Nauvoo, Illinois, in the 1840s and even then did not fully evolve until the church had removed to Utah.

8. Howe, *Mormonism Unvailed*, p. 203.

9. Clark, *Gleanings by the Way*, p. 347.

10. Tucker, *Origin, Rise, and Progress of Mormonism*, p. 16.

11. Arrington, "James Gordon Bennett's 1831 Report on 'The Mormonites,'" pp. 357–58.

12. Howe, *Mormonism Unvailed*, pp. 232–67.

13. Tucker, *Origin, Rise, and Progress of Mormonism*, p. 75; Hunt, *Mormonism*, p. 95.

14. Turner, *Mormonism in All Ages*, pp. 220–21.

15. Arrington, "James Gordon Bennett's 1831 Report," pp. 361–62.

16. Howe, *Mormonism Unvailed*, pp. 287–90.

17. Turner, *Mormonism in All Ages*, p. 301.

18. Ibid., p. 163.

19. Clark, *Gleanings by the Way*, p. 346.

20. Brodie, *No Man Knows My History*, pp. 442–56.

21. Orr, *Mormonism Dissected*, p. 1.

22. Caswall, *The City of the Mormons*, p. 50.

23. Howe, *Mormonism Unvailed*, p. 260.

24. Ibid., p. 112.

25. Tucker, *Origin, Rise, and Progress of Mormonism*, p. 132.

26. Orr, *Mormonism Dissected*, p. 1.

27. Cyrus Smalling, as quoted in Lee, *The Mormons; or, Knavery Exposed*, p. 15.

28. Joseph Smith, *History of the Church*, 1:89–91.

29. Turner, *Mormonism in All Ages*, p. 228.

30. Tucker, *Origin, Rise, and Progress of Mormonism*, p. 136.

31. Donna Hill, *Joseph Smith*, p. 146.

32. Howe, *Mormonism Unvailed*, p. 125.

33. Ford, *A History of Illinois*, 2:215.

34. See, for example, Turner, *Mormonism in All Ages*, pp. 303–34.

35. "Statement of J.C. Dowen," 1885. Mormons and Mormonism. Papers, 1832–1954. Chicago Historical Society.

36. *Niles' Weekly Register*, July 16, 1831.

37. Turner, *Mormonism in All Ages*, p. 229; Howe, *Mormonism Unvailed*, p. 115.

38. Turner, *Mormonism in All Ages*, p. 36.

39. The best-known account of these activities was written by the Campbellite minister Mathew S. Clapp and appeared in the *Painesville Telegraph*, February 15, 1831.

40. Young, "Autobiography," p. 102.

41. Walker, *Elder William Holmes Walker*, p. 5.

42. Reprinted in the *Painesville Telegraph*, May 20, 1836.

43. Howe, *Mormonism Unvailed*, p. 126.

44. Ibid., p. 74.

45. Ibid., pp. 178–79.

46. *Messenger and Advocate*, January 1836.

47. Tyler, "Incidents of Experience," p. 24.

48. *New York Herald*, April 3, 1842; reprinted in *Times and Seasons*, May 2, 1842.

49. See Bunker and Bitton, "Mesmerism and Mormonism," pp. 146–70.

50. *Painesville Telegraph*, May 20, 1836.

51. Belnap, "Autobiography," p. 30.

52. Doctrine and Covenants, Sec. 6:5.

53. Brown, "Testimonies for the Truth," p. 61.

54. Howe, *Mormonism Unvailed*, p. 191.

55. *Messenger and Advocate*, March 1837.

56. Ibid.

57. Doctrine and Covenants, Sec. 6:4.

58. Ibid., Sec. 4:14.

59. *Messenger and Advocate*, December 1835.
60. Ibid., October 1836.
61. Ibid., January 1837.
62. Ibid., February 1837.
63. *Evening and Morning Star*, July 1834.
64. Doctrine and Covenants, Sec. 97:10.
65. *Evening and Morning Star*, July 1834.
66. Ibid.
67. Parley Parker Pratt, *Key to the Science of Theology*, p. 76.
68. For representative Mormon opinion, see Parley Parker Pratt, *The Autobiography of Parley P. Pratt*, pp. 80–81; *Evening and Morning Star*, July 1834; *Messenger and Advocate*, February 1837. For an overview of Protestant opinion, see Marty, *Righteous Empire*, pp. 46–56, and passim.
69. Joseph Smith, *History of the Church*, 6:289.
70. Howe, *Mormonism Unvailed*, p. 14. This evidence has persuaded Marvin Hill that the Saints' rejection of American society implied a political rejection as well as a religious one, and that the church intended to rule at least just prior to the advent of the millennium. (Marvin S. Hill, "The Shaping of the Mormon Mind," p. 369. See also his more extended treatment of this idea in "The Role of Christian Primitivism," pp. 69–74.) In the above quote from Sidney Rigdon, Hill added the sentence, "When God sets up a system of salvation, he sets up a system of government . . . that shall rule over temporal and spiritual affairs." This would strengthen Hill's case, but a closer reading of Rigdon's speech reveals that Rigdon was no longer talking of 1830, but had returned to matters at hand in Nauvoo in 1844. Rigdon's entire speech may be found in Joseph Smith, *History of the Church*, 6:288–92.
71. Hill correctly believes that the Saints lost faith in man's ability to govern himself, but this came only in the 1840s when the persistent battering of the church drove them to this unhappy conclusion. Marvin S. Hill, "The Role of Christian Primitivism," pp. 69–70.
72. In the "Mormon War" in Missouri in 1838, many Saints briefly envisioned winning political power by force of arms, but they understandably abandoned the idea after their defeat.
73. Joseph Smith, *History of the Church*, 1:450–51.
74. *Northern Times*, October 2, 1835.
75. *Painesville Telegraph*, April 17, 1835.
76. Ibid.
77. Ibid.
78. Howe, *Mormonism Unvailed*, p. 145.
79. Oaks and Hill, *Carthage Conspiracy*, pp. 6–7.
80. *Painesville Telegraph*, March 22, 1831.
81. Howe, *Mormonism Unvailed*, p. 201.
82. Ibid., p. 145.
83. *Painesville Telegraph*, April 17, 1835.
84. Ibid., January 27, 1837.
85. Ibid., August 16, 1833; Howe, *Mormonism Unvailed*, p. 144.
86. Fielding, "The Growth of the Mormon Church," pp. 79–80.

Chapter 5

1. A Book of Commandments, 48:59–64.
2. Ibid., 54:43.
3. Ibid., 30:9.

4. Doctrine and Covenants, Sec. 27:1.

5. For a longer discussion of these problems, see Fielding, "The Growth of the Mormon Church," pp. 48–55.

6. Joseph Smith, *History of the Church*, 1:189.

7. *Evening and Morning Star*, January 1834.

8. In Anderson, "Early Mormon Descriptions," p. 276.

9. Corrill, *A Brief History of the Church*, pp. 18–19.

10. Joseph Smith, *History of the Church*, 1:381–82.

11. Ibid., p. 396.

12. Lucas, "Jackson County," pp. 96, 94.

13. Joseph Smith, *History of the Church*, 1:375.

14. The specific charges against the clergy may be found in ibid., pp. 372–73, 392.

15. Ibid., p. 398.

16. A Book of Commandments, 44:32.

17. Ibid., 64:30–32.

18. Joseph Smith, *History of the Church*, 1:382.

19. Ibid., p. 396.

20. Howe, *Mormonism Unvailed*, p. 197.

21. As quoted in Jennings, "Isaac McCoy," pp. 73–74.

22. Joseph Smith, The Book of Mormon, p. 497.

23. Joseph Smith, *History of the Church*, 1:419.

24. Ibid., p. 347.

25. *Evening and Morning Star*, July 1833.

26. Joseph Smith, *History of the Church*, 1:379.

27. Ibid., p. 397.

28. Howe, *Mormonism Unvailed*, p. 195.

29. Jennings, "Isaac McCoy," p. 73.

30. Joseph Smith, *History of the Church*, 1:397.

31. Ibid.

32. As quoted in Jennings, "Destruction of the Mormon Press," pp. 69–70.

33. Joseph Smith, *History of the Church*, 1:396.

34. Ibid., p. 374.

35. Ibid., p. 396.

36. Gregg, *Commerce of the Prairies*, p. 95.

37. Joseph Smith, *History of the Church*, 1:395, 398.

38. Ibid., p. 398.

39. Ibid., p. 399.

40. Doctrine and Covenants, Sec. 85.

41. Joseph Smith, *History of the Church*, 1:415.

42. Ibid., pp. 423–24.

43. *Messenger and Advocate*, August 1836.

44. *Evening and Morning Star*, June 1834.

45. Ibid., August 1834.

46. Ibid., January 1834.

47. Ibid., December 1834.

48. Ibid., June 1834; *Messenger and Advocate*, August 1836.

49. *Evening and Morning Star*, June 1834.

50. Ibid., February 1834.

51. Ibid., August 1834.

52. Doctrine and Covenants, Sec. 47:12.

53. For a treatment of the motives behind Zion's Camp, see Crawley and Anderson, "Zion's Camp," pp. 406–20.

54. *Niles' Weekly Register*, July 26, 1834.

55. Joseph Smith, *History of the Church*, 2:121.
56. Ibid., pp. 97–98.
57. Ibid., p. 145.
58. Stokes, "The Wilson Letters," pp. 504–5.
59. Ibid., p. 508.
60. Ibid., p. 506.
61. Joseph Smith, *History of the Church*, 2:449–52.
62. Ibid., pp. 452–54.
63. Ibid., p. 462.

Chapter 6

1. Peck, *The Reed Peck Manuscript*, p. 9.
2. William Smith, *William Smith on Mormonism*, p. 24.
3. John Whitmer, *John Whitmer's History*, p. 17.
4. Howe, *Mormonism Unvailed*, p. 163.
5. Joseph Smith, *History of the Church*, 2:144.
6. Marvin S. Hill, "Cultural Crisis," pp. 287–88.
7. Brown, "Testimonies for the Truth," p. 65.
8. Joseph Young to Phineas Richards, October 26, 1836, Richards Family Correspondence, Sources of Mormon History in Illinois, Microfilm Collection, Southern Illinois University–Edwardsville; original at the Huntington Library.
9. Jesse, "Diary of Wilford Woodruff," p. 381.
10. Ibid., p. 391.
11. Benjamin F. Johnson, *My Life's Review*, pp. 27–28.
12. For economic conditions in Kirtland, see Hill, Rooker, and Winmer, "The Kirtland Economy Revisited," pp. 391–475; for specific discussion of the Kirtland Safety Society Anti-Banking Company, see pp. 431–59.
13. Marvin S. Hill, "Cultural Crisis," pp. 286–87.
14. Ibid., p. 296.
15. Corrill, *A Brief History of the Church*, p. 27. The Saints who remained faithful to Joseph Smith argued with the dissenters that the church had indeed trafficked too much in the things of the world, but because of the deep involvement of the prophet in these events, they were loath to dwell on the issue.
16. Jesse, "Diary of Wilford Woodruff," p. 382.
17. Ibid., p. 383.
18. For a more extended discussion of the growing centralization of the church, see O'Dea, *The Mormons*, pp. 160–62. In January 1832, Joseph Smith dropped his title of first elder of ordination as president of the High Priesthood. (The priesthood already had its graded offices.) In March 1833, the First Presidency of the church was established with Smith as president and Sidney Rigdon and Fredrick G. Williams (also called presidents) as his counselors. In December 1833, the prophet made his father, Joseph Smith, Sr., the first patriarch of the church. In February 1834, the church created the standing High Council of Kirtland to handle judiciary affairs, but it took on the running of the routine governmental affairs of the state. In February 1835, the Quorum of the Twelve Apostles and the First Quorum of the Seventy appeared. By 1835, the church government was fully developed.
19. Oliver Cowdery, *Rehearsal of My Grounds*, p. 4.
20. David Whitmer, *An Address to All Believers*, all quotes pp. 33–34.
21. Ibid., p. 59.
22. Ibid., p. 59, p. 35.
23. Ibid., p. 61.

24. Ibid., p. 62.
25. A Book of Commandments, pp. 28–41.
26. Pollack, "In Search of Security," pp. 346–47.
27. Joseph Smith, *History of the Church*, 2:509–10.
28. *Painesville Telegraph*, February 15, 1838.
29. *Messenger and Advocate*, July 1837.
30. Benjamin F. Johnson, *My Life's Review*, p. 28.
31. A Book of Commandments, 40:22.
32. See, for example, Sidney Rigdon's scurrilous and adolescent attacks on the Kirtland dissenters in the *Elders' Journal*, August 1838; and Joseph Smith's accusation that Saints who refused Kirtland bank money were "traitors" and "covenant breakers" who undermined the kingdom "for which they [would] feel the wrath of God" in Jesse, "Diary of Wilford Woodruff," p. 394.
33. Lucy Mack Smith, *Biographical Sketches*, pp. 211–13. The quote is on pp. 212–13. See also Fielding, "The Growth of the Mormon Church," pp. 248–50.
34. Fielding, "The Growth of the Mormon Church," pp. 255–57.
35. Ibid., pp. 258–63.
36. As quoted in Gentry, "History of the Latter-day Saints," pp. 129, 127–28.
37. Ibid., p. 129.
38. Ibid., p. 128.
39. Ibid., p. 127.
40. Joseph Smith, *History of the Church*, 3:17–18.
41. Ibid., p. 11.
42. Corrill, *A Brief History of the Church*, p. 31.
43. Peck, *The Reed Peck Manuscript*, p. 10.
44. Corrill, *A Brief History of the Church*, p. 32.
45. Peck, *The Reed Peck Manuscript*, p. 8.
46. John Whitmer, *John Whitmer's History*, pp. 21–22; see also Corrill, *A Brief History of the Church*, p. 31.
47. Peck, *The Reed Peck Manuscript*, pp. 6–7.
48. John Whitmer, *John Whitmer's History*, p. 22.
49. Corrill, *A Brief History of the Church*, pp. 24–25.
50. Peck, *The Reed Peck Manuscript*, p. 8.
51. Ibid., pp. 7–8.
52. Ibid., p. 8.
53. Corrill, *A Brief History of the Church*, p. 30.
54. Peck, *The Reed Peck Manuscript*, pp. 8–9.
55. Ibid., p. 12.
56. Corrill, *A Brief History of the Church*, p. 32.
57. Peck, *The Reed Peck Manuscript*, p. 13.
58. Joseph Smith, *History of the Church*, 3:66.

Chapter 7

1. *Elders' Journal*, May 1838.
2. Corrill, *A Brief History of the Church*, p. 31.
3. Peck, *The Reed Peck Manuscript*, p. 10.
4. Ibid., p. 11.
5. Joseph Smith, *History of the Church*, 3:180–81.
6. Schindler, *Orrin Porter Rockwell*, p. 42.
7. Joseph Smith, *History of the Church*, 3:41.
8. Crawley, "Two Rare Missouri Documents," p. 527.

9. Swartznell, *Mormonism Exposed*, p. 13.

10. Ibid., p. 17. Swartznell subsequently became a rabid anti-Mormon and is a somewhat unreliable source. His statements, nevertheless, accurately reflect Wight's temperament and are supported by other sources. See, for example, Corrill, *A Brief History of the Church*, p. 28.

11. Corrill, *A Brief History of the Church*, p. 29.

12. Parley Parker Pratt, *History of the Late Persecution*, p. 27.

13. *The Return*, October 1889.

14. Ibid., November 1889.

15. Joseph Smith, *History of the Church*, 3:56–57.

16. Ibid., p. 56; Lee, *Mormonism Unveiled*, pp. 56–58.

17. Lee, *Mormonism Unveiled*, p. 60.

18. Joseph Smith, *History of the Church*, 3:59–60.

19. Ibid., p. 61.

20. Ibid., p. 64.

21. Swartznell, *Mormonism Exposed*, p. 32; see also Marvin S. Hill, "The Role of Christian Primitivism," p. 208.

22. Peck, *The Reed Peck Manuscript*, p. 15.

23. Lucy Mack Smith, *Biographical Sketches*, p. 222.

24. Lee, *Mormonism Unveiled*, p. 66.

25. Parley Parker Pratt, *The Autobiography of Parley P. Pratt*, pp. 174–75.

26. Corrill, *A Brief History of the Church*, p. 28.

27. Pocock, *The Machiavellian Moment*.

28. Lee, *Mormonism Unveiled*, p. 67.

29. As quoted in Mulder and Mortensen, *Among the Mormons*, p. 98.

30. Missouri General Assembly, *Document Containing the Correspondence*, p. 34.

31. Ibid., p. 40.

32. Joseph Smith, *History of the Church*, 3:157.

33. Albert Rockwood to his sister, October 7, 1838. Rockwood's "letters" were not conventional letters, but a running journal that he eventually intended to send to his family. Thus, the actual date of his writing is best determined by his commentary on passing events rather than by the date supplied on the letter's head. Albert Rockwood Letters in Sources of Mormon History in Illinois, Microfilm Collection, Southern Illinois University–Edwardsville.

34. Ibid.

35. I have reconstructed this speech from accounts given in Peck, *The Reed Peck Manuscript*, pp. 18–20, and in Thomas Marsh's affidavit and the testimony of Sampson Avard, Maurice [Morris?] Phelps, John Corrill, Reed Peck, and George Hinkle in Missouri General Assembly, *Document Containing the Correspondence*, pp. 57–58, 98–99, 110, 111, 119–20, 128, and passim.

36. Peck, *The Reed Peck Manuscript*, p. 19. Punctuation added.

37. Thomas Marsh in Missouri General Assembly, *Document Containing the Correspondence*, p. 58.

38. See Dan. 2:44–45.

39. Sampson Avard and Reed Peck in Missouri General Assembly, *Document Containing the Correspondence*, pp. 99, 129.

40. Lee, *Mormonism Unveiled*, p. 71.

41. Benjamin F. Johnson, *My Life's Review*, pp. 42–43.

42. Stout, "Autobiography of Hosea Stout," pp. 336–37.

43. Joseph Smith, *History of the Church*, 3:168, 172.

44. Missouri General Assembly, *Document Containing the Correspondence*, p. 61.

45. Albert Rockwood to his father, October 29, 1838.

46. Corrill, *A Brief History of the Church*, p. 41; Peck, *The Reed Peck Manuscript*, p. 24.

47. Joseph Smith, *History of the Church*, 3:203–4.
48. Missouri General Assembly, *Document Containing the Correspondence*, p. 92.
49. Parley Parker Pratt, *History of the Late Persecution*, p. 53.
50. See, for example, Parley Parker Pratt, *Appeal to the Inhabitants*, pp. 1–2; and Packard, *Memorial*, p. 9.
51. *The Wasp*, April 30, 1842; see also Joseph Smith, *History of the Church*, 4:25.
52. Packard, *Memorial*, p. 4.
53. Rigdon, *An Appeal to the American People*, p. 14; Packard, *Memorial*, p. 4.
54. Packard, *Memorial*, p. 4.
55. Rigdon, *An Appeal to the American People*, pp. 15, 18.
56. Joseph Smith, *History of the Church*, 4:85–86.
57. Parley Parker Pratt, *The Autobiography of Parley P. Pratt*, p. 181; for similar comments on the militia by Joseph Smith, see his *History of the Church*, 3:229–30.
58. Parley Parker Pratt, *History of the Late Persecution*, p. 50.
59. Ibid., p. 26.
60. Ibid.
61. Joseph Smith, *History of the Church*, 3:310–11.
62. Ibid., pp. 320, 332.
63. Ibid., p. 332.
64. *The Wasp*, April 23, 1842.
65. Owen, *Memorial of Ephraim Owen, Jr.*, p. 5.
66. Parley Parker Pratt, *An Appeal to the Inhabitants*, p. 2.
67. Parley Parker Pratt, *History of the Late Persecution*, p. 69.
68. Packard, *Memorial*, p. 10.
69. Joseph Smith, *History of the Church*, 3:332.
70. Parley Parker Pratt, *An Appeal to the Inhabitants*, pp. 5–6.
71. Joseph Smith, *History of the Church*, 3:320–21.

Chapter 8

1. As quoted in Greene, *Facts Relative to the Expulsion*, pp. 5–6; see also Parley Parker Pratt, *The Autobiography of Parley P. Pratt*, pp. 286–90.
2. As quoted in Greene, *Facts Relative to the Expulsion*, p. 9.
3. Joseph Smith, *History of the Church*, 3:301.
4. Ibid.
5. Ibid., pp. 360–61.
6. Gentry, "History of the Latter-day Saints," p. 636.
7. Marvin S. Hill, "The Role of Christian Primitivism," p. 247.
8. See, for example, Joseph Smith, *History of the Church*, 4:212, 338; and *Times and Seasons*, September 15, 1841.
9. Joseph Smith, *History of the Church*, 3:304.
10. Ibid., 4:74; Flanders, *Nauvoo*, pp. 128, 283.
11. Smith had interviews with Van Buren on December 29, 1839, and February 6, 1840; Joseph Smith, *History of the Church*, 4:40, 80.
12. Ibid., p. 80.
13. *Quincy Whig*, October 17, 1840.
14. Joseph Smith, *History of the Church*, 4:91.
15. Ibid., p. 107.
16. Ibid., p. 108.
17. *Times and Seasons*, March 15, 1841.
18. Joseph Smith, *History of the Church*, 4:89.
19. Ibid., p. 145.

20. *Times and Seasons*, September 1840.

21. Joseph Smith, *History of the Church*, 4:269, 268.

22. For a more extended discussion of the charter's passage and its provisions, see Flanders, *Nauvoo*, pp. 96–101.

23. Ford, *History of Illinois*, 2:67–68.

24. Flanders, *Nauvoo*, p. 104.

25. Ibid., pp. 12–22; Brodie, *No Man Knows My History*, pp. 258–59.

26. For a general treatment of the origins of Mormon and anti-Mormon politics, see Flanders, *Nauvoo*, pp. 211–22.

27. *Warsaw Signal*, July 7, 1841.

28. Ibid., May 19, 1841.

29. Ibid., July 28, 1841.

30. Ibid., June 9, 1841.

31. Brodie, *No Man Knows My History*, p. 270.

32. *Warsaw Signal*, June 9, 1841.

33. Ibid., July 7, 1841.

34. John Nevis letter, May 2, 1841. Sources of Mormon History in Illinois, Microfilm Collection, Southern Illinois University–Edwardsville.

35. *Warsaw Signal*, July 7, 1841.

36. Ibid., September 15, 1841. In actuality, Smith was an invited guest to watch, not review, the parade, and he attended in civilian dress. *Times and Seasons*, October 1, 1841.

37. *Warsaw Signal*, July 7, 1841.

38. Ibid., June 9, 1841.

39. Ibid., July 7, 1841.

40. Joseph Smith, *History of the Church*, 4:480.

41. Johannsen, *Stephen A. Douglas*, pp. 105–8.

42. *Quincy Whig*, January 22, 1842; see also the *Sangamo Journal*, January 21, 1842.

43. Ford, *History of Illinois*, 2:73.

44. Reprinted in *Times and Seasons*, June 1, 1842. Duncan's interpretation of the ordinance was rather freewheeling. The ordinance provided for the fining and/or imprisonment of any person found guilty of disrupting a religious meeting or ridiculing or abusing the faith of another individual. Designed as a defensive measure, it explicitly offered protection to all denominations. Duncan, however, would not be the last gentile to see the ordinance as a symbol of Mormon tyranny. The ordinance is reprinted in Joseph Smith, *History of the Church*, 4:306.

45. Joseph Smith, *History of the Church*, 4:306.

46. Ibid., 5:4–5.

47. For an excellent discussion of the origins of polygamy among the Mormons, see Foster, *Religion and Sexuality*, pp. 123–80.

48. Joseph Smith, *History of the Church*, 5:20.

49. Ibid., pp. 11, 13.

50. Bennett, *The History of the Saints*, pp. 6–7.

51. Ibid., p. 278.

52. Ibid., p. 218. Shorn of its racy flamboyance, Bennett's description of early polygamy has been shown by modern historians to be surprisingly accurate. See Foster, *Religion and Sexuality*, pp. 170–74.

53. Bennett, *The History of the Saints*, p. 217.

54. Ibid., pp. 148–49.

55. Ibid., p. 281.

56. Ibid., pp. 5–6.

57. Ibid., p. 293.

58. Ibid., p. 302.

59. Ibid., pp. 191–92.

60. Ibid., p. 149.

61. Ibid., p. 307.

62. For a discussion of James Gordon Bennett's peculiar relationship with the Mormons, see Brodie, *No Man Knows My History*, pp. 270, 284, 309, and passim, and *Niles' National Register*, August 16, 1842; the article by "An Officer of the U. S. Artillery" may be found in Bennett, *The History of the Saints*, pp. 155–57.

63. Flanders, *Nauvoo*, p. 230.

64. *Warsaw Signal*, August 6, 1842.

65. *Times and Seasons*, September 1, 1841.

66. *Nauvoo Wasp*, July 16, 1842.

67. Ibid., May 7, 1842.

68. Joseph Smith, *History of the Church*, 5:55–56.

69. *Times and Seasons*, August 2, 1841.

70. Ibid., December 15, 1842; Joseph Smith, *History of the Church*, 5:34.

71. Joseph Smith, *History of the Church*, 5:32–34.

72. *Times and Seasons*, December 15, 1842.

73. Ibid., May 5, 1841, January 1, 1842, June 1, 1842, December 15, 1842; *Nauvoo Wasp*, January 14, 1843; *Nauvoo Neighbor*, May 10, 1843.

74. *Times and Seasons*, December 15, 1842.

75. Joseph Smith, *History of the Church*, 5:87–88.

76. Ibid., p. 154; for the complete exchange of letters, see pp. 115–17, 130–31, 132–34, 153–55.

77. *Warsaw Signal*, August 13, 1842.

78. *Nauvoo Wasp*, August 27, 1842.

79. Joseph Smith, *History of the Church*, 5:93.

80. Ibid., p. 232.

81. *Nauvoo Wasp*, January 28, 1843.

82. Joseph Smith, *History of the Church*, 5:287.

83. Fielding, "The Nauvoo Journal of Joseph Fielding," p. 144.

84. Joseph Smith, *History of the Church*, 5:466–68.

85. Ford, *History of Illinois*, 2:150–52.

86. Reprinted in Joseph Smith, *History of the Church*, 5:513–15.

87. *Nauvoo Neighbor*, August 2, 1843.

88. Joseph Smith, *History of the Church*, 5:526.

89. Pease, *Illinois Election Returns*, p. 140.

90. Ford, *History of Illinois*, 2:153–55.

91. Ibid., p. 153.

92. Flanders, "The Kingdom of God in Illinois," pp. 32–33. Flanders properly underscores the role Mormon inconsistency played in generating hostility toward the church, but he goes too far, in my opinion, in downplaying the Saints' clannishness as the basic source of anti-Mormon feeling.

93. Hampshire, "Thomas Sharp and Anti-Mormon Sentiment," pp. 89–90.

94. *Warsaw Message*, September 13, 1843.

95. Ibid.

96. *Nauvoo Neighbor*, "Extra," December 9, 1843.

97. Joseph Smith, *History of the Church*, 6:110–11.

98. *Nauvoo Neighbor*, December 27, 1843.

99. Ford, *History of Illinois*, 2:155–56.

100. Joseph Smith, *History of the Church*, 6:130–31.

Chapter 9

1. Among those historians emphasizing the Saints' imperial ambitions are Hansen, in *Mormonism and the American Experience*, esp. Chaps. 2–3, and *Quest for Empire*, and Flanders, "To Transform History," pp. 108–17, and his *Nauvoo*. The most prominent historian to argue that the Mormons' posture was essentially defensive is Marvin S. Hill, "Quest for Refuge," pp. 3–20; see also his "Mormon Religion in Nauvoo," pp. 170–80.

2. A favorite Mormon text. For examples, see *Times and Seasons*, December 1839 and September 1, 1841.

3. Partridge, "'The Death of a Mormon Dictator,'" p. 591.

4. Fielding, "The Nauvoo Journal of Joseph Fielding," pp. 143, 148.

5. Ibid., p. 144.

6. *Times and Seasons*, September 1, 1841.

7. Ibid., October 15, 1842.

8. *Nauvoo Wasp*, November 5, 1842.

9. *Times and Seasons*, June 1, 1841.

10. Joseph Smith, *History of the Church*, 6:56–57.

11. Ibid., 5:61–65.

12. Parley Parker Pratt, *The Autobiography of Parley P. Pratt*, p. 330.

13. Parley Parker Pratt, *The Angel of the Prairies*, pp. 6–7.

14. Ibid., p. 10.

15. Ibid., pp. 10–11.

16. Ibid., p. 11.

17. Ibid., p. 14.

18. Ibid.

19. Ibid., p. 15.

20. Ibid., p. 16.

21. Ibid.

22. Ibid., pp. 16–17.

23. Ibid., p. 17.

24. Ibid., pp. 18–19.

25. Ibid., pp. 19–20.

26. Ibid., p. 20.

27. Ibid., p. 21.

28. Ibid., pp. 23–24.

29. Joseph Smith, *History of the Church*, 6:293–95.

30. Ibid., p. 306.

31. Ibid., p. 365.

32. Ehat, "'Heaven Began on Earth,'" pp. 254–57.

33. Flanders, *Nauvoo*, p. 288.

34. Hansen, *Quest for Empire*, pp. 59–60.

35. Joseph Smith, *History of the Church*, 6:222.

36. Ibid., pp. 255–60.

37. Miller, *Correspondence*, p. 20.

38. Joseph Smith, *History of the Church*, 6:260.

39. As quoted in Ehat, "'Heaven Began on Earth,'" p. 254.

40. Lee, *A Mormon Chronicle*, 1:80.

41. Council member Bishop William Marks later wrote, "I was also a witness of the introduction of a kingly form of government, to which Joseph suffered himself to be ordained a king; to reign over the house of Israel forever." Letter June 15, 1853; reprinted in *The Return*, November 1890.

42. Regrettably, transcripts of the teaching are still unavailable to scholars. Quinn, "Council of Fifty," pp. 163–64, 192.

43. Lee, *Mormonism Unveiled*, p. 173.

44. As quoted in Ehat, "'Heaven Began on Earth,'" p. 259.

45. Ibid., pp. 261, 264.

46. Ibid., pp. 258, 266.

47. *Times and Seasons*, October 1, 1843.

48. Joseph Smith, *The Voice of Truth*, p. 21.

49. Joseph Smith wrote letters to John C. Calhoun, Henry Clay, Martin Van Buren, Lewis Cass, and Richard Johnson. His letters to Calhoun and Clay are reprinted in *The Voice of Truth*, pp. 21–26, 51–59.

50. *Nauvoo Neighbor*, February 15, 1844.

51. Brodie, *No Man Knows My History*, p. 362.

52. Hansen, *Mormonism and the American Experience*, p. 140.

53. *Nauvoo Neighbor*, February 14, 1844.

54. Joseph Smith, *History of the Church*, 6:188.

55. Ibid., p. 243.

56. Ibid., p. 516. The Mormons' decision to run electors in each of the states and in Wisconsin Territory is further evidence of the seriousness with which they took Joseph Smith's candidacy. Ibid., p. 340.

57. *The Prophet*, June 8, 1844.

58. Joseph Smith, *The Voice of Truth*, pp. 27–34; *Nauvoo Neighbor*, April 17, 1844, May 15, 1844, June 12, 1844; *The Prophet*, June 15, 1844.

59. Joseph Smith, *The Voice of Truth*, p. 33.

60. *Nauvoo Neighbor*, June 12, 1844.

61. Ibid.

62. Joseph Smith, *The Voice of Truth*, pp. 28–32.

63. Ibid., p. 32.

64. *The Prophet*, June 8, 1844.

65. Joseph Smith, *The Voice of Truth*, pp. 32–33.

66. Ibid., p. 28.

67. *Nauvoo Neighbor*, June 12, 1844.

68. *The Prophet*, June 8, 1844.

69. Ibid., June 15, 1844.

70. Ibid.

71. *Nauvoo Neighbor*, May 15, 1844.

72. *The Prophet*, June 8, 1844.

73. Ibid., June 15, 1844.

74. *Nauvoo Neighbor*, June 15, 1844.

75. Ibid., May 15, 1844.

76. Ibid.; see also the issues for May 1 and June 12, 1844.

77. Ibid., June 26, 1844.

78. *The Prophet*, June 8, 1844.

79. Joseph Smith, *The Voice of Truth*, p. 50.

80. *Times and Seasons*, March 15, 1844.

81. *Nauvoo Neighbor*, June 26, 1844.

82. Joseph Smith, *The Voice of Truth*, pp. 34–36.

83. Hansen, *Quest for Empire*, pp. 78–79; Flanders, *Nauvoo*, pp. 302–3; Donna Hill, *Joseph Smith*, pp. 377–78.

84. *Nauvoo Neighbor*, April 24, 1844.

85. Miller, *Correspondence*, p. 21.

86. Joseph Smith, *History of the Church*, 6:404. In another effort to broaden their base, the Mormons attempted to find a gentile to run as their vice presidential candi-

date. The Saints' first choice fell upon New York publisher James Arlington Bennett. Bennett, however, was born in Ireland, and therefore ineligible. Sidney Rigdon was subsequently added to the ticket. Ibid., 6:231–32, 244–45.

87. *Nauvoo Neighbor*, April 3, 1844.

88. Joseph Smith, *History of the Church*, 6:232.

89. Ibid., pp. 325–26.

90. Ingals, "Autobiography of Dr. Ephraim Ingals," p. 295.

91. Ford, *History of Illinois*, 2:156–57.

92. Cartwright, *The Autobiography of Peter Cartwright*, p. 228.

93. Roberts, ed. *History of the Church*, 7:116; for similar comments, see Joseph Smith, *History of the Church*, 6:605–6; *Times and Seasons*, August 15, 1844.

Chapter 10

1. Hampshire, "Thomas Sharp and Anti-Mormon Sentiment," p. 90.

2. *Warsaw Signal*, February 14, 1844.

3. Joseph Smith, *History of the Church*, 6:152.

4. Robert Flanders presents a detailed discussion of economic affairs in *Nauvoo*, pp. 120–79.

5. Joseph Smith, *History of the Church*, 5:285–86.

6. Lawrence Foster provides an intriguing account of the religious justification for this practice in *Religion and Sexuality*, pp. 159–66.

7. Joseph Smith, *History of the Church*, 6:225, 236–40, 272, 278–80.

8. *The Nauvoo Expositor*, June 7, 1844.

9. Ibid.

10. Ibid.

11. Ibid.

12. Joseph Smith, *History of the Church*, 6:443.

13. Ibid.

14. Ibid., pp. 441–42.

15. Ibid., p. 447. Curiously, William Phelps had edited the Mormon newspaper *Evening and Morning Star* when it was destroyed by a Missouri mob eleven years before.

16. *Warsaw Signal*, April 25, 1844.

17. Ibid., May 29, 1844.

18. Roberts, ed., *History of the Church*, 7:67.

19. *Warsaw Signal*, June 12, 1844.

20. *Warsaw Signal*, "Extra," June 14, 1844.

21. Ibid.

22. Joseph Smith, *History of the Church*, 6:499.

23. Ibid., p. 518.

24. George Rockwell letter to [?], June 22, 1844. Newberry Library, Chicago, Ill.

25. A ubiquitous claim. For example, see *Times and Seasons*, July 1, 15, 1844.

26. *The Niles National Register*, July 13, 1844.

27. Ellsworth, "Mobocracy and the Rule of Law," pp. 71–82.

28. *Warsaw Signal*, August 28, 1844; see also the issue for December 18, 1844.

29. Ibid., September 18, 1844.

30. Ibid., July 10, 1844.

31. Ibid.

32. Ibid., July 31, 1844.

33. Ibid., August 7, 1844.

34. Ibid., July 10, 1844.

35. Ibid., September 18, 1844.

36. Davis, *An Authentic Account*, p. 18.
37. Ibid., p. 29.
38. Ibid., p. 38.
39. Ibid., p. 47.
40. Reprinted in *Warsaw Signal*, August 28, 1844.
41. Reprinted in ibid., May 14, 1844.
42. Davis, *An Authentic Account*, p. 41.
43. Ford, *History of Illinois*, 2:217.
44. *Warsaw Signal*, May 21, 1845; Ford, *History of Illinois*, 2:219–20.
45. Tucker, *Origin, Rise, and Progress of Mormonism*, pp. 198–99.
46. *Warsaw Signal*, May 21, 1845.
47. Ibid., April 9, 1845.
48. Ford, *History of Illinois*, 2:174.
49. *Warsaw Signal*, August 21, 1844.
50. Ibid., July 24, 1844.
51. Oaks and Hill, *Carthage Conspiracy*, pp. 33–34.
52. Ibid., pp. 35–36.
53. Ford, *History of Illinois*, 2:233–34.
54. Greater biographical information on the conspirators and their motivation is found in Oaks and Hill, *Carthage Conspiracy*, pp. 53–59. An excellent account of their trial follows in Chaps. 5–10.
55. *Warsaw Signal*, December 19, 1844.
56. Hay, "The Mormon Prophet's Tragedy," p. 678.
57. Quinn, "The Mormon Succession Crisis of 1844," pp. 187–233.
58. Esplin, "Joseph, Brigham and the Twelve," pp. 301–44. The power struggle that followed the prophet's death continued until the Saints left Nauvoo: different groups cast off Young's leadership at different times. Although the Twelve Apostles firmly controlled Nauvoo, they still had to fight, often on terms of greater equality, for the loyalty of the thousands of ungathered Mormons in the East. At first, it seemed that Sidney Rigdon offered the most potent threat to Young's regime, but his following remained small and he soon drifted into obscurity. Lyman Wight, George Adams, and other dissenters met the same fate. A bit more successful were the followers of James J. Strang. A recent convert, the charismatic Strang established a viable Mormon splinter community on Beaver Island, Michigan, which was even more unorthodox than the church it had left. A more permanent establishment developed from the large inchoate number of moderate Saints who remained in the Midwest. In the early 1850s, these former church members gradually coalesced around the prophet's son, Joseph Smith III, to found the Reorganized Church of Jesus Christ of the Latter Day Saints.
59. *Laws of the State of Illinois*, pp. 139–40.
60. Stout, *On the Frontier*, 1:18.
61. Flanders, *Nauvoo*, pp. 324–26; see also Moody, "Nauvoo's Whistling and Whittling Brigade," pp. 480–90.
62. Ford, *History of Illinois*, 2:224.
63. *Nauvoo Neighbor*, July 23, 1845; see also the issue for October 23, 1844.
64. Ibid., July 9, 1845; the *Nauvoo Neighbor* responded to attacks upon the Saints for not observing Independence Day in the July 23, 1845 issue.
65. Ibid., August 6, 1844.
66. Ibid., December 18, 1844.
67. *Times and Seasons*, January 15,1845.
68. *Nauvoo Neighbor*, September 11, 1844; see also the issue for December 11, 1844.
69. Ibid., November 6, 1844.
70. *The Prophet*, February 15, 1845.
71. *Nauvoo Neighbor*, November 6, 1844.

72. *The Prophet*, February 15, 1845.

73. *Nauvoo Neighbor*, December 11, 1844.

74. Ibid., April 30, 1845.

75. *Times and Seasons*, August 1, 1845.

76. Roberts, ed., *History of the Church*, 7:404.

77. Quoted in Durham, "A Political Interpretation of Mormon History," p. 141.

78. See the remarks of Apostles Orson Hyde and Amasa Lyman in *Times and Seasons*, August 15, 1845.

79. *Nauvoo Neighbor*, September 10, 17, 1845.

80. Roberts, ed., *History of the Church*, 7:479.

81. Snow, Journal, 3:58.

82. Roberts, ed., *History of the Church*, 7:515.

83. Stout, *On the Frontier*, pp. 73–74.

84. *Times and Seasons*, November 1, 1845.

85. O'Dea, *The Mormons*, p. 115.

86. The most famous of these morale-building efforts is William Clayton's "Come, Come ye Saints"; see also Martha Haven's poem in Partridge, "'The Death of a Mormon Dictator,'" p. 610, and Pratt's poem in *The Autobiography of Parley P. Pratt*, pp. 348–53.

87. Roberts, ed., *History of the Church*, 7:463.

88. Originally, a number of Mormons attempted to remain behind: those who detested Brigham Young, who had no taste for western emigration, or who were too sick, aged, or otherwise infirm to make the trek west. By May the state militia forces charged with keeping the peace had become so infected with anti-Mormonism that they began to expel many of those who stayed behind. Worse was to follow. After the exodus had begun, "the better sort" abandoned the anti-Mormon struggle to men of more base instincts. On September 11, between seven and eight hundred men led by a ruffian named Thomas Brockman laid siege to Nauvoo. The following day they accepted the city's surrender and immediately began driving out the remaining church members and a good number of the "new citizens" who had purchased Mormon homes.

89. Roberts, ed., *History of the Church*, 7:603.

Bibliography

Primary Sources

Newspapers

Elders' Journal
The Evening and Morning Star
The Gospel Reflector
The Hancock Eagle
Latter Day Saints' Messenger and Advocate
The Nauvoo Expositor
The Nauvoo Neighbor
The Nauvoo Wasp
The Niles' National Register
The Niles' Weekly Register
Northern Times
Painesville Telegraph
The Prophet
The Return
The Times and Seasons
The Warsaw Message
The Warsaw Signal
The Wasp
The Western World

Books, Pamphlets, and Personal Papers

Aitken, W. A. *Journey up the Mississippi River from Its Mouth to Nauvoo, the City of the Latter Day Saints.* Ashton-under-Lyne, 1845.

Anderson, Richard Lloyd, ed. "Jackson County in Early Mormon Descriptions." *Missouri Historical Review* 65 (1971): 270–93.

Anti-Mormon Almanac, for 1842 . . . Showing that Mormonism Authorizes the Crimes of Theft, Robbery, High Treason, and Murder. . . . New York, [1841].

Arrington, Leonard J. "James Gordon Bennett's 1831 Report on 'The Mormonites.'" *Brigham Young University Studies* 10 (1970): 353–64.

Asbury, Henry. *Reminiscences of Quincy, Illinois, Containing Historical Events, Anecdotes, Matters Concerning Old Settlers and Old Times, Etc.* Quincy, Ill., 1882.

Austin, Emily M. *Mormonism; or, Life Among the Mormons.* Madison, Wis., 1882.

Bacheler, Origen. *Mormonism Exposed, Internally and Externally.* New York, 1838.

Baird, Robert. *Religion in America; or, An Account of the Origin, Progress, Relation to the State, and Present Condition of the Evangelical in the United States with Notices of the Unevangelical Denominations.* New York, 1844.

Belnap, Gilbert. "Autobiography." In *Centennial Issue in Honor of Utah Pioneer Gilbert Belnap, 1850–1950,* compiled by Della A. Belnap. N.p., n.d.

Bennett, John C. *The History of the Saints; or, an Exposé of Joe Smith and Mormonism.* Boston, 1842.

A Book of Commandments for the Government of the Church of Christ. Zion [Independence, Mo.], 1833.

Britton, Rollin J. "Early Days on Grand River and the Mormon War." *Missouri Historical Review* 13 (1918–1919): 112–34, 287–310, 388–98.

Brown, Benjamin. "Testimonies for the Truth." In *Four Faith Promoting Classics.* Salt Lake City: Bookcraft, 1968.

Burgess, Harrison. "Sketch of a Well-Spent Life." In *Classic Experiences and Adventures.* Salt Lake City: Bookcraft, 1969.

Call, Anson. "The Life Record of Anson Call." Archives of the Church of Jesus Christ of Latter-day Saints in Salt Lake City, Utah.

Campbell, Alexander. *Delusions. An Analysis of the Book of Mormon; with an Examination of Its Internal and External Evidences, and a Refutation of Its Pretenses to Divine Authority.* Boston, 1832.

Cartwright, Peter. *The Autobiography of Peter Cartwright.* New York: Abingdon Press, 1956.

Caswall, Rev. Henry, M.A. *The City of the Mormons; or, Three Days at Nauvoo in 1842.* London, 1843.

Clark, John A. *Gleanings by the Way.* Philadelphia, 1842.

Clayton, William. *Manchester Mormons: The Journal of William Clayton, 1840–1842.* Edited by James B. Allen and Thomas G. Alexander. Santa Barbara, Calif.: B. Peregine Smith, 1974.

Cook, Lyndon W. "'Brother Joseph is Truly a Wonderful Man, He is All We Could Wish a Prophet to Be': Pre-1844 Letters of William Law." *Brigham Young University Studies* 20 (1980): 207–18.

Corrill, John. *A Brief History of the Church of Christ of Latter-day Saints . . . With the Reasons of the Author for Leaving the Church.* St. Louis, 1839.

Cowdery, Oliver. *Defense in a Rehearsal of My Grounds for Separating Myself from the Latter Day Saints.* Norton, Ohio, 1839.

Crary, Christopher. *Pioneer and Personal Reminiscences.* Marshalltown, Iowa, 1893.

Crawley, Peter. "Two Rare Missouri Documents." *Brigham Young University Studies* 14 (1974): 502–27.

Davis, George T. M. *An Authentic Account of the Massacre of Joseph Smith, the Mormon Prophet.* St. Louis, 1844.

Dibble, Philo. "Philo Dibble's Narrative." In *Four Faith Promoting Classics.* Salt Lake City: Bookcraft, 1968.

The Doctrine and Covenants of the Church of Latter Day Saints, Containing Revelations Given to Joseph Smith, the Prophet. . . . Kirtland, Ohio, 1835.

Douglas, Stephen A. *The Letters of Stephen A. Douglas.* Edited by Robert W. Johannsen. Urbana: University of Illinois Press, 1961.

Fielding, Joseph. "'They Might Have Known That He Was Not a Fallen Prophet'—The Nauvoo Journal of Joseph Fielding." Transcribed and edited by Andrew F. Ehat. *Brigham Young University Studies* 19 (1979): 133–66.

Ford, Thomas. *A History of Illinois: From Its Commencement as a State in 1818 to 1847.* Edited by Milo Quaife. 2 vols. Chicago: The Lakeside Press, 1945.

Gooch, John. *Death of the Prophets Joseph and Hyrum Smith.* . . . Boston, 1844.

Grant, Jedediah M. *A Collection of Facts, Relative to the Course Taken by Elder Sidney Rigdon, in the States of Ohio, Missouri, Illinois and Pennsylvania.* Philadelphia, 1844.

Greene, John P. *Facts Relative to the Expulsion of the Mormons, or Latter Day Saints, from the State of Missouri Under the "Exterminating Order."* Cincinnati, 1839.

Gregg, Josiah. *Commerce of the Prairies; or, The Journal of a Santa Fe Trader.* New York, 1844; Vol. 20 in *Early Western Travels, 1774–1846,* edited by Reuben Gold Thwaites. Cleveland: Arthur H. Clark, 1905.

Gunnison, J. W. *The Mormons or Latter-day Saints in the Valley of the Great Salt Lake: A History of Their Rise and Progress, Peculiar Doctrines, Present Condition and Prospects.* Philadelphia, 1856.

Hall, William. *The Abominations of Mormonism Exposed; Containing Many Facts and Doctrines Concerning That Singular People, During Seven Years Membership with Them: From 1840 to 1847.* Cincinnati, 1852.

Hampshire, Annette P. "Thomas Sharp and Anti-Mormon Sentiment in Illinois, 1842–1845." *Journal of the Illinois State Historical Society* 72 (1979): 82–100.

Hancock, Mosiah Lyman. *The Life Story of Mosiah Lyman Hancock.* N.p., n.d.

Harris, William. *Mormonism Portrayed; Its Errors and Absurdities Exposed, and the Spirit and Designs of Its Authors made Manifest.* . . . Warsaw, Ill., 1841.

Hay, John. "The Mormon Prophet's Tragedy." *Atlantic Monthly,* December 1869, pp. 669–78.

Himes, Joshua Vaughn. *Mormon Delusions and Monstrosities.* Boston, 1842.

The History of Jackson County Missouri. . . . Kansas City, 1881.

Holt, James. "The Reminiscences of James Holt: A Narrative of the Emmett Company." Edited by Dale L. Morgan. *Utah Historical Quarterly* 23 (1955): 1–33, 150–79.

Howe, E. D. *Mormonism Unvailed: or, A Faithful Account of That Singular*

Imposition and Delusion, from Its Rise to the Present Time. Painesville, Ohio, 1834.

Hoyt, William D. "A Clay Countian's Letters of 1834." *Missouri Historical Review* 45 (1951): 349–53.

Hunt, James H. *Mormonism: Embracing the Origin, Rise and Progress of the Sect.* . . . St. Louis, 1844.

Hunter, Edward. "Autobiography." *Our Pioneer Heritage* 6 (1963): 317–26.

Huntress, Keith, ed. *Murder of an American Prophet: Events and Prejudices Surrounding the Killing of Joseph and Hyrum Smith; Illinois, June 27, 1844.* San Francisco: Chandler, 1960.

Ingals, Ephraim. "Autobiography of Dr. Ephraim Ingals." *Journal of the Illinois State Historical Society* 28 (1936): 279–308.

Jackson, Joseph H. *A Narrative of the Adventures and Experience of Joseph H. Jackson, in Nauvoo.* . . . Warsaw, Ill., 1844.

Jacob, Norton. *The Record of Norton Jacob.* Rev. ed. Edited by C. Edward and Ruth S. Jacob. N.p.: The Norton Family Association, 1953.

Jacobs, Zina Diantha Huntington. "'All Things Move in Order in the City': The Nauvoo Diary of Zina Diantha Huntington." Edited by Maureen Ursenbach Beecher. *Brigham Young University Studies* 19 (1979): 285–320.

Jennings, Warren A. "Two Iowa Postmasters View Nauvoo: Anti-Mormon Letters to the Governor of Missouri." *Brigham Young University Studies* 11 (1971): 275–92.

Jesse, Dean C. "The Early Accounts of Joseph Smith's First Vision." *Brigham Young University Studies* 9 (1969): 275–94.

———. "The Kirtland Diary of Wilford Woodruff." *Brigham Young University Studies* 12 (1972): 365–99.

Johnson, Benjamin F. *My Life's Review.* Independence, Mo.: Zion's Press, 1947.

Johnson, Joel. *A Portrait of the Missouri Mob.* [Nauvoo, Ill.?], 1842.

Kennedy, J. H. *Early Days of Mormonism: Palmyra, Kirtland, and Nauvoo.* London, 1888.

Knight, Newel. "Journal." In *Classic Experiences and Adventures.* Salt Lake City: Bookcraft, 1965.

Laub, George. "George Laub's Nauvoo Journal." Edited by Eugene England. *Brigham Young University Studies* 18 (1978): 151–78.

Law, William. "'Brother Joseph is Truly a Wonderful Man, He is All We Could Wish a Prophet to Be': Pre-1844 Letters of William Law." Edited by Lyndon W. Cook. *Brigham Young University Studies* 20 (1980): 207–18.

Laws of the State of Illinois, Passed by the Fourteenth General Assembly. Springfield, Ill., 1845.

Leavitt, Sarah Studevant. *History of Sarah Studevant.* N.p., n.d.

Lee, E. G. *The Mormons; or, Knavery Exposed.* Philadelphia, 1841.

Lee, John Doyle. *A Mormon Chronicle: The Diaries of John D. Lee, 1848–1876.* 2 vols. Edited by Robert Glass Cleland and Juanita Brooks. San Marino, Calif.: Huntingdon Library, 1955.

_____. *Mormonism Unveiled; or, The Life and Confessions of the Late Mormon Bishop.* . . . St. Louis, 1877.

"Letters of a Proselyte: The Hascall-Pomeroy Correspondence." *Utah Historical Quarterly* 25 (1957): 53–70, 133–51, 237–57, 339–57.

Lewis, Catherine. *Narrative of Some of the Proceedings of the Mormons; Giving an Account of Their Iniquities.* . . . Lynn, Mass., 1848.

Lightner, Mary E. *The Life and Testimony of Mary E. Lightner.* N.p., n.d.

Livesay, Richard. *An Exposure of Mormonism, Being a Statement of Facts Relating to the Self-Styled "Latter Day Saints" and the Origin of the Book of Mormon.* Preston, Mass., 1838.

Lucas, Samuel. "Jackson County." In *Gazetteer of the State of Missouri*, compiled by Alphonso Wetmore. St. Louis, 1837.

Lyne, Thomas A. *A True and Descriptive Account of the Assassination of Joseph and Hyrum Smith.* . . . New York, 1844.

McGee, Major Joseph. *Story of the Grand River, 1821-1905.* Gallatin, Mo.: North Missourian Press, 1909.

Majors, Alexander. *Seventy Years on the Frontier: Alexander Majors' Memoirs of a Lifetime on the Border.* Chicago, 1893.

Marsh, Eudoria. "Mormons in Hancock County: A Reminiscence." Edited by Douglas L. Wilson and Rodney O. Davis. *Journal of the Illinois State Historical Society* 64 (1971): 22–65.

Merkley, Christopher. *Biography of Christopher Merkley.* Salt Lake City, 1887.

Miller, George. *Correspondence of Bishop George Miller with the Northern Islander: From His Acquaintance with Mormonism up to Near the Close of His Life.* Burlington, Wis., [1916?].

Missouri General Assembly. *Document Containing the Correspondence, Orders, &c. in Relation to the Disturbance with the Mormons.* . . . Fayette, Mo., 1841.

Mormons and Mormonism. Papers, 1832–1954. Chicago Historical Society.

Olney, Oliver. *The Absurdities of Mormonism Portrayed.* Hancock County, Ill., 1843.

Orr, Adrian Van Brocklin. *Mormonism Dissected; or, Knavery "On Two Sticks" Exposed.* Bethania, Pa., 1841.

Owen, Ephraim, Jr. *Mormons. Memorial of Ephraim Owen, Jr.* . . . *Asking of Congress to Afford Protection to the People Called Mormons, in the Enjoyment of Their Civil Rights as Citizens of the United States.* . . . Washington, 1838.

Packard, Noah. *Memorial to the Honorable, the Governor, Senate and House of Representatives of Massachusetts, in Legislative Capacity Assembled.* Boston, 1844.

Page, John E. *Slander Refuted.* N.p., [1842?].

Parsons, Tyler. *Mormon Fanaticism Exposed.* Boston, 1841.

Partridge, George F., ed. "'The Death of a Mormon Dictator': Letters of Massachusetts Mormons, 1843–1848." *New England Quarterly* 9 (1936): 583–617.

Peck, Reed. *The Reed Peck Manuscript*. Salt Lake City: Modern Microfilm, n.d.

Perkins, James H. *Annals of the West*. Cincinnati, 1847.

Porter, Larry C., and Jan Shipps, eds. "The Colesville, New York, 'Exodus' Seen from Two Documentary Perspectives." *New York History* 62 (1981): 201–11.

Pratt, Orson. *The Prophetic Almanac*. New York, 1845.

Pratt, Parley Parker. *The Angel of the Prairies; or, A Dream of the Future*. Salt Lake City, 1880.

————. *An Appeal to the Inhabitants of the State of New York; Letter to Queen Victoria; The Fountain of Knowledge; Immortality of the Body, and Intelligence and Affection*. Nauvoo, Ill., 1841.

————. *The Autobiography of Parley P. Pratt*. Salt Lake City: Deseret Book Company, 1938.

————. *History of the Late Persecution Inflicted by the State of Missouri Upon the Mormons. . . .* Detroit, 1839.

————. *Key to the Science of Theology*. Liverpool, 1855.

————. *Mormonism Unveiled: Zion's Watchman Unmasked and Its Editor, Mr. LaRoy Sunderland, Exposed. . . .* New York, 1842.

————. *A Voice of Warning and Instruction to All People*. N.p.: Hawkes Publishing, n.d.

The Proceedings of a Convention, held at Carthage, in Hancock County, Ill., on Tuesday and Wednesday, October 1st and 2nd, 1845. N.p., 1845.

Quincy, Josiah. *Figures of the Past: From the Leaves of Old Journals*. Boston, 1883.

Rigdon, Sidney. *An Appeal to the American People: Being an Account of the Persecutions of the Church of Latter Day Saints; and of the Barbarities Inflicted upon Them by the Inhabitants of the State of Missouri*. Cincinnati, 1840.

Rupp, I. Daniel, comp. *An Original History of the Religious Denominations at Present Existing in the United States*. Philadelphia, 1844.

Shurtliff, Luman Andros. *Journal of Luman Andros*. N.p., n.d.

Smith, Joseph, Jr. The Book of Mormon: An Account Written by the Hand of Mormon, upon Plates taken from the Plates of Nephi. Palmyra, New York, 1830.

————. *Correspondence between Joseph Smith, the Prophet, and Col. John Wentworth . . . Gen. James Arlington Bennett . . . and Hon. John C. Calhoun . . . in Which is Given a Sketch of the Life of Joseph Smith, the Rise and Progress of the Church of Latter Day Saints. . . .* New York, 1844.

————. *History of the Church of Jesus Christ of Latter-day Saints*. Edited by B. H. Roberts. 7 vols. Salt Lake City: Deseret Book Company, 1978.

————. *Joseph Smith's 1832 Account of His Early Life*. Salt Lake City: Modern Microfilm, 1979.

————. *Joseph Smith's Diary, 1832–34*. Salt Lake City: Modern Microfilm, 1979.

————. *Joseph Smith's Diary, 1835–36*. Salt Lake City: Modern Microfilm, 1979.

_____. *Joseph Smith's 1838–39 Diaries*. Salt Lake City: Modern Microfilm, 1982.

_____. *The Voice of Truth, Containing the Public Writings, Portrait, and Last Sermon of President Joseph Smith*. Nauvoo, Ill., 1845.

Smith, Lucy Mack. *Biographical Sketches of Joseph Smith the Prophet, and His Progenitors for Many Generations*. Liverpool, 1853.

Smith, William. *William Smith on Mormonism*. Lamoni, Iowa, 1883.

Smoot, A. O. "Early Experience of A. O. Smoot." In *Four Faith Promoting Classics*. Salt Lake City: Bookcraft, 1968.

Snow, Eliza R. "Letter from Missouri." *Brigham Young University Studies* 13 (1973): 544–52.

Snow, Erastus. Journal. Vols. 1–3. N.d. Archives of the Church of Jesus Christ of Latter-day Saints in Salt Lake City, Utah.

Snow, Lorenzo. "The Iowa Journals of Lorenzo Snow." Edited by Maureen Ursenbach Beecher. *Brigham Young University Studies* 24 (1984): 261–73.

Sources of Mormon History in Illinois. Microfilm Collection, Southern Illinois University–Edwardsville.

Stenhouse, T. B. H. *The Rocky Mountain Saints: A Full and Complete History of the Mormons, from the First Vision of Joseph Smith to the Last Courtship of Brigham Young*. New York, 1872.

Stokes, Durward T., ed. "The Wilson Letters, 1835–1849." *Missouri Historical Review* 60 (1966): 495–517.

Stout, Hosea. "Autobiography of Hosea Stout 1810 to 1844." Edited by Reed A. Stout. *Utah Historical Quarterly* 30 (1962): 53–75, 149–74, 237–61, 333–44.

_____. *On the Frontier: The Diary of Hosea Stout*. Edited by Juanita Brooks. 2 vols. Salt Lake City: University of Utah Press, 1964.

Sunderland, LaRoy. *Mormonism Exposed and Refuted*. New York, 1838.

Swartznell, William. *Mormonism Exposed, Being a Journal of Residence in Missouri from the 28th of May to the 20th of August, 1838*. Pittsburgh, 1840.

Taylor, John. *A Short Account of the Murders, Roberies [sic], Burnings, Thefts, and Other Outrages Committed by the MOB and MILITIA of the State of Missouri Upon the Latter Day Saints. . . .* Springfield, [Ill.?], 1839.

Thorp, Joseph. *Early Days in the West: Along the Missouri One Hundred Years Ago*. Liberty, Mo.: Liberty Tribune, 1924.

Townsend, John K. *Narrative of Journey across the Rocky Mountains to the Columbia River*. Philadelphia, 1839.

Tucker, Pomeroy. *Origin, Rise, and Progress of Mormonism. Biography of Its Founders and History of Its Church. Personal Remembrances and Historical Collections Hitherto Unwritten*. New York, 1867.

Turner, J. B. *Mormonism in All Ages: or, The Rise, Progress, and Causes of Mormonism; with the Biography of Its Author and Founder, Joseph Smith, Junior*. New York, 1842.

Tyler, Daniel. "Incidents of Experience." In *Classic Experiences and Adventures*. Salt Lake City: Bookcraft, 1968.

Walker, William Holmes. *The Life Incidents and Travels of Elder William Holmes Walker*. N.p.: Elizabeth Walker Piepgrass, n.d.

Westbrook, G. W. *The Mormons in Illinois; with an Account of the Late Disturbances, which Resulted in the Assassination of Joseph & Hyrum Smith. . . .* St. Louis, 1844.

Weston, George. Letters. Newberry Library, Chicago, Ill.

Wetmore, Alphonso, comp. *Gazetteer of the State of Missouri*. St. Louis, 1837.

Whitmer, David. *An Address to All Believers in Christ By a Witness to the Divine Authenticity of the Book of Mormon*. Richmond, Mo., 1887.

Whitmer, John. *John Whitmer's History*. Salt Lake City: Modern Microfilm, n.d.

Woodruff, Wilford. *Leaves from My Journal*. Salt Lake City, 1881.

Young, Emily Dow Partridge. "Autobiography." *Woman's Exponent* 13 (1884–1885): 102–3; 14 (1885–1886): 3.

Young, Joseph. *History of the Organization of the Seventies. . . .* Salt Lake City, 1878.

Young, Lorenzo Dow. "Lorenzo Dow Young's Narrative." In *Four Faith Promoting Classics*. Salt Lake City: Bookcraft, 1968.

Secondary Sources

Books

Ahlstrom, Sydney E. *A Religious History of the American People*. vol. 1. Garden City, N.Y.: Image Books, 1975.

Allen, James B., and Glen M. Leonard. *The Story of the Latter-day Saints*. Salt Lake City: Deseret Book Company, 1976.

Arrington, Leonard J. *Brigham Young: American Moses*. New York: Alfred A. Knopf, 1985.

————. *Charles C. Rich: Mormon General and Western Frontiersman*. Provo, Utah: Brigham Young University Press, 1974.

————. *Great Basin Kingdom: Economic History of the Latter-day Saints, 1830–1900*. Lincoln, Neb.: University of Nebraska Press, 1966.

Arrington, Leonard J., and Davis Bitton. *The Mormon Experience: A History of the Latter-day Saints*. New York: Alfred A. Knopf, 1979.

Bercovitch, Sacvan. *The American Jeremiad*. Madison, Wis.: University of Wisconsin Press, 1978.

Berthoff, Rowland. *An Unsettled People: Social Order and Disorder in American History*. New York: Harper & Row, 1971.

Brodie, Fawn M. *No Man Knows My History: The Life of Joseph Smith*. 2d ed., rev. New York: Alfred A. Knopf, 1971.

Brooks, Juanita. *John Doyle Lee: Zealot-Pioneer Builder-Scapegoat*. Glendale, Calif.: Arthur H. Clark Company, 1972.

Bushman, Richard L. *Joseph Smith and the Beginnings of Mormonism*. Urbana, Ill.: University of Illinois Press, 1984.

Cook, Lyndon W. *Joseph Smith and the Law of Consecration*. Provo, Utah: Grandin Book Company, 1985.

Cross, Whitney. *The Burned-Over District: The Social and Intellectual History of Enthusiastic Religion in Western New York, 1800–1850*. Ithaca, N.Y.: Cornell University Press, 1950.

Diggins, John P. *The Lost Soul of American Politics: Virtue, Self-Interest, and the Foundations of Liberalism*. Chicago: University of Chicago Press, 1984.

Douglas, Ann. *The Feminization of American Culture*. New York: Alfred A. Knopf, 1977; Avon Books, 1978.

England, Breck. *The Life and Thought of Orson Pratt*. Salt Lake City: University of Utah Press, 1985.

Ericksen, Ephraim Edward. *The Psychological and Ethical Aspects of Mormon Group Life*. Salt Lake City: University of Utah Press, 1922.

Feldberg, Michael. *The Turbulent Era: Riot and Disorder in Jacksonian America*. New York: Oxford University Press, 1980.

Flanders, Robert Bruce. *Nauvoo: Kingdom on the Mississippi*. Urbana, Ill.: University of Illinois Press, 1965.

Foster, Lawrence. *Religion and Sexuality: Three American Communal Experiments of the Nineteenth Century*. New York: Oxford University Press, 1981.

Gregg, Thomas. *The Prophet of Palmyra: Mormonism Reviewed and Examined in the Life, Character, and Career of its Founder*. New York, 1890.

Gross, Robert A. *The Minutemen and Their World*. New York: Hill and Wang, 1976.

Gunn, Stanley R. *Oliver Cowdery: Second Elder and Scribe*. Salt Lake City: Bookcraft, 1962.

Hansen, Klaus J. *Mormonism and the American Experience*. Chicago: University of Chicago Press, 1981.

———. *Quest for Empire: The Political Kingdom of God and the Council of Fifty in Mormon History*. East Lansing, Mich.: Michigan State University Press, 1967.

Hill, Donna. *Joseph Smith: The First Mormon*. Garden City, N.Y.: Doubleday, 1977.

Johannsen, Robert W. *Stephen A. Douglas*. New York: Oxford University Press, 1973.

Johnson, Paul E. *A Shopkeeper's Millennium: Society and Revivals in Rochester, New York, 1815–1837*. New York: Hill and Wang, 1978.

Jones, Wesley M. *A Critical Study of Book of Mormon Sources*. Detroit: Harlo Press, 1964.

Kern, Louis J. *An Ordered Love. Sex Roles and Sexuality in Victorian Utopias: The Shakers, the Mormons, and the Oneida Community*. Chapel Hill: University of North Carolina Press, 1981.

Kimball, Stanley B. *Heber C. Kimball: Mormon Patriarch and Pioneer*. Urbana, Ill.: University of Illinois Press, 1981.

Larson, Andrew Karl. *Erastus Snow: The Life of a Missionary and Pioneer for the Early Mormon Church*. Salt Lake City: University of Utah Press, 1971.

Leone, Mark P. *Roots of Modern Mormonism*. Cambridge, Mass.: Harvard University Press, 1979.

LeSueur, Stephen C. *The 1838 Mormon War in Missouri*. Columbia: University of Missouri Press, 1987.

Linn, William Alexander. *The Story of the Mormons: From the Date of Their Origin to the Year 1901*. New York: MacMillan, 1902.

McKiernan, F. Mark. *The Voice of One Crying in the Wilderness: Sidney Rigdon, Religious Reformer, 1793–1876*. Lawrence, Kans.: Coronado Press, 1971.

McKiernan, F. Mark, Alma R. Blair, and Paul M. Edwards, eds. *The Restoration Movement: Essays in Mormon History*. Lawrence, Kans.: Coronado Press, 1973.

McLaughlin, William G. *Revivals, Awakenings, and Reform: An Essay on Religion and Social Change in America, 1607–1977*. Chicago: University of Chicago Press, 1978.

Marty, Martin E. *Righteous Empire: The Protestant Experience in America*. New York: Harper Torchbooks, 1970.

Moore, R. Laurence. *Religious Outsiders and the Making of Americans*. New York: Oxford University Press, 1986.

Morgan, Edmund S. *The Challenge of the American Revolution*. New York: W. W. Norton, 1976.

Mulder, William, and A. Russell Mortensen, eds. *Among the Mormons: Historic Accounts by Contemporary Observers*. New York: Alfred A. Knopf, 1958.

Oaks, Dallin H., and Marvin S. Hill. *Carthage Conspiracy: The Trial of the Accused Assassins of Joseph Smith*. Urbana, Ill.: University of Illinois Press, 1975.

O'Dea, Thomas F. *The Mormons*. Chicago: University of Chicago Press, 1957.

Parrish, William E. *David Rice Atchison of Missouri: Border Politician*. Columbia: University of Missouri Press, 1961.

Pease, Theodore Calvin, ed. *Illinois Election Returns: 1818–1848*. Springfield, Ill.: Trustees of the Illinois State Historical Library, 1923.

Pocock, J. G. A. *The Machiavellian Moment: Florentine Political Thought and the Atlantic Republican Tradition*. Princeton: Princeton University Press, 1975.

Richards, Leonard. *"Gentlemen of Property and Standing": Anti-Abolitionist Mobs in Jacksonian America*. New York: Oxford University Press, 1970.

Roberts, B. H. *A Comprehensive History of the Church of Jesus Christ of Latter-day Saints*. 6 vols. Provo, Utah: Brigham Young University Press, 1957.

———. *The Missouri Persecutions*. Salt Lake City, 1900.

———. *Studies of the Book of Mormon*. Edited and with an Introduction by Brigham D. Madsen. Urbana: University of Illinois Press, 1985.

Ryan, Mary P. *Cradle of the Middle Class: The Family in Oneida County, New York, 1790–1865*. Cambridge: Cambridge University Press, 1981.

Schindler, Harold. *Orrin Porter Rockwell: Man of God/Son of Thunder*. Salt

Lake City: University of Utah Press, 1966.

Shipps, Jan. *Mormonism: The Story of a New Religious Tradition.* Urbana: University of Illinois Press, 1985.

Somkin, Fred. *Unquiet Eagle: Memory and Desire in the Idea of American Freedom, 1815–1860.* Ithaca, N.Y.: Cornell University Press, 1967.

Tuveson, Ernest Lee. *Redeemer Nation: The Idea of America's Millennial Role.* Chicago: University of Chicago Press, 1968.

Van Wagoner, Richard S. *Mormon Polygamy: A History.* Salt Lake City: Signature Books, 1986.

West, Ray B., Jr. *Kingdom of the Saints: The Story of Brigham Young and the Mormons.* New York: Viking Press, 1957.

Articles

Alexander, Thomas G. "Historiography and the New Mormon History: A Historian's Perspective." *Dialogue: A Journal of Mormon Thought* 19 (1986): 25–49.

Anderson, Richard Lloyd. "Joseph Smith's New York Reputation Reappraised." *Brigham Young University Studies* 10 (1970): 283–314.

_____. "The Mature Joseph Smith and Treasure Searching." *Brigham Young University Studies* 24 (1984): 489–560.

Appleby, Joyce. "Republicanism and Ideology." *American Quarterly* 37 (1985): 461–73.

Arrington, Leonard. "Early Mormon Communitarianism: The Law of Consecration and Stewardship." *Western Humanities Review* 7 (1953): 341–69.

_____. "Mormonism: From Its New York Beginnings." *New York History* 61 (1980): 387–410.

Arrington, Leonard J., and Jon Haupt. "Intolerable Zion: The Image of Mormonism in Nineteenth Century American Literature." *Western Humanities Review* 22 (1968): 243–60.

_____. "The Missouri and Illinois Mormons in Antebellum Fiction." *Dialogue: A Journal of Mormon Thought* 5 (1970): 37–50.

Baker, Jean. "From Belief into Culture: Republicanism in the Antebellum North." *American Quarterly* 37 (1985): 532–50.

Banning, Lance. "Jeffersonian Ideology Revisited: Liberal and Classical Ideas in the New American Republic." *William and Mary Quarterly* 43 (1986): 3–34.

Barnow, Erik. "The Benson Exodus of 1833: Mormon Converts and the Westward Movement." *Vermont History* 54 (1986): 133–48.

Berthoff, Rowland. "Independence and Attachment, Virtue and Interest: From Republican Citizen to Free Enterpriser, 1787–1837." In *Uprooted Americans: Essays to Honor Oscar Handlin*, edited by Richard Bushman et al. Boston: Little, Brown, 1979.

_____. "Peasants and Artisans, Puritans and Republicans: Personal Liberty and Communal Equality in American History." *The Journal of American History* 69 (1982): 579–98.

Berthoff, Rowland, and John M. Murrin. "Feudalism, Communalism, and the Yeoman Freeholder: The American Revolution Considered as a Social Accident." In *Essays on the American Revolution*, edited by Stephen G. Kurtz and James H. Hutson. New York: W. W. Norton, 1973.

Bitton, Davis. "The Waning of Mormon Kirtland." *Brigham Young University Studies* 12 (1972): 455–64.

Bunker, Gary L., and Davis Bitton. "Mesmerism and Mormonism." *Brigham Young University Studies* 15 (1975): 146–70.

Bushman, Richard L. "The Book of Mormon and the American Revolution." *Brigham Young University Studies* 17 (1976): 3–20.

_____. "The Character of Joseph Smith: Insights from His Holographs." *Ensign* 7 (1977): 10–13.

_____. "The Historians and Mormon Nauvoo." *Dialogue: A Journal of Mormon Thought* 5 (1970): 51–61.

Cannon, Mark W. "The Crusades Against the Masons, Catholics, and Mormons: Separate Waves of a Common Current." *Brigham Young University Studies* 3 (1961): 23–40.

Clark, James R. "The Kingdom of God, the Council of Fifty, and the State of Deseret." *Utah Historical Quarterly* 26 (1958): 131–48.

Clebsch, William A. "Each Sect the Sect to End All Sects." *Dialogue: A Journal of Mormon Thought* 1 (1966): 84–89.

Crawley, Peter, and Richard L. Anderson. "The Political and Social Realities of Zion's Camp." *Brigham Young University Studies* 14 (1974): 406–20.

Davis, David Brion. "The New England Origins of Mormonism." *The New England Quarterly* 27 (1953): 148–63.

_____. "Some Themes of Countersubversion: An Analysis of Anti-Masonic, Anti-Catholic, and Anti-Mormon Literature." *Mississippi Valley Historical Review* 47 (1960): 204–24.

DePillis, Mario S. "The Quest for Religious Authority and the Rise of Mormonism." *Dialogue: A Journal of Mormon Thought* 1 (1966): 68–88.

_____. "The Social Sources of Mormonism." *Church History* 38 (1968): 50–79.

Durham, G. Homer. "A Political Interpretation of Mormon History." *Pacific Historical Review* 13 (1944): 136–50.

Durham, Reed C. "The Election Day Battle at Gallatin." *Brigham Young University Studies* 13 (1972): 36–61.

Ehat, Andrew F. "'It Seems Like Heaven Began on Earth': Joseph Smith and the Constitution of the Kingdom of God." *Brigham Young University Studies* 20 (1980): 253–80.

Ellsworth, Paul D. "Mobocracy and the Rule of Law: American Press Reaction to the Murder of Joseph Smith." *Brigham Young University Studies* 20 (1979): 71–82.

Esplin, Ronald K. "Joseph, Brigham, and the Twelve: A Succession of Continuity." *Brigham Young University Studies* 21 (1981): 301–44.

Flanders, Robert Bruce. "The Kingdom of God in Illinois: Politics in Utopia." *Dialogue: A Journal of Mormon Thought* 5 (1970): 26–36.

―――. "Some Reflections on the New Mormon History." *Dialogue: A Journal of Mormon Thought* 9 (1974): 34–41.

―――. "To Transform History: Early Mormon Culture and the Concept of Time and Space." *Church History* 40 (1971): 108–17.

Gayler, George R. "Attempts by the State of Missouri to Extradite Joseph Smith, 1841–1843." *Missouri Historical Review* 58 (1963): 21–36.

―――. "Governor Ford and the Death of Joseph and Hyrum Smith." *Journal of the Illinois State Historical Society* 50 (1957): 391–411.

―――. "The Mormons and Politics in Illinois: 1839–1844." *Journal of the Illinois State Historical Society* 49 (1956): 48–66.

Gentry, Leland H. "The Danite Band of 1838." *Brigham Young University Studies* 14 (1974): 421–50.

Godfrey, Kenneth W. "Joseph Smith and the Masons." *Journal of the Illinois State Historical Society* 64 (1971): 79–90.

Grimsted, David. "Rioting in Its Jacksonian Setting." *American Historical Review* 77 (1972): 361–97.

Hammett, Theodore. "Two Mobs of Jacksonian Boston: Ideology and Interest." *The Journal of American History* 62 (1976): 845–68.

Hansen, Klaus. "Joseph Smith and the Political Kingdom of God." *The American West* 5 (1968): 20–24, 63.

―――. "The Political Kingdom of God as a Cause for Mormon-Gentile Conflict." *Brigham Young University Studies* 2 (1960): 241–60.

―――. "The World and the Prophets." *Dialogue: A Journal of Mormon Thought* 1 (1966): 103–7.

Hatch, Nathan O. "The Christian Movement and the Demand for a Theology of the People." *The Journal of American History* 67 (1980): 545–67.

Hill, Marvin S. "Brodie Revisited: A Reappraisal." *Dialogue: A Journal of Mormon Thought* 7 (1972): 72–85.

―――. "Cultural Crisis in the Mormon Kingdom: A Reconsideration of the Causes of Kirtland Dissent." *Church History* 49 (1980): 286–97.

―――. "Joseph Smith and the 1826 Trial: New Evidence and New Difficulties." *Brigham Young University Studies* 13 (1972): 223–33.

―――. "Joseph Smith the Man: Some Reflections on a Subject of Controversy." *Brigham Young University Studies* 21 (1981): 175–86.

―――. "Money-Digging Folklore and the Beginnings of Mormonism: An Interpretive Suggestion." *Brigham Young University Studies* 24 (1984): 473–88.

―――. "Mormon Religion in Nauvoo: Some Reflections." *Utah Historical Quarterly* 44 (1976): 170–80.

―――. "A Note on Joseph Smith's First Vision and Its Import in the Shaping of Early Mormonism." *Dialogue: A Journal of Mormon Thought* 12 (1979): 90–99.

―――. "The 'Prophet Puzzle' Assembled; or, How to Treat Our Historical Diplopia Toward Joseph Smith." *Journal of Mormon History* 3 (1976): 101–5.

―――. "Quest for Refuge: An Hypothesis as to the Social Origins and Nature of the Mormon Political Kingdom." *Journal of Mormon History* 2 (1975): 3–20.

——. "The Rise of Mormonism in the Burned-Over District: Another View." *New York History* 61 (1980): 411–30.

——. "Secular or Sectarian History?: A Critique of *No Man Knows My History*." *Church History* 43 (1974): 78–96.

——. "The Shaping of the Mormon Mind in New England and New York." *Brigham Young University Studies* 9 (1969): 351–72.

——. "Survey: The Historiography of Mormonism." *Church History* 28 (1959): 418–26.

Hill, Marvin S.; C. Keith Rooker; and Larry T. Wimmer. "The Kirtland Economy Revisited: A Market Critique of Sectarian Economics." *Brigham Young University Studies* 17 (1977): 391–475.

Huntress, Keith. "Governor Thomas Ford and the Murderers of Joseph Smith." *Dialogue: A Journal of Mormon Thought* 4 (1969): 41–52.

Irving, Gordon. "The Mormons and the Bible in the 1830s." *Brigham Young University Studies* 13 (1973): 473–88.

Jennings, Warren A. "The Army of Israel Marches into Missouri." *Missouri Historical Review* 62 (1968): 107–35.

——. "The Expulsion of the Mormons from Jackson County, Missouri." *Missouri Historical Review* 64 (1969): 41–63.

——. "Factors in the Destruction of the Mormon Press in Missouri, 1833." *Utah Historical Quarterly* 35 (1967): 57–76.

——. "Importuning for Redress." *The Missouri Historical Society Bulletin* 27 (1970): 15–29.

——. "Isaac McCoy and the Mormons." *Missouri Historical Review* 61 (1966): 62–82.

Jesse, Dean C. "New Documents and Mormon Beginnings." *Brigham Young University Studies* 24 (1984): 397–428.

——. "The Reliability of Joseph Smith's History." *Journal of Mormon History* 13 (1976): 23–46.

Kelly, Robert. "Ideology and Political Culture from Jefferson to Nixon." *American Historical Review* 82 (1977): 531–62.

Kimball, James L., Jr. "The Nauvoo Charter: A Reinterpretation." *Journal of the Illinois State Historical Society* 64 (1971): 66–78.

——. "A Wall to Defend Zion: The Nauvoo Charter." *Brigham Young University Studies* 15 (1975): 491–97.

Kimball, Stanley B. "The Mormons in Illinois, 1838–1846: A Special Introduction." *Journal of the Illinois State Historical Society* 64 (1971): 4–21.

——. "Thomas Barnes: Coroner of Carthage." *Brigham Young University Studies* 11 (1971): 141–47.

Kloppenberg, James T. "The Virtues of Liberalism: Christianity, Republicanism, and Ethics in Early American Political Discourse." *Journal of American History* 74 (1987): 9–33.

Kramnick, Isaac. "Republican Revisionism Revisited." *American History Review* 87 (1982): 629–64.

Lyon, Edgar T. "Independence, Missouri, and the Mormons, 1827–1833." *Brigham Young University Studies* 13 (1972): 10–19.

McNiff, William John. "The Kirtland Phase of Mormonism." *The Ohio State Archaeological and Historical Quarterly* 50 (1941): 261–68.

Moody, Thurmon Dean. "Nauvoo's Whistling and Whittling Brigade." *Brigham Young University Studies* 15 (1975): 480–90.

Moore, R. Laurence. "Insiders and Outsiders in American Historical Narrative and American History." *American Historical Review* 87 (1982): 390–412.

Mulder, William. "Mormonism's Gathering: An American Doctrine with a Difference." *Church History* 23 (1954): 248–64.

———. "The Mormons in American History." *Bulletin of the University of Utah* 48 (1957): 7–36.

Oaks, Dallin H. "The Suppression of the Nauvoo Expositor." *Utah Law Review* 9 (1965): 862–905.

Parkin, Max H. "Mormon Political Involvement in Ohio." *Brigham Young University Studies* 9 (1969): 484–502.

Paul, Rodman W. "The Mormons as a Theme in Western Historical Writing." *The Journal of American History* 54 (1967): 511–23.

Poll, Richard D. "Nauvoo and the New Mormon History: A Bibliographical Survey." *Journal of Mormon History* 5 (1978): 105–23.

Quinn, D. Michael. "The Council of Fifty and Its Members, 1844 to 1945." *Brigham Young University Studies* 20 (1980): 163–97.

———. "The Mormon Succession Crisis of 1844." *Brigham Young University Studies* 16 (1976): 187–233.

Richards, Paul. "Missouri Persecution: Petition for Redress." *Brigham Young University Studies* 13 (1973): 520–43.

Robertson, R. J., Jr. "The Mormon Experience in Missouri, 1830–1839." Pt. 1. *Missouri Historical Review* 68 (1974): 280–98.

———. "The Mormon Experience in Missouri, 1830–1839." Pt. 2. *Missouri Historical Review* 68 (1974): 393–415.

Ross, Dorothy. "The Liberal Tradition Revisited and the Republican Tradition Addressed." In *New Directions in American Intellectual History*, edited by John Higham and Paul K. Conkin. Baltimore: Johns Hopkins University Press, 1979.

Shalhope, Robert E. "Republicanism and Early American Historiography." *Willliam and Mary Quarterly* 49 (1982): 334–56.

———. "Toward a Republican Synthesis: The Emergence of an Understanding of Republicanism in American Historiography." *William and Mary Quarterly* 29 (1972): 49–80.

Shipps, Jan. "The Prophet Puzzle: Suggestions Leading Toward a More Comprehensive Interpretation of Joseph Smith." *Journal of Mormon History* 1 (1974): 3–20.

Smith, Timothy L. "The Book of Mormon in a Biblical Culture." *Journal of Mormon History* 7 (1980): 3–21.

Taylor, Alan. "Rediscovering the Context of Joseph Smith's Treasure Seeking." *Dialogue: A Journal of Mormon Thought* 19 (1986): 18–28.

Underwood, Grant. "Re-visioning Mormon History." *Pacific Historical Review* 55 (1986): 403–26.

——. "'Saved or Damned': Tracing a Persistent Protestantism in Early Mormon Thought." *Brigham Young University Studies* 26 (1986): 85–103.

Van Wagoner, Richard S. "Mormon Polyandry in Nauvoo." *Dialogue: A Journal of Mormon Thought* 18 (1985): 67–83.

Walker, Ronald W. "Joseph Smith: The Palmyra Seer." *Brigham Young University Studies* 24 (1984): 461–72.

——. "Martin Harris: Mormonism's Early Convert." *Dialogue: A Journal of Mormon Thought* 19 (1986): 29–43.

——. "The Persisting Idea of American Treasure Hunting." *Brigham Young University Studies* 24 (1984): 429–59.

Wilson, Douglas. "Prospects for the Study of the Book of Mormon as a Work of American Literature." *Dialogue: A Journal of Mormon Thought* 3 (1968): 29–41.

Wilson, John F. "Some Comparative Perspectives on the Early Mormon Movement and the Church-State Question, 1830–1845." *Journal of Mormon History* 8 (1971): 63–77.

Wood, Gordon. "Evangelical America and Early Mormonism." *New York History* 61 (1980): 359–86.

Yorgason, Laurence M. "Preview on a Study of the Social and Geographical Origins of Early Mormon Converts, 1830–1845." *Brigham Young University Studies* 10 (1970): 279–82.

Dissertations and Theses

Fielding, Robert Kent. "The Growth of the Mormon Church in Kirtland, Ohio." Ph.D. dissertation, Indiana University, 1957.

Gentry, Leland Homer. "A History of the Latter-day Saints in Northern Missouri from 1836 to 1839." Ph.D. dissertation, Brigham Young University, 1965.

Godfrey, Kenneth W. "Causes of Mormon–Non-Mormon Conflict in Hancock County, Illinois, 1839–1846." Ph.D. dissertation, Brigham Young University, 1967.

Hill, Marvin S. "The Role of Christian Primitivism in the Origin and Development of the Mormon Kingdom, 1830–1844." Ph.D. dissertation, University of Chicago, 1968.

Pollock, Gordon Douglas. "In Search of Security: The Mormons and the Kingdom of God on Earth, 1830–1844." Ph.D. dissertation, Queen's University, 1977.

Shipps, JoAnn Barnett. "The Mormons in Politics: The First Hundred Years." Ph.D. dissertation, University of Colorado, 1965.

Zahiser, Patricia A. "Violence in Missouri, 1831–1839: The Case of Mormon Persecution." M.A. thesis, Florida Atlantic University, 1973.

Index